The Profundity and Bifurcation of Change

The Intelligent Social Change Journey

Part V: *Living the Future*

MQIPress (2020)
Frost, West Virginia
ISBN 978-0-9985147-9-6

The Consciousness Series

*The human experience is a neuronal dance with the Universe, with each of us
in the driver's seat selecting our partners and directing our dance steps.*

"Experiencing as we are the Anthropocene and Post-truth Era, the urge to seek balance through knowledge and consciousness becomes imperative. This is a timely wake-up call to responsibly face our existential risks before it is too late, as much as a lucid and serene reflection on a path to wisdom." – Francisco Javier Carrillo, President, The World Capital Institute

"I read the book with great excitement and the authors have achieved a consilient publication like none other. This book serves as a roadmap, a rearview mirror, a societal plea, a sign that humanity is evolving, and is a call for love. It is about knowledge, decision making, virtue, beauty, alchemy, compassion and hope. It is about Oneness and the mystery of the Myst. What a fine result. This book puts such light into the Universe!" –Susan Dreiband, Chief Knowledge Officer & Senior Policy Analyst, US Forest Service, Retired; US Forest Service, Change Management Champion & Consultant, Retired; Reiki Master and Energy Healer

"My mind is numb (in a positive way) from a cursory reading of the book (I need to reread it more closely.) I can summarize my thoughts in one word: WOW!! I—who have a Bachelor's in Philosophy; minor in Shakespeare; three Masters' in: Systems Management, Education, and International Relations; a Law Degree, and a Doctorate in Engineering Management; and three careers in the military, business, and academia—have never quite seen a work of such ambition, scope, and consilience. Clearly, it could be overwhelming for a reader only schooled in one or two areas. The convergence of all our knowledge/experiences in the conscious and subconscious realms, and their relation to Change, is not an easy task.

*This book is more than one on CHANGE. You have here a **'tour de force'** on human-kind itself on our planet, giving us a vocabulary and models which enable a deeper understanding and appreciation of the many complex forces that underpin the way we use knowledge for change."* – Michael Stankosky, DSc, Professorial Lecturer, Knowledge Management, George Washington University

"Another insightful and powerful book from the Bennets and colleagues! A deep scientific, social and psychological analysis and reflection on various ways to create change in the complex world in which we currently live. A great thought-provoking book that you will read and re-read!" – Dr. Vincent Ribiére, Managing Director, Institute for Knowledge and Innovation Management-Southeast Asia, Bangkok University

Original release (as eBook): 2017
Second printing (soft cover): 2020

Copyright © 2020 MQIPress. All rights reserved.
In the spirit of collaborative advantage, with attribution,
any part of this book may be copied and distributed freely.

MQIPress
Frost, West Virginia
303 Mountain Quest Lane
Marlinton, WV 24954
United States of America
Telephone: 304-799-7267

alex@mountainquestinstitute.com
www.mountainquestinstitute.com
www.mountainquestinn.com
www.MQIPress.com
www.Myst-art.com

ISBN 978-0-9985147-9-6

Man considering the Universe of which he is a unit, sees nothing but change in matter, forces and mental states. He sees that nothing really is, but that everything is becoming and changing. Nothing stands still. Everything is being born, growing, dying. At the very instant a thing reaches its height, it begins to decline. The law of rhythm is in constant operation. There is no fixed reality, enduring quality or substantiality in anything –nothing is permanent but Change. Man sees all things evolve from other things and resolve into other things; a constant action and reaction, inflow and outflow, building up and tearing down, creation and destruction, birth, growth and death. Nothing endures but Change. And if he is a thinking man, he realizes that all of these changing things must be outward appearances or manifestations of some underlying power, some Substantial Reality.
The Kybalion (1940, p. 53)

Part V: *Living the Future**

Table of Contents

Table of Contents | i

Tables and Figures | iv

Appreciation | vi

Preface | viii

Introduction to the Intelligent Social Change Journey | 1
  THE OVERARCHING ISCJ MODEL | 4
  COGNITIVE-BASED ORDERING OF CHANGE | 8
  HOW TO BEST USE THIS MATERIAL | 11

Part V Introduction | 15

Chapter 31: The Alchemy of Change | 22
  THE SEVEN STEPS OF TRANSFORMATION | 24
  THE METAMORPHOSIS | 27
  OUR CURRENT CYCLE OF CHANGE | 31
  WHERE CAN WE GO FROM HERE AS WE LIVE THE FUTURE? | 37

Chapter 32: Balancing and Sensing | 40
  THE SENSE OF BALANCE | 42
  SELF-BALANCING | 44
  BALANCING THE SENSES | 51
  DYNAMIC BALANCING | 52
  FINAL THOUGHTS | 53

Chapter 33: The Harmony of Beauty | 54
  SENSING BEAUTY | 56
  BEAUTY IN OUR THINKING | 57
  BEAUTY IN ART | 59
  HEALTH AS A WORK OF ART | 64
  SHARING BEAUTY | 67
  BEAUTY AS TRANSCENDENCE | 71
  FINAL THOUGHTS | 72

Chapter 34: Virtues for Living the Future | 73
BEAUTY, GOODNESS AND TRUTH | 73
GOOD CHARACTER | 75
GOOD CHARACTER IS ACTIONABLE | 78
EXPLORING GOOD CHARACTER THROUGH CORE VALUES | 80
ALL PEOPLE ARE NOT CREATED EQUAL | 83
FINAL THOUGHTS | 85

Chapter 35: Conscious Compassion | 86
TOWARDS A GLOBAL ETHIC | 86
MOVING INTO COMPASSION | 88
JUDGING AND COMPASSION | 90
DEVELOPING CONSCIOUS COMPASSION | 95
COMPASSION AS A TOOL FOR CHANGE | 97
FINAL THOUGHTS | 97

Chapter 36: The Changing Nature of Knowledge | 99
KNOWLEDGE AS A MEASURE OF SELF GROWTH | 101
SPREADING THE KNOWLEDGE MOVEMENT | 103
IT'S GLOBAL | 106
THE SPIRITUAL NATURE OF KNOWLEDGE | 108
KNOWING | 111
ONENESS | 113
FINAL THOUGHTS | 117

Chapter 37: Consciousness Rising | 118
INFORMATION FIELDS AS CONSCIOUSNESS FIELDS | 119
EXTRAORDINARY CONSCIOUSNESS | 127
NEW ROLE FOR PERSONALITY | 130
BEYOND ASSOCIATIVE PATTERNING | 136
ASSOCIATIVE ATTRACTING | 141
THE HOLOGRAPHIC UNIVERSE | 144
FINAL THOUGHTS | 146

Chapter 38: The Bifurcation | 147
FREEDOM AND CHOICE | 151
CHOOSING BEYOND DUALITY | 154
THE SPLIT IN THE ROAD | 156
IS HUMANITY READY FOR THE CREATIVE LEAP? | 159
CLOSING THOUGHTS | 165

ADDENDUM: Manifesting Our Choice | 169
by David and Alex Bennet

APPENDICES:
Appendix A: The Overarching ISCJ Model | 176
Appendix B: The Table of Contents for All Parts | 177
Appendix D: Engaging Tacit Knowledge | 183
Appendix E: Knowing | 195

Endnotes | 215

References | 216

Index | 227

About Mountain Quest | 234

About the Authors | 236

* This book is Part V of *The Profundity and Bifurcation of Change*, available from Amazon.com in hard copy and Kindle format, and in PDF format from MQIPress.net

Part V
Tables, Figures, and Tools

TABLE

ISCJ-1. The three Phases from the viewpoints of the nature of knowledge, points of reflection and cognitive shifts | 7
ISCJ-2. Comparison of Phases of the Intelligent Social Change Journey with Levels of Learning | 10

35-1. A conceptual merging of "conscious" and "compassion" | 96

37-1. Relationship of the Phases of the Intelligent Social Change Journey and the Levels of Consciousness | 122

FIGURES

ISCJ-1. The Baseline Model | 2
[The Overarching ISCJ Model in Appendix A.]
ISCJ-2. Relationship of Parts and Phases of the ISCJ | 11

31-1. The Caduceus is a well-known example of Alchemical symbolism still in use today | 23
31-2. As imaginal cells unite within the alchemical soup, they gain strength in numbers | 27

32-1. In the words sung by Janis Joplin: "Freedom is another word for nothin' left to lose." | 50
32-2. The balancing of the planes, the senses and time | 52

33-1. The Art of Reefka Schneider | 62
33-2. The Art of Cindy Taylor | 62
33-3. The Art of Corbie Crouse | 63
33-4. The Art of Jackie Urbanovic | 64
33-5. Sharing the beauty of life at Mountain Quest | 69
33-6. A *Myst* picture entitled: "Crowned with Light." *The majesty of communing in the Myst: One voice, one song, one heart* | 70

35-1. From sympathy to unconditional love: a continuum with an increasing depth of connection | 90
35-2. As judging grows to awareness with discernment, compassion grows | 93

36-1. The shifting perception of knowledge as we move through the ISCJ | 100
36-2. Thought bite: "*KM is significant because it fits right upon this historical opportunity.*" | 109
36-3. Growing through change | 116

37-1. Conceptual model relating knowledge and consciousness | 129
37-2. Consciousness Rising | 137
37-3. Resonance is a quality of the Field | 140

38-1. The human journey of choice | 153
38-2. Can humanity advance at the same pace without the push of need, fear and survival? | 157
38-3. Complexity begets complexity, from which emerges simplicity 164

The Bifurcation (Original painting by Cindy Taylor) | 167

TOOLS

32-1. The Lokahi Triangle and The Life Triangle | 43
32-2. Holding Neurovascular Reflect Points | 48
33-1. Choosing Beauty | 66
34-1. Developing a Good Character Action Set | 82
35-1. Discerning Judgment | 92
35-2. Achieving Zero Limits through *Ho'oponopono* | 94

In Appreciation

Hundreds of people, named and unnamed, have contributed thousands of ideas to this book in the context of conversations and dialogues, articles and books, and quotes and stories. We are all indeed one, sharing ideas in groups and communities, face-to-face and virtual, appearing and connecting where we will, in an ever-looping creative embrace and continuous expansion toward intelligent activity.

Our deep appreciation to our co-authors, who each bring a unique focus and value to this work. These are Arthur Shelley, Theresa Bullard, and John Lewis. It is our sincere hope that each of them—who now are co-creators with us—will share this work largely in their day-to-day lives. Also, our appreciation to Donna Panucci, Maik Fuellmann, Jackie Urbanovic and Barbara Wheeler for their contributing and expanding thoughts, and to Mark Boyes, who co-created the thought-provoking image in Chapter 10.

Across our consilience approach, there are a handful of authors whose work has both inspired our thinking and excited our creativity. *Life's Hidden Meaning* by Niles MacFlouer provides insights from Ageless Wisdom, just coming into our realms of understanding. Serving as an example of committed knowledge sharing, MacFlouer has hosted a weekly radio show on Ageless Wisdom since 2004! This massive and incredibly insightful body of work is available on the Internet at http://www.agelesswisdom.com/archives_of_radio_shows.htm Over the past year we have listened, reflected, associated and created connections to this work, such that it is nearly impossible to follow these connections. In this regard, we try to err on the side of over-referencing, and since there is not one specific reference, but, rather, a way of thinking, we have referenced this body of work as MacFlouer (2004-16). We encourage those who resonate with this material to explore it more fully.

In 1996, Ken Wilber wrote *A Brief History of Everything*, and his brilliance continues to emerge from that point. While we applaud his continuing search for a simple and elegant theory of everything, we would be reluctant to eliminate *any* of the rich truths and theories explored in his dozens of books. *Paths of Change* by Will McWhinney served as a baseline for exploring world views and combinations of reality in the change journey. *Spontaneous Evolution: Our Positive Future* by Bruce H. Lipton and Steve Bhaerman is inspirational and informative from the viewpoint of cell biology. Jean Houston's *Jump Time* was way ahead of its time, and is a must read for any decision-maker in today's environment, and that is all of us. And where would we be as a humanity without the brilliance and wisdom of Bohm, Cozolino, Csikszentmihalyi, Damasio, Edelman, Gardner, Goleman, Goswami, Handy,

Hawkins, Kant, Kolb, Kurzweil, Laszlo, McTaggart, Polanyi, Stonier, Templeton, Tiller, Wilber, and so many others! Our appreciation to all of the contributors called out in our references, and to those who may not be in our references but whose thought has seeped into our minds and hearts in the course of living.

Our continued thanks to the professionals, colleagues and thought leaders who participated in the KMTL study and follow-on Sampler Call. These include: Dorothy E. Agger-Gupta, Verna Allee, Debra Amidon, Ramon Barquin, Surinder Kumar Batra, Juanita Brown, John Seely Brown, Frada Burstein, Francisco Javier Carrillo, Robert Cross, Tom Davenport, Ross Dawson, Steve Denning, Charles Dhewa, Nancy Dixon, Leif Edvinsson, Kent Greenes, Susan Hanley, Clyde Holsapple, Esko Kilpi, Dorothy Leonard, Geoff Malafsky, Martha Manning, Carla O'Dell, Edna Pasher, W. Barnett Pearce, Larry Prusak, Madanmohan Rao, Tomasz Rudolf, Melissie Rumizen, Hubert Saint-Onge, Judi Sandrock, Charles Seashore, Dave Snowden, Milton Sousa, Michael Stankosky, Tom Stewart, Michael J.D. Sutton, Karl-Erik Sveiby, Doug Weidner, Steve Weineke, Etienne Wenger-Trayner and Karl Wiig.

There are very special people who assisted in ensuring the quality of this work. Kathy Claypatch with Ageless Wisdom Publishers served as a conduit to assure consistency with that work; Ginny Ramos, a rehabilitation counselor and Alex's daughter, served in the role of editor; and four readers played instrumental roles in assuring consistent and understandable concepts. These are Joyce Avedisian, Susan Dreiband, Denise Sumner and Deb Tobiasson, all knowledgeable explorers in the journey of life.

A special thanks to our families who ground us: from David to Steve, Melanie, John, Cindy, Jackson, Rick, Chris and the grandchildren that help to keep us young; from Alex to Ginny, Bill and Andrew and her long-lost new family; from Arthur to Joy, Cath and Helen; from Theresa to Barbara and Jay, as well as to Dennis H. and Gudni G. and her MMS friends and family; and from John to Mary, Shannon and Jonathan. Thank you to all our friends who support this work in so many ways, and who have supported Mountain Quest since its 2001 beginnings. And our continuing thankfulness to Cindy Taylor and Theresa Halterman, part of our MQI Team, and for our son Andrew Dean, who keeps Mountain Quest running while we play with thoughts and words and dive into the abyss of the unknown.

With Appreciation and Love, Alex, David, Arthur, Theresa and John.

Preface

As we move in and out of life situations, there are verbal cues, often conveyed by signs, that catch our attention and somehow miraculously remain in memory throughout our lives, popping in and out as truisms. Although we may not realize how true they were at the time, one of those sayings in an early office setting was: "Change. Your life depends on it!" Then, some 10 years later, a sign appearing on the check-in desk of the dental clinic on Yokosuka Naval Base, clearly referring to our teeth, read: "Ignore them, and they will go away."

So often we feel like victims, with some new challenge emerging from here or there, something interrupting our best laid plans, some stress or weight that sprouts discomfort or confusion. Yet we have a choice to be pulled along into the fray, dive into the flow and fully participate in the decisions and actions, or even to be the wave-setters, co-creating the reality within which we live and breathe.

Never in the history of humanity has the *need to change* so clearly manifested itself into our everyday existence. While the potential for catastrophic destruction has loomed over us since the mid-20th century, we are still *here*, admittedly a world in turmoil on all fronts—plagued with economic, political, eco-system, social, cultural and religious fragmentation—but also a humanity that is awakening to our true potential and power. Just learning how to co-evolve with an increasingly changing, uncertain and complex external environment, we are now beginning to recognize that it is the change available *within* our internal environment *and energetic connections to each other and the larger whole* that offer up an invitation to an incluessent future, that state of Being far beyond the small drop of previous possibility accepted as true, far beyond that which we have known to dream (Dunning, 2015).

In this work, we introduce the overarching concepts of **profundity** and **bifurcation** as related to change. Profundity comes from the Old French term *profundite* which emerges from the late Latin term *profunditas* or *profundus*, meaning profound (Encarta, 1999). Profundity insinuates an intellectual complexity leading to great understanding, perceptiveness and knowledge. There is a focus on greatness in terms of strength and intensity and in depth of thought. We believe that the times in which we live and the opportunity to shape the future of humanity demand that each of us look within, recognizing and utilizing the amazing gifts of our human mind and heart to shape a new world.

Bifurcation comes from the Latin root word *bifurcare*, which literally means to fork, that is, split and branch off into two separate parts (Encarta, 1999). In terms of change, this concept alludes to a pending decision for each decision-maker, each human, and perhaps humanity at large. We live in two worlds, one based on what we understand from Newtonian Physics and one based on what we don't understand but are able to speculate and feel about the Quantum Field. As change continues with every breath we take and every action we make, there is choice as to how we engage our role as co-creator of reality.

In this book, we explore very different ways to create change, each building on the former. There is no right or wrong—choice is a matter of the lessons we are learning and the growth we are seeking—yet it is clear that there is a split ahead where we will need to choose our way forward. One road continues the journey that has been punctuated by physical dominance, bureaucracy, hard competition and a variety of power scenarios. A second road, historically less-traveled, recognizes the connections among all humans, embracing the value of individuation and diversity as a contribution to the collective whole and the opportunities offered through creative imagination. This is the road that recognizes the virtues of inclusiveness and truth and the power of love and beauty, and moves us along the flow representing Quantum entanglement.

A number of themes are woven throughout this work; for example, the idea of "NOW", the use of forces as a tool for growth, the power of patterns, earned and revealed intuition, bisociation and creativity, stuck energy and flow, the search for truth, and so many more. We take a consilience approach, tapping into a deep array of research in knowledge and learning, with specific reference to recent neuroscience understanding that is emerging, pointing the reader to additional resources. And we look to psychology, physics, cell biology, systems and complexity, cognitive theory, social theory and spirituality for their contributions. Humans are holistic, that is, the physical, mental, emotional and intuitional are all at play and working together. Recognize that you are part of one entangled intelligent complex adaptive learning system (Bennet et al., 2015b), each overlapping and affecting the other, whether consciously or unconsciously, in every instant of life. As we move from science to philosophy, facts to psychology, management to poetry, and words to pictures, you will no doubt feel a tugging in the mind/brain, and perhaps some confusion. Such was the case for one of the authors when studying micro-economics and Shakespeare tragedies back to back! The good news is that this can result in a great deal of expansion and availability of a wide variety of frames of reference from which to process incoming information.

Through the past half a century, all of the authors have engaged in extensive research—much of it experiential in nature—which has led us to break through life-long perceived limits and shift and expand our beliefs about Life and the world of which we are a part. The advent of self-publishing virtual books has opened the door to share this learning globally. The concepts forwarded in the earlier works of all of the authors lay the foundation for this book.

While this book is quite large, it wrote itself. In the movie Amadeus (1984), when a complaint is lodged against his work saying there are just too many notes, Mozart responds that there are just exactly as many notes as are needed. In this book, there are exactly as many chapters as are needed, no more, no less. As you move through the information and concepts available in this text, we ask that you stay open to new ideas, ways of thinking and perceiving, and—using the discernment and discretion emerging from your unique life experiences—reflect on how these ideas might fit into your personal theory of the world. It is our hope that these ideas will serve as triggers for a greater expansion of thought and consciousness, which every individual brings to the larger understanding of who we are and how, together as One, we operate in the world.

To begin, we offer the following assumptions:

Assumption 1: Everything—at least in our physical reality—is energy and patterns of energy. We live in a vast field of energy in which we are continuously exchanging information, which is a form of energy.

Assumption 2: Creativity—nurtured by freedom, purpose and choice—is a primary urge of the human. Knowledge serves as an action lever for co-creating our experiences.

Assumption 3: Knowledge is partial and incomplete. Knowledge produces forces, whether those forces are used to push forward an idea that benefits humanity, or whether those forces are to push against another's beliefs and values (knowledge), which can escalate to warfare.

Assumption 4: The human mind is an associative patterner, that is, continuously re-creating knowledge for the situation at hand. Knowledge exists in the human brain in the form of stored or expressed neural patterns that may be selected, activated, mixed and/or reflected upon through thought. Incoming information is associated with stored information. From this mixing process, new patterns are created that may represent understanding, meaning and the capacity to anticipate (to various degrees) the results of potential actions. Thus, knowledge is context sensitive and situation dependent, with the mind continuously growing, restructuring and creating increased organization (information) and knowledge for the moment at hand.

Assumption 5: The unconscious mind has a vast store of tacit knowledge available to us. It has only been in the past few decades that cognitive psychology and neuroscience have begun to seriously explore unconscious mental life. Polanyi felt that tacit knowledge consisted of *a range* of conceptual and sensory information and images that could be used to make sense of a situation or event (Hodgkin, 1991; Smith, 2003). He was right. The unconscious mind is incredibly powerful, on the order of 700,000 times more processing speed than the conscious stream of thought.

The challenge is to make better use of our tacit knowledge through creating greater connections with the unconscious, building and expanding the resources stored in the unconscious, deepening areas of resonance, connecting to the larger information field, and learning how to share our tacit resources with each other.

Assumption 6: People are multidimensional, and rarely do they hold to a single belief, a consistent logic, or a specific worldview. As identified in the recent model of experiential learning (Bennet et al, 2015b), there are five primary modes of thinking, each of us with our preferences—concrete experience, reflective observation, abstract conceptualization, active experimentation and social engagement—and each of us has a dozen or more subpersonalities offering a variety of diverse thoughts and feelings that rise to the occasion when triggered by our external and internal environments (Bennet et al., 2015a). *The human experience is a neuronal dance with the Universe, with each of us in the driver's seat selecting our partners and directing our dance steps.*

Assumption 7: We are social creatures who live in an entangled world; our brains are linked together. We are in continuous interaction with those around us, and the brain is continuously changing in response. Thus, in our expanded state we are both individuated and One, bringing all our diversity into collaborative play for the greater good of humanity.

Assumption 8: We live in times of extreme change in the human mind and body, in human-developed systems, and of the Earth, our human host. Through advances in science and technology, most of what we need to learn and thrive in these times is already available. We need only to open our minds and hearts to the amazing potential of our selfs.

There are still vast workings of the human mind and its connections to higher-order energies that we do not understand. The limitations we as humans place on our capacities and capabilities are created from past reference points that have been developed primarily through the rational and logical workings of the mechanical functioning of our mind/brain, an understanding that has come through extensive intellectual effort. Yet we now recognize that *knowledge is a living form of information*, tailored by our minds specifically for situations at hand. The totality of knowledge can no easier be codified and stored than our feelings, nor would it be highly beneficial to do so in a changing and uncertain environment. Thus, in this book, given the limitations of our own perceptions and understanding, we do not even pretend to cover the vast amount of information and knowledge available in the many fields connected to change. We *do* choose to consider and explore areas and phenomena that move beyond our paradigms and beliefs into the larger arena of knowing, and to move beyond the activity of our cognitive functions to consider the larger energy patterns within which humanity is immersed.

This extensive book is initially being published in five Parts as five separate books, which will be available in both kindle (from Amazon) and PDF (from MQIPress) formats. In support of the Intelligent Social Change Journey, these Parts are:

Part I: Laying the Groundwork

Part II: Learning from the Past

Part III: Learning in the Present

Part IV: Co-Creating the Future

Part V: Living in the Future

Each part has a separate focus, yet they work together to support your full engagement in the Intelligent Social Change Journey. A Table of Contents for all five parts is Appendix B. An overarching model of the ISCJ is Appendix A. This model can also be downloaded for A4 printing at the following location: www.mqipress.net

Workshops on all five Parts of *The Profundity and Bifurcation of Change* or, specifically, on The Intelligent Social Change Journey facilitated by the authors are available. Contact alex@mountainquestinstitute.com ... arthur.shelley@rmit.edu.au ... Theresa@quantumleapalchemy.com ... or John@ExplanationAge.com

The Drs. Alex and David Bennet live at the Mountain Quest Institute, Inn and Retreat Center situated on a 430-acre farm in the Allegheny Mountains of West Virginia. See www.mountainquestinn.com and www.mountainquestinstitute.com They may be reached at alex@mountainquestinstitute.com Dr. Arthur Shelley is the originator of *The Organizational Zoo*, Dr. Theresa Bullard is the Founder of the Quantra Leadership Academy as well as an International Instructor for the Modern Mystery School, and Dr. John Lewis is author of *The Explanation Age.* Taking a consilience approach, this eclectic group builds on corroborated resources in a diversity of fields while simultaneously pushing the edge of thought, hopefully beyond your comfort zone, for that is where our journey begins.

Introduction to
The Intelligent Social Change Journey

The Intelligent Social Change Journey (ISCJ) is a developmental journey of the body, mind and heart, moving from the heaviness of cause-and-effect linear extrapolations, to the fluidity of co-evolving with our environment, to the lightness of breathing our thought and feelings into reality. Grounded in development of our mental faculties, these are phase changes, each building on and expanding previous learning in our movement toward intelligent activity.

We are on this journey together. This is very much a *social* journey. Change does not occur in isolation. The deeper our understanding in relationship to others, the easier it is to move into the future. The quality of sympathy is needed as we navigate the linear, cause-and-effect characteristics of Phase 1. The quality of empathy is needed to navigate the co-evolving liquidity of Phase 2. The quality of compassion is needed to navigate the connected breath of the Phase 3 creative leap. See the figure below.

In the progression of learning to navigate change represented by the three phases of the ISCJ, we empower our selfs, individuating and expanding. In the process, we become immersed in the human experience, a neuronal dance with the Universe, with each of us in the driver's seat selecting our partners and directing our dance steps. Let's explore that journey a bit deeper.

In Phase 1 of the Journey, *Learning from the Past*, we act on the physical and the physical changes; we "see" the changes with our sense of form, and therefore they are real. Causes have effects. Actions have consequences, both directly and indirectly, and sometimes delayed. Phase 1 reinforces the characteristics of how we interact with the simplest aspects of our world. The elements are predictable and repeatable and make us feel comfortable because we know what to expect and how to prepare for them. While these parts of the world do exist, our brain tends to automate the thinking around them and we do them with little conscious effort. The challenge with this is that they only remain predictable if all the causing influences remain constant ... and that just doesn't happen in the world of today! The linear cause-and-effect phase of the ISCJ (Phase 1) calls for sympathy. Supporting and caring for the people involved in the change helps to mitigate the force of resistance, improving the opportunity for successful outcomes.

As we expand toward Phase 2, we begin to recognize patterns; they emerge from experiences that repeat over and over. Recognition of patterns enables us to

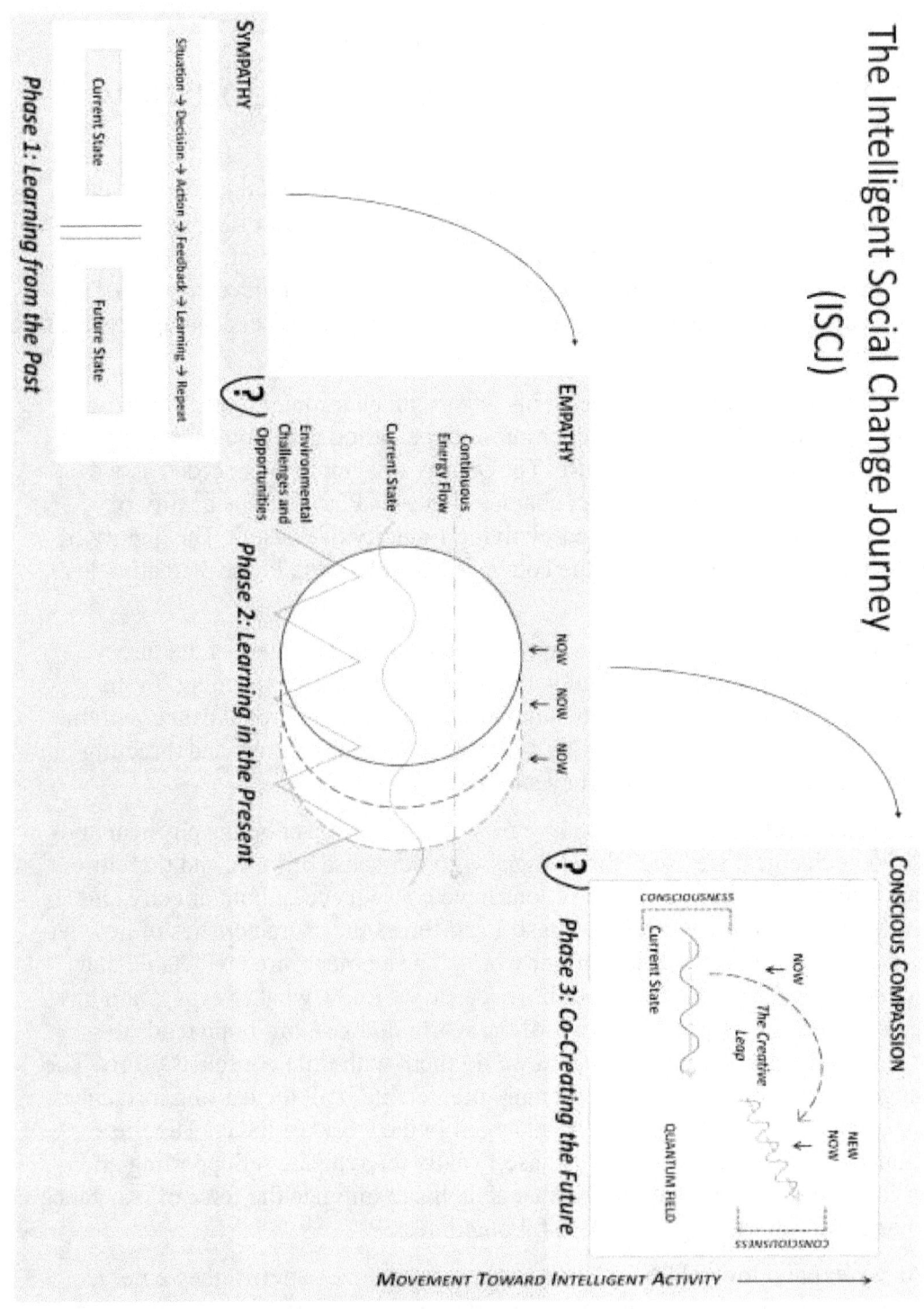

Figure ISCJ-1. *The Baseline Model.*

"see" (in our mind's eye) the relationship of events in terms of time and space, moving us out of an action and reaction mode into a position of co-evolving with our environment, and enabling us to better navigate a world full of diverse challenges and opportunities. It is at this stage that we move from understanding based on past cause-and-effect reactions to how things come together, to produce new things both in the moment at hand and at a future point in time.

Phase 2, *Learning in the Present*, takes us to the next level of thinking and feeling about how we interact with our world, including the interesting area of human social interactions. Although complex, the somewhat recognizable patterns enable us to explore and progress through uncertainty and the unknown, making life more interesting and enjoyable. In Phase 2 patterns grow into concepts, higher mental thought, and we begin the search for a higher level of truth. Sustainability in the co-evolving state of Phase 2 requires empathy, which provides a direct understanding of another individual, and a heightened awareness of the context of their lives and their desires and needs in the moment at hand. While not yet achieving the creative leap of the intuitional (represented in Phase 3), we are clearly developing higher mental faculties and instinctive knowledge of the workings of the Universe, which helps cultivate intuition and develop insights in service to our self and society.

The creative leap of Phase 3, *Co-Creating the Future*, requires the ability to tap into the larger intuitional field that energetically connects all people. This can only be accomplished when energy is focused outward in service to the larger whole, requiring a deeper connection to others. Compassion deepens that connection. Thus, each phase of the Intelligent Social Change Journey calls for an increasing depth of connection to others, moving from sympathy to empathy to compassion.

<<<<<<<>>>>>>>

INSIGHT: **Each phase of the Intelligent Social Change Journey calls for an increasing depth of connection to others, moving from sympathy to empathy to compassion.**

<<<<<<<>>>>>>>

The ISCJ Baseline Model accents the phase changes as each phase builds on/expands from the previous phase. As the journeyer moves from Phase 1 to Phase 2 and prepares for the creative leap of Phase 3, the mental faculties are developing, the senses are coming into balance, and there are deepening connections to others. This will feel familiar to many travelers, for this is the place where we began. The model shows our journey is a significant change of mind, body and spirit as we operate on different cognitive and emotional planes as we progress through the developmental phases. Some people are aware of the changes they are undergoing and seek to accelerate the learning, while others resist the development, hoping (perhaps somewhat naively) to simplify the way they interact with the world.

Babies are born connected, to their mothers and families, and to the larger energies surrounding them and within them. This represents Phase 3. As one author exclaimed when exploring this reversal of the Phase 1, 2 and 3 models, "This really brings it all together for me. There is something that we admire in babies that we would like to become, and this framework makes sense of that feeling." If, and when, we return to Phase 3 in the round-trip journey of life, it will be with experience in our backpack and development of the mental faculties under our cap.

Sometime around the fourth grade, as most grade school teachers will attest, the ego pokes its head out, and, through social interactions, the process of individuation has begun, with a focus on, and experiencing in, the NOW. This represents Phase 2 of our change model, a state of co-evolving. In the pre-adolescent child, intuitional connections are subsumed by a physical focus accompanied by emotional flare-ups as the child is immersed in learning experiences, interacting and learning from and with their environment.

By the time the mid-teens come around, the world has imposed a level of order and limits, with a focus on cause-and-effect. In some families and cultures this may take the form of physical, mental or emotional manipulation and control, always related to cause-and-effect. If you do that, this will happen. For others, cultural or religious aspects of expectations and punishment may lead to the cause-and-effect focus. For the mid-teen perceived as overactive and unruly in the schoolroom, the limiting forces may be imposed through Ritalin or other drugs, which may have even started at a much earlier age. Regardless of how it is achieved, learning from the past—the Phase 1 model—becomes the starting point of our lives as we move into adulthood. From this starting point, we begin to develop our mental faculties.

The Overarching ISCJ Model

To help connect the dots, we have prepared a larger version of the Intelligent Social Change Journey, which is at Appendix A. The Overarching ISCJ Model focuses on the relationships of the phases with other aspects of the journey. For example, three critical movements during our journey, consistent with our movement through the phases, are reflected in expanded consciousness, reduction of forces and increased intelligent activity. *Consciousness* is considered a state of awareness and a private, selective and continuous change process, a sequential set of ideas, thoughts, images, feelings and perceptions and an understanding of the connections and relationships among them and our self. *Forces* occur when one type of energy affects another type of energy in a way such that they are moving in different directions, pressing against each other. Bounded (inward focused) and/or limited knowledge creates forces.

Intelligent activity represents a state of interaction where intent, purpose, direction, values and expected outcomes are clearly understood and communicated among all parties, reflecting wisdom and achieving a higher truth. We will repeat this definition where appropriate throughout the book.

<<<<<<<>>>>>>>

INSIGHT: **The ISCJ is a journey toward intelligent activity, which is a state of interaction where intent, purpose, direction, values and expected outcomes are clearly understood and communicated among all parties, reflecting wisdom and achieving a higher truth.**

<<<<<<<>>>>>>>

Immediately below each phase of the Overarching ISCJ model are characteristics related to each phase. These are words or short phrases representing some of the ideas that will be developed in each section supporting each phase. **Phase 1**, *Learning from the Past*, characteristics are: linear and sequential, repeatability, engaging past learning, starting from current state, and cause and effect relationship. **Phase 2**, *Learning in the Present*, characteristics are: Recognition of patterns; social interaction; and co-evolving with the environment through continuous learning, quick response, robustness, flexibility, adaptability and alignment. **Phase 3**, *Co-Creating Our Future*, characteristics are: Creative imagination, recognition of global Oneness, mental in service to the intuitive; balancing senses; bringing together time (the past, present and future); knowing; beauty; and wisdom.

Still exploring the overarching model, at the lower part of the graphic we see three areas related to knowledge in terms of the nature of knowledge, areas of reflection, and cognitive shifts necessary for each phase of change. For ease of reference, we have also included the content of these three areas in Table ISCJ-1.

In Phase 1, *Learning from the Past*, the nature of knowledge is characterized as a product of the past and, as we will learn in Chapter 2, knowledge is context sensitive and situation dependent, and partial and incomplete. Reflection during this phase of change is on reviewing the interactions and feedback, and determining cause-and-effect relationships. There is an inward focus, and a questioning of decisions and actions as reflected in the questions: What did I intend? What really happened? Why were there differences? What would I do the same? What would I do differently? The cognitive shifts that are underway during this phase include: (1) recognition of the importance of feedback; (2) the ability to recognize systems and the impact of external forces; (3) recognition and location of "me" in the larger picture (building conscious awareness); and (4) pattern recognition and concept development. These reflections are critical to enabling the phase change to *co-evolving*.

In Phase 2, *Learning in the Present*, the nature of knowledge is characterized in terms of expanded cooperation and collaboration, and knowledge sharing and social learning. There is also the conscious *questioning of why*, and the *pursuit of truth*. Reflection includes a deepening of conceptual thinking and, through cooperation and collaboration, the ability to connect the power of diversity and individuation to the larger whole. There is an increasing outward focus, with the recognition of different world views and the exploration of information from different perspectives, and expanded knowledge capacities. Cognitive shifts that are underway include: (1) the ability to recognize and apply patterns at all levels within a domain of knowledge to predict outcomes; (2) a growing understanding of complexity; (3) increased connectedness of choices, recognition of direction you are heading, and expanded meaning-making; and (4) an expanded ability to bisociate ideas resulting in increased creativity.

In Phase 3, *Co-Creating Our Future*, the nature of knowledge is characterized as a recognition that with knowledge comes responsibility. There is a conscious pursuit of larger truth, and knowledge is selectively used as a measure of effectiveness. Reflection includes the valuing of creative ideas, asking the larger questions: How does this idea serve humanity? Are there any negative consequences? There is an openness to other's ideas, a questioning with humility: What if this idea is right? Are my beliefs or other mental models limiting my thought? Are hidden assumptions or feelings interfering with intelligent activity?

Cognitive shifts that are underway include: (1) a sense and knowing of Oneness; (2) development of both the lower (logic) and upper (conceptual) mental faculties, which work in concert with the emotional guidance system; (3) recognition of self as a co-creator of reality; (4) the ability to engage in intelligent activity; and (5) a developing ability to tap into the intuitional plane at will.

Time and space play a significant role in the phase changes. Using Jung's psychological type classifications, feelings come from the past, sensations occur in the present, intuition is oriented to the future, and thinking embraces the past, present *and* future. Forecasting and visioning work is done at a point of change (McHale, 1977) when a balance is struck continuously between short-term and long-term survival. Salk (1973) describes this as a shift from Epoch A, dominated by ego and short-term considerations, to Epoch B, where both *Being and ego co-exist*. In the ISCJ, this shift occurs somewhere in Phase 2, with Beingness advancing as we journey toward Phase 3. Considerable focus to time and space occurs later in the book (Chapter 16/Part III).

Phase of the Intelligent Social Change Journey	ISCJ: Nature of Knowledge	ISCJ: Points of Reflection	ISCJ: Cognitive Shifts
PHASE 1: Cause and Effect (Requires Sympathy) • Linear, and Sequential • Repeatable • Engaging past learning • Starting from current state • Causal relationships	• A product of the past • Knowledge is context-sensitive and situation-dependent • Knowledge is partial and incomplete	• Reviewing the interactions and feedback • Determining cause-and-effect relationships; logic • Inward focus • Questioning of decisions and actions: What did I intend? What really happened? why were there differences? What would I do the same? What would I do differently?	• Recognition of the importance of feedback • Ability to recognize systems and the impact of external forces • Recognition and location of "me" in the larger picture (building conscious awareness) • Beginning pattern recognition and early concept development
PHASE 2: Co-Evolving (Requires Empathy) • Recognition of patterns • Social interaction • Co-evolving with environment through continuous learning, quick response, robustness, flexibility, adaptability, alignment.	• Engaging knowledge sharing and social learning • Engaging cooperation and collaboration • Questioning of why? • Pursuit of truth	• Deeper development of conceptual thinking (higher mental thought) • Through cooperation and collaboration ability to connect the power of diversity and individuation to the larger whole • Outward focus • Recognition of different world views and exploration of information from different perspectives • Expanded knowledge capacities	• The ability to recognize and apply patterns at all levels within a domain of knowledge to predict outcomes • A growing understanding of complexity • Increased connectedness of choices • Recognition of direction you are heading • Expanded meaning-making • Expanded ability to bisociate ideas resulting in increased creativity
PHASE 3: Creative Leap (Requires Compassion) • Creative imagination • Recognition of global Oneness • Mental in service to the intuitive • Balancing senses • Bringing together past, present and future • Knowing; Beauty; Wisdom	• Recognition that with knowledge comes responsibility • Conscious pursuit of larger truth • Knowledge selectively used as a measure of effectiveness	• Valuing of creative ideas • Asking the larger questions: How does this idea serve humanity? Are there any negative consequences? • Openness to other's ides; questioning with humility: What if this idea is right Are my beliefs or other mental models limiting my thought? Are hidden assumptions or feelings interfering with intelligent activity?	• A sense and knowing of Oneness • Development of both the lower (logic) and upper (conceptual) mental faculties, which work in concert with the emotional guidance system • Applies patterns across domains of knowledge for greater good • recognition of self as a co-creator of reality • The ability to engage in intelligent activity • Developing the ability to tap into the intuitional plane at will

Table ISCJ-Table 1. *The three Phases from the viewpoints of the nature of knowledge, points of reflection and cognitive shifts.*

Cognitive-Based Ordering of Change

As a cognitive-based ordering of change, we forward the concept of logical levels of learning consistent with levels of change developed by anthropologist Gregory Bateson (1972) based on the work in logic and mathematics of Bertrand Russell. This logical typing was both a mathematical theory and a law of nature, recognizing long before neuroscience research findings confirmed the relationship of the mind/brain which show that we literally create our reality, with thought affecting the physical structure of the brain, and the physical structure of the brain affecting thought.

Bateson's levels of change range from simplistic habit formation (which he calls Learning I) to large-scale change in the evolutionary process of the human (which he calls Learning IV), with each higher-level synthesizing and organizing the levels below it, and thus creating a greater impact on people and organizations. This is a hierarchy of logical levels, ordered groupings within a system, with the implication that as the levels reach toward the source or beginning **there is a sacredness, power or importance informing this hierarchy of values** (Dilts, 2003). This structure is consistent with the phase changes of the Intelligent Social Change Journey.

<<<<<<<>>>>>>>

INSIGHT: **Similar to Bateson's levels of change, each higher phase of the Intelligent Social Change Journey synthesizes and organizes the levels below it, thus creating a greater impact in interacting with the world.**

<<<<<<<>>>>>>>

With Learning 0 representing the status quo, a particular behavioral response to a specific situation, Learning I (first-order change) is stimulus-response conditioning (cause-and-effect change), which includes learning simple skills such as walking, eating, driving, and working. These basic skills are pattern forming, becoming habits, which occur through repetitiveness without conceptualizing the content. For example, we don't have to understand concepts of motion and movement in order to learn to walk. Animals engage in Learning I. Because it is not necessary to understand the concepts, or underlying theories, no questions of reality are raised. Learning I occurs in Phase 1 of the ISCJ.

Learning II (second-order change) is deuteron learning and includes creation, or a change of context inclusive of new images or concepts, or shifts the understanding of, and connections among, existing concepts such that meaning may be interpreted. These changes are based on mental constructs that *depend on a sense of reality* (McWhinney, 1997). While these concepts may represent real things, relations or qualities, they also may be symbolic, specifically created for the situation at hand.

Either way, they provide the means for reconstructing existing concepts, using one reality to modify another, from which new ways of thinking and behaviors emerge. Argyris and Schon's (1978) concept of double loop learning reflects Level II change. Learning II occurs in Phase 2 of the ISCJ.

Learning III (third-order change) requires thinking beyond our current logic, calling us to change our system of beliefs and values, and offering different sets of alternatives from which choices can be made. Suggesting that Learning III is learning about the concepts used in Learning II, Bateson says,

> In transcending the promises and habits of Learning II, one will gain "a freedom from its bondages," bondages we characterize, for example, as "drive," "dependency," "pride," and "fatalism." One might learn to change the premises acquired by Learning II and to readily choose among the roles through which we express concepts and thus the "self." Learning III is driven by the "contraries" generated in the contexts of Learning I and II. (Bateson, 1972, pp. 301-305)

<<<<<<<>>>>>>>

INSIGHT: **There is a freedom that occurs as we leave behind the thinking patterns of Phase 2 and open to the new choices and discoveries of Phase 3.**

<<<<<<<>>>>>>>

Similarly, Berman (1981, p. 346) defines Learning III as, "an experience in which a person suddenly realizes the arbitrary nature of his or her own paradigm." This is the breaking open of our personal mental models, our current logic, losing the differential of subject/object, blending into connection while simultaneously following pathways of diverse belief systems. Learning III occurs as we move into Phase 3 of the ISCJ.

Learning IV deals with revolutionary change, getting outside the system to look at the larger system of systems, awakening to something completely new, different, unique and transformative. This is the space of *incluessence*, a future state far beyond that which we know to dream (Dunning, 2015). As Bateson described this highest level of change:

> The individual mind is immanent but not only in the body. It is immanent in pathways and messages outside the body; and there is a larger Mind of which the individual mind is only a sub-system. This larger Mind is comparable to God and is perhaps what people mean by "God," but it is still immanent in the total interconnected social system and planetary ecology. (Bateson, 1972, p. 465)

Table ISCJ-2 below is a comparison of the Phases of the Intelligent Social Change Journey and the four Levels of Learning espoused by Bateson (1972) based on the work in logic and mathematics of Bertrand Russell, and supported by Argyris and Schon (1978), Berman (1981), and McWhinney (1997).

Phase of the Intelligent Social Change Journey	Level of Learning [NOTE: LEARNING 0 represents the status quo; a behavioral response to a specific situation.]
PHASE 1: Cause and Effect (Requires Sympathy) • Linear, and Sequential • Repeatable • Engaging past learning • Starting from current state • Cause and effect relationships	**LEARNING i:** (First order change) • Stimulus-response conditioning • Incudes learning simple skills such as walking, eating, driving and working • Basic skills are pattern forming, becoming habits occurring through repetitiveness without conceptualizing the content • No questions of reality
PHASE 2: Co-Evolving (Requires Empathy) • Recognition of patterns • Social interaction • Co-evolving with environment through continuous learning, quick response, robustness, flexibility, adaptability, alignment	**LEARNING II (Deutero Learning)** (Second order change) • Includes creation or change of context inclusive of new images or concepts • Shifts the understanding of, and connections among, existing concepts such that meaning may be interpreted • Based on mental constructions that depend on a sense of reality
[Moving into Phase 3] **PHASE 3: Creative Leap** (Requires Compassion) • Creative imagination • Recognition of global Oneness • Mental in service to the intuitive • Balancing senses • Bringing together past, present and future • Knowing; Beauty; Wisdom	**LEARNING III:** (Third order change) • Thinking beyond current logic • Changing our system of beliefs and values • Different sets of alternatives from which choices can be made • Freedom from bondages **LEARNINNG IV:** • Revolutionary change • Getting outside the system to look at the larger system of systems • Awakening to something completely new, different, unique and transformative • Tapping into the large Mind of which the individual mind is a sub-system

Table ISCJ-Table 2. *Comparison of Phases of the ISCJ with Levels of Learning.*

An example of Learning IV is Buddha's use of intuitional thought to understand others. He used his ability to think in greater and greater ways to help people cooperate and share together, and think better. Learning IV is descriptive of controlled intuition in support of the creative leap in Phase 3 of the ISCJ, perhaps moving beyond what we can comprehend at this point in time, perhaps deepening the connections of sympathy, empathy and compassion to unconditional love.

How to Best Use this Material

This book has, quite purposefully, been chunked into five smaller books, referred to as Parts, which are both independent and interdependent. Chunking is a methodology for learning. The way people become experts involves the chunking of ideas and concepts and creating understanding through development of significant patterns useful for identifying opportunities, solving problems and anticipating future behavior within the focused domain of knowledge. Figure ISCJ-2 shows the relationship of the Parts of this book and their content to the Intelligent Social Change Journey. *Remember*: the ISCJ is a journey of expansion, with each Phase building on—and inclusive of—the former Phase as we develop our mental faculties in service to the intuitional, and move closer to intelligent activity. As such, one needs to experience the earlier phases in order to elevate to the upper levels. Early life experiences and educational development during these earlier stages create the foundation and capacity to develop into higher levels of interactions and ways of being.

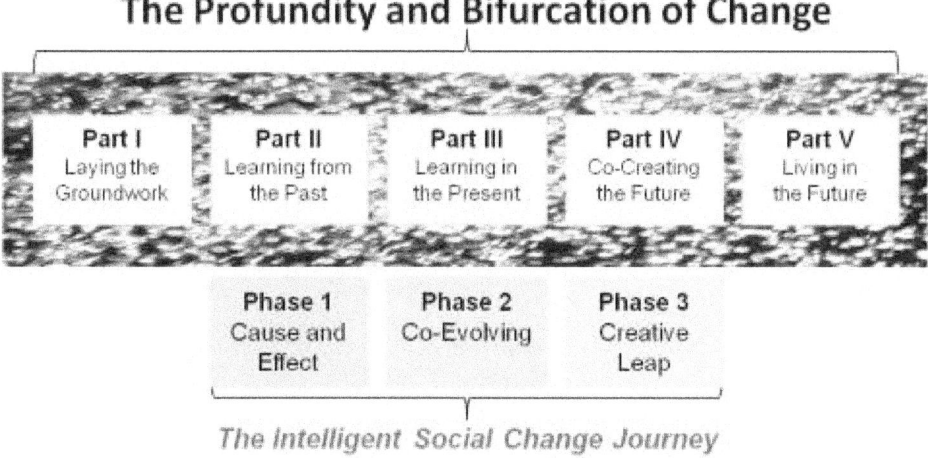

Figure ISCJ-2. *Relationship of Parts and Phases of the ISCJ.*

While many different ideas have been introduced in the paragraphs of this Introduction to the Intelligent Social Change Journey, you will discover that all of these ideas are addressed in depth during the course of this book, and each Part is inclusive of tools, references, insights and reflective questions provided in support of your personal learning journey. We also cross-reference, both within the Parts, and across all of the Parts.

This is a journey, and as such *the learning is in the journey*, the reflecting on and application of the learning, not in achieving a particular capability or entering the next Phase at a specific point in time. Similar to the deepening of relationships with others, the growth of understanding and expansion of consciousness takes its own time, twisting and curving forwards and backwards until we have learned all we can from one frame of reference, and then jump to another to continue our personal journey. That said, we suggest that those who are impatient to know the topics within this book, but reluctant to read such an extended text, jump to Chapter 11/Part III, which provides readiness assessment statements and related characteristics reflecting the high-level content of this book.

For your reference, the Overarching ISCJ model can be downloaded for printing in A3 format at www.MQIPress.net The corresponding author may be reached at alex@mountainquestinstitute.com

PART V

Living the Future

Introduction to Part V

By now we all agree that we are far more than our physical body, and we've explored our energetic connections and the power of our thoughts and emotions. While experiencing in the physical, we are simultaneously focused on the mental, feeling (and sometimes emoting) the gifts of the emotional plane, and, when we are open to it, sensing the "forever" energy of the spiritual swirling within and without. We also recognize that our mind/brain is continuously selecting, integrating and complexing streams of incoming information through our five senses of form and two primary inner senses, all operating on the physical, mental and emotional planes. As we become more of the co-creators that we are, we also have greater access to the intuitional plane.

Moving into a future of choice, let's take a few minutes to review our journey as multidimensional beings through the lens of the three phases of the Intelligent Social Change Journey. Now, you probably think we're going to start with the Phase 1 cause-and-effect, linear stream, logic-focused change model. Nope. We're going to start at Phase 3, only, if truth be told and as hinted along the path, that *IS* where we as humans started! If you've read the introduction in previous books, then you know where we are going with this. Babies are born connected to their mothers and families, and to the larger energies surrounding them and within them. This represents Phase 3. Sometime around the fourth grade, there is a focus on social interaction in the NOW, which represents Phase 2. Then, as the mid-teens come round, the world has imposed limits with a focus on cause-and-effect, which represents Phase 1. As we move into adulthood we begin the Intelligent Social Change Journey at Phase 1 in order to, through experience, more fully develop our mental faculties in support of expanding consciousness.

From the frame of reference of biogeochemistry emerging from the work of Vernadsky (1998), and bringing in our understanding of the Noosphere, during the ISCJ we expand our focus from the geosphere (the physical, spherical regions of matter making up the Earth) to the biosphere (Earth system supporting and part of living organisms) to the Noosphere (thought and consciousness). Through this lens we recognize that life is a geological force which literally changes Earth's landforms, climate and atmosphere (Vernadsky, 1998). With ever-deepening connections to others, if and when we return to Phase 3 in the round-trip journey of life, it will be with experience of the physical world in our backpack and development of the mental faculties under our cap. See the Introduction to the ISCJ for a deeper discussion of this cycle. (See also Figure 38-1 in Chapter 38.)

<<<<<<<>>>>>>>

INSIGHT: **If and when we return to Phase 3 in the round-trip journey of life, it will be with experience of the physical in our backpack and development of the mental faculties under our cap.**

<<<<<<<>>>>>>>

Giving Yourself Permission

In this developmental Journey, choice becomes more and more important. This is not just the choice of interactivity with the world, but the choice of who we are and how we think and feel. (See Chapter 26/Part IV on The Mental Fabric and Chapter 19/Part III on emotions as a Guidance System.)

As a tool of self-development, "giving yourself permission" has been a technique used by psychologists for many years, although more recently the value of the technique has become recognized by the general public, and books related to this concept have emerged in the popular press. Giving yourself permission is an intentional act. While it requires letting go of the past in terms of paradigms, mental models, behaviors, etc., it is far more than letting go. Recall in the calibrated levels of consciousness identified by Hawkins (2002) that there was a level that represented "neutrality", which rose from "courage" and was followed by "willingness." Thus, "letting go" precedes the setting of intent. This same progression is a part of presencing, that which occurs between "letting go" and "letting come" (see Chapter 22/Part IV).

Murray (2013) says giving yourself permission is *allowing yourself to confront and push against the brink of what you've been conditioned to believe are your limits in thought, belief, skill, and resources*. This statement gets right to the crux of the issue. The permission we refer to is permission to break through past conditioning AND *move beyond perceived limits*, with a specific focus on thoughts and beliefs, and the actions driven by those thoughts and beliefs.

When we are young we seek permission from parents, teachers, and others playing authoritative roles in our lives. Then, seeking permission transforms into "asking the boss" or "checking in with the spouse." Even if there is no question about the activity in which you are choosing to engage or that for which you are seeking permission, *there's a sense of freedom that comes with seeking permission*. For example, in a work situation, while you may have lots of leave, asking permission to take that leave at a specific time enables planning so that there is no disruption of work flow. When such is the case, there is no need to worry about things at the office while you are on vacation. Similarly, asking permission of your spouse to go to a poker night or on a shopping spree is a way of ensuring there are no family plans during that time, or time-sensitive issues that need to be resolved at home.

Much like the power of positive affirmations, the very act of focusing required by giving yourself permission is a strong step toward accomplishing the desired behaviors or feelings. For example, reflect on those things that might make your life a bit brighter, and write them down in terms of permissions: I give myself permission to play ... I give myself permission to laugh at myself ... I give myself permission to take a nap ... I give myself permission to be happy ... I give myself permission to say "no"... and so forth. The clarity of writing these statements helps bring them into focus. Once in your focus (attention), now you can purposefully *set your intention* to act accordingly. (See Chapter 25/Part IV on Attention and Intention.) However, giving yourself permission moves beyond the power of affirmations because it includes acknowledgement that *YOU are the co-creator of your life*, that YOU have the power to shift and change your feelings and activities.

###############

A Reflective Moment

As introduced in Chapter 17/Part III, one of the main jobs of consciousness is to tie our life together into a coherent story, a concept of self (LeDoux, 1996). The idea of who we are, the image we have of ourselves and where we fit socially, is built up over years of experience and being continuously remodeled in our thought. Thus, the story of you lives in the mind, with our reflective moments of life review forever searching for a higher truth in terms of purpose and meaning. From an individuated viewpoint, the short story below captures one such reflective moment along the Intelligent Social Change Journey.

I am creative. From the very beginning this was clear, or so my grandmother told me over and over again as she entertained my children with kiddie tales of the early days. I wasn't alone in any of those tales! It was Dimple John next door who came up with selling grass-fed sugar-coated slugs for Valentine's Day, and Little Mary down the street who got us to tear our clothes into strips to weave a colorful flag for our community holiday picnic.

Those early activities cracked open the door to a flood of creativity that actually began to make sense by the time my teen years rolled around. We rigged a bell-ringing system on the side of Dimple John's granddad's wheelchair, complete with three different tones, with different sequences communicating different needs or wants. Then, we developed a neighborhood map, which included all the special talents and skills neighbors were always offering to share with each other.

That's about when I was gifted with a set of oil paints and several canvases that changed my life! At first the colors didn't make sense, the dimensions weren't clear, the relationships were wrong. But the smell of the paints drew me back again and again. The feel of the brush in my hand as I dabbled and stroked the canvas tingled all the way up to my heart, and a splash of beauty began to emerge here and there. And when I saw it, my eyes would water, and the ringing and singing in my ears left a taste of sweetness in my mouth.

Through the many years since I've worked with youngsters as they discovered their creative genius. I could feel their inner selfs emerge and expand as, together, they expressed through art and writing and playing. Filling their environment with new sounds and smells as they explored diverse collections of art-bound materials, they were free to experiment and experience. One of them wound up authoring that new bestselling cookbook, Living a Life of Taste and Love; another developed new mental gym approaches for children; and another was awarded the Nobel Prize in Science last year. That creating just kept expanding. They did good.

Dimple John didn't follow the same track as those kids. In adulthood, he struggled with self-doubts, feeling worthless and talentless. When he finally rallied, it was to focus all his energy on get-rich-quick schemes, which never panned out. Forces always seemed to be pushing against him, although he took every opportunity to push against others as well! He actually got kind of arrogant. Always telling others what was right and never listening to anyone else. Seems to be a lot of that in the world today. But haven't seen him or heard from him in quite awhile. He sort of dropped off the Earth as my life moved on.

Little Mary, who grew up quite tall and slim, had a heart of gold, which skipped a beat and stopped a few years back. She was a giving person who knew **how** to give. Wise giving. Oh, nothing big, not in the newspapers or any such thing. Everyday kind of stuff, always offering the extra dollar when someone in the Dollar Store line was a bit short, or bringing over a hot dinner when she knew someone was working on a short deadline, or capturing a small happy slice of someone's life in a poem and leaving it in their mailbox. Then, there were the pictures. We didn't know about them until she was gone. Had no idea! She told me once my painting had inspired her, but **she** was the true artist. Her expression started a whole new genre of beauty, starting with splashes of color and morphing into joyful experiences of life! As I think of her now, I can feel her love. She's here in my heart.

Me? As I created my self, my truth came in slowly, taking a number of circuitous routes, yet always seeming to head me the same direction. And bit by bit, ever so slowly, I began to listen to my self, and things began to make sense.

###############

The Larger Journey

Our final chapter will reflect on the choice facing humanity today. In a book entitled *Jump Time*, anthropologist and social scientist Jean Houston (2000) says that we are at a time in the eternal life cycle when a shift in every aspect of our experience is taking place. This shift is such a fundamental change that literally *nothing* will ever be the same.

We live in an endless world of possibilities. As Mulford recognized as early as 1889,

> There are more and more possibilities in Nature, in the elements, and in man and out of man; and they come as fast as man sees and knows how to use the forces in Nature and in himself. Possibilities and miracles mean the same thing. (Mulford, 1889-2007, p. 74)

What those possibilities (and miracles) are, may well be decided in this very instant of your thought! There are choices to make and actions to take.

<<<<<<<>>>>>>>

INSIGHT: **The possibilities and miracles of your life may well be decided in this very instant of your thought!**

<<<<<<<>>>>>>>

As promised above, before launching into the chapters related to Part V: Living the Future, we provide the **Introduction to the Intelligent Social Change Journey** (ISCJ), which was primary in *The Profundity and Bifurcation of Change Part I*. The ISCJ is a journey toward intelligent activity, which is a state of interaction where intent, purpose, direction, values and expected outcomes are clearly understood and communicated among all parties, reflecting wisdom and achieving a higher truth. This is the journey which has brought us to where we are today and beckons toward the future.

With all this in mind, we explore the possibilities of today by first taking a look at the ancient tradition of Alchemy, which holds some of the keys to the transformational process of humanity underway. Part V includes ...

Chapter 31: The Alchemy of Change. Alchemy is the art and science of transformation and transmutation, of changing something into something even better. Through this lens, we explore how to *consciously* and *intentionally* speed up evolution to enhance outcomes.

Chapter 32: Balancing and Sensing. Consciousness is out of balance in our world of today. In our acceleration of development of the mental faculties—which we've done quite well—we have focused on the material world and suppressed our inner spiritual senses. Humanity is growing up, and it is time for us to bring all that we are to the table, so to speak, to become the fullness of who we are—physical, mental, emotional and spiritual—and bring ourselves into balance.

Chapter 33: The Harmony of Beauty. Beauty is a transcendent state which can bring all of our senses into harmony. We build on the work of Plato, who suggests that there is an ordering, that the beauties of the earth were to be used as stepping stones moving humanity upwards through fair forms to fair practices to fair notes and, ultimately, to absolute beauty, fair living.

Chapter 34: Virtues for Living the Future. Long ago philosophers such as Socrates, Plato and Aristotle reflected on those things which were a crucial part of living a good life. At the very core were the virtues of beauty, goodness and truth, which provide the foundation for development of good character. In this chapter we explore the concept—and pragmatic actions—that form good character.

Chapter 35: Conscious Compassion. Compassion, a virtue, is introduced as a state of being connected to morality and good character. Beyond a concept, it is inclusive of a state of acting, *giving selfless service*, a conscious compassion. We discover that compassion is part of a larger continuum, moving across the three phases of the Intelligent Social Change Journey and beyond—from sympathy to empathy to compassion to the unconditional love of the advanced human.

Chapter 36: The Changing Nature of Knowledge. Should we choose, just as the mental is in service to the intuitive, knowledge is in service to intelligent activity, and that intelligent activity supports freedom of thought and more learning and knowledge that, when creatively engaged, leads to innovation. This flow connects people and connects thoughts, and has the potential to expand the consciousness of all those joining together. In this chapter we explore the future through the eyes of Knowledge Management thought leaders.

Chapter 37: Consciousness Rising. We explore the new role of the personality, for with the consciousness expanding of self the personality is no longer focused on survival, pleasure and avoidance of pain. We then take a leap (creative?) to the holographic Universe and the superconscious, considering the staggering implications and the coalescing of our spiritual beliefs and scientific understanding, which is moving ever closer.

Chapter 38: The Bifurcation. We are there; we have reached the fork in the road. Choice is simultaneously in the hands of the individual and in the embrace of humanity. *We have the freedom to choose*. Will we stay in the safety of the known and keep repeating the past, or will we, as a humanity, take the creative leap? Are we content to live in Plato's shadows on the wall of the cave, or will be move out into the light of consciousness?

Addendum: Manifesting Our Choice. "We are both onlookers and actors in the great drama of existence" (Niels Bohr, 1961, p. 119). In this addendum, we share the Bennets' miraculous story that continues to push them through their personal limits and paradigms to explore the wonder and diversity of the Universe.

We begin.

Chapter 31
The Alchemy of Change

*An example of change through an ancient tradition
that calls for full participation of humanity
in the transformation process.*

SUBPARTS: THE SEVEN STEPS OF TRANSFORMATION ... THE METAMORPHOSIS ... OUR CURRENT CYCLE OF CHANGE ... WHERE CAN WE GO FROM HERE AS WE LIVE THE FUTURE?

FIGURES: **31-1**. THE CADUCEUS IS A WELL-KNOWN EXAMPLE OF ALCHEMICAL SYMBOLISM STILL IN USE TODAY ... **31-2**. AS IMAGINAL CELLS UNITE WITHIN THE ALCHEMICAL SOUP, THEY GAIN STRENGTH IN NUMBERS.

As we make the creative leap into this new reality, we go through an alchemical process of purifying and raising our existence to a new, higher level of being. Alchemy is an ancient tradition that holds some of the keys to what the transformational process involves. The concept of participating in our own evolution, in order to accelerate its progress, is central to the tradition of alchemy. Real Alchemy is the art and science of how to consciously and intentionally speed up evolution. Alchemy is the epitome of integrating science, spirit and consciousness together. For purposes of this discussion, Alchemy is considered *the art and science of transformation and transmutation; of changing something into something even better* (Hauck, 1999, p. 4-5).

While many people think of Alchemy as some archaic fringe science focused on turning lead into gold, historically some of the most innovative scientists bringing the greatest inventions and discoveries to humanity were Alchemists. For example, scientific giants such as Isaac Newton, Roger Bacon, Robert Fludd, Leonardo DaVinci, Robert Boyle, Paracelsus, Tycho Brahe, Nicola Tesla and Wolfgang Pauli all studied and were inspired by Alchemy (Linden, 2003). Modern sciences such as physics, chemistry, astronomy, biology, allopathic medicine, pharmacology, psychology, as well as oriental medicine and other holistic health remedies developed out of the ancient traditions of Alchemy. However, where modern sciences have taken a purely materialistic and reductionist approach, Alchemy is intimately connected with the philosophies and practices of Hermeticism, mythology and spirituality. Because of this, Alchemy not only holds the secretes to understanding and harnessing the process of transformation at many different levels, it also holds a key to bridging the fields of science, spirit and consciousness.

Part of why Alchemy became so misunderstood is that symbolism and metaphor have been used to communicate the teachings of alchemy in a language of images and symbols rather than a language of words. Some such symbols are still in use today. For example, one to the most prominent Alchemical symbols is the Caduceus, used by today's medical industry. The Caduceus is the staff with wings, knob on top, and either one or two serpents intertwining up the staff. The former (one serpent) is the Staff of Asclepius, while the latter (two serpents) is the Staff of Hermes. Asclepius was the Greek god of medicine; Hermes, son of Zeus, was the god of wisdom. Asclepius was also a student of Hermes Trismagistus. While today's medical industry seems to have forgotten the roots of this symbol, it is waiting there to reveal its secrets again when people are ready to start looking and remembering that there is a deeper meaning behind it.

Figure: 31-1. *The Caduceus is a well-known example of Alchemical symbolism still in use today.*

When it comes to the Alchemical change process, the most important ingredient that differentiates it from simple change is that alchemical change is driven by *consciousness and informed intention and knowledge.* As forwarded throughout this book, with the discoveries of Neuroscience, Quantum Physics, and other newly emerging sciences, we have finally recognized that consciousness plays an important role in our experience of reality. Alchemists never lost touch with this fact. Instead of dying out hundreds of years ago, as many assumed, the field of Alchemy has continued to live on and develop its art, waiting for the day the world would be ready for its wisdom and power again. That time is now.

The Seven Steps of Transformation

Through the study of nature, Alchemists learned that the evolutionary process of transformation is broken down into seven stages. This process is a natural one that we go through all the time and you may recognize these stages in your own life, organization, or in society as a whole. However, when left to Nature alone, it usually takes a long time for things to naturally evolve.

By focusing on ways to harness consciousness and understanding the natural process of evolution, Alchemists learn to intentionally work with Nature and speed up the evolutionary process. Through intention and skillful interaction with evolution, Alchemy can lead to some amazing results that, by ordinary standards, might be considered "miracles". The key to skillfully interacting with evolution to speed it up is to understand the underlying principles of these seven stages and how to harness this process. At the most fundamental levels, the alchemical process is one of breaking apart or separating out the various components, purifying them, and then recombining into a harmonious whole. Several rounds of this separating-purifying-recombining takes place through the seven stages of Alchemy. The seven stages are Calcination, Dissolution, Separation, Conjunction, Fermentation, Distillation and Coagulation. As presented in Bullard (2013), these stages are briefly described below. While there is a similarity to our Phase 1 Change Model—unfreeze/break and implement change/refreeze and stabilize—there is the added element of something entirely new that emerges from the process. Using the same evolutionary, transformational ingredients, the creative leap to something new is similarly prominent in our Phase III Change Model.

<<<<<<<>>>>>>>

INSIGHT: **At the most fundamental levels, the alchemical process is one of breaking apart or separating out the various components, purifying them, and then recombining in into a harmonious whole.**

<<<<<<<>>>>>>>

Calcination. This first stage is about breaking things down and burning them to ash. This is where we take our first step at eliminating whatever dense impurities or problems are plaguing a system. This is accomplished by burning or breaking down the whole object. At a personal level, this is when our ego gets burned or we experience an intense or traumatic event that shakes our foundation. It is a rather searing, caustic approach, but that is the fastest way to get rid of the impurities. The whole system is bound up with and polluted by those impurities, so the whole system must get thrown into the fire to set the essential parts free from the parts that weigh it down.

Dissolution. The second step is a stirring-of-the-pot. During a physical process you put the remains of the calcination in water and let them dissolve into a homogeneous mixture. At a personal level, dissolution can bring up a swirl of emotions or the reactionary disillusionment that comes after our ego gets burned. Typically in this stage, there is a lack of clarity and we are not sure what is actually going on or what the right approach is to deal with it and so we are left to our gut-reactions. This connects us with the deeper stirring of our subconscious, that part of us that is based on our patterned or habitual way of being, determined by past programming and indoctrination. The subconscious is also the storehouse of our unresolved issues of the past that still trigger us and leads to imbalances in our foundation in life. This is the part of our deeper psyche that must be purified and brought into a greater balance.

Separation. In this third stage you let the mixture sit undisturbed for a bit and things will naturally start to separate out because they have different densities. Once the layers or various elements become separated and more clearly identifiable, you start picking out the pieces of what to keep and what to discard, what is pure or essential, what is impure or toxic. After the various parts that are essential to keep have been separated out, they must go through their own purification processes to bring them into a greater state of clarity and balance before they can successfully be brought back together.

Conjunction. This is the half-way point where you bring the purified parts back together in harmonious proportion and reunite them. At this stage we find a working combination between the essential ingredients and, in bringing them back together, a new vision and sense of clarity for how to proceed is established. Continuing onward from here requires a strong sense of connection and dedication to accomplishment of the new vision.

Fermentation. The fifth stage brings another operation of separating and burning, but it is at a much more subtle level. Here you let something mature in a warm, slow process, by gently keeping the pressure or heat on, in order to eliminate any final impurities or more subtle imbalances. Fermenting means to allow something to mature to the point where anything that is corruptible or transitory will rot away. It is driven by more of an internal fire flamed by a higher vision of purpose. Any impurities that make it to this stage are not as obvious and take more soul-searching to root out. Simultaneously the new unified whole with its new vision is maturing and taking deeper root to replace the old parts that are dying away.

During laboratory Alchemy, the end of the Fermentation stage is indicated by a rainbow-colored film that forms on the surface of the ferment. This colorful film is called the Peacock's Tail. New life is born out of the ferment. Something innovative emerges and a whole new epiphany or revelation comes through. The dark stages are done. Transformation has occurred.

Distillation. From the sixth stage on, everything that remains is of essence and must be kept. So, the task now switches from one of purification to one of refinement and elevation. Here you go through several cycles of "evaporating and re-condensing". During this stage you are elevating the vibration, expanding consciousness, raising its energy into a more refined state, infusing life energy and wisdom into it, and then letting it come back down into a denser, more grounded and practical state. You go through several rounds of this refining process, and with each round of elevating to a higher level, you capture more of the subtle energies within it, then you let it re-condense into a more tangible state.

In laboratory Alchemy, to distill something means to take what emerges out of the ferment, dissolve it again into watery solution, and then heat it so that it evaporates into air. Still containing the vapor within our distillation apparatus, the evaporated essence is dispersed to the invisible realms where it can interact with more subtle energy influences. This is the stage where we work to harness the subtle energies and infuse consciousness into our substance. After evaporating or elevating to higher realms and capturing spirit energy or consciousness, we then re-condense back into solution to anchor those subtle energies into tangible form.

Coagulation. This final stage is a crystallization process, where everything congeals into a final perfected form. Typically, you have to go through several rounds of the previous six steps before you will actually reach your end goal, your *philosopher's stone*.

This seven-step process is universal and can therefore be applied in many different ways. For example, it can be applied to your personal life and how you have grown mentally, emotionally and spiritually through various life experiences. It can be applied at a practical level in a laboratory setting to create medicine from plants and herbs (the basis of both modern pharmacology and age-old herbal remedies). It can even be applied to the societal changes that we're going through right now.

In fact, Alchemy has been used to conduct social experiments. Significant shifts in social tenor such as those seen during the Renaissance and other times of great social transformation were often the result of applying alchemical principles to the social standards of the day. For example the Medici's, who were the Fathers of the Renaissance, were scholars of Alchemy and the ancient classics that influenced the development of Alchemical thought.

The Metamorphosis

A metaphor that has been used to describe the process of alchemical change is the metamorphosis of a caterpillar into a butterfly. In metamorphosis, the old form of the caterpillar completely breaks down in the cocoon before the butterfly emerges as an entirely new form and takes flight. In its cocoon, the caterpillar undergoes the **Calcination** stage, which can last anywhere from a couple of weeks to seven months, dependent on the amount of light and heat present. The old structure of the caterpillar is broken down and goes through a form of death.

Entering the **Dissolution** stage, cells dissolve into a soupy mess. We can recognize the effects of this stage in our current cycle of societal evolution, with all of the old paradigm systems—from financial to government to education to various other structures our society is built upon—dissolving. They are starting to crumble and lose their foothold as unique identities.

As old cells and structures break down and expire, there simultaneously appear new types of cells called *imaginal cells*. Seemingly out of nowhere, these imaginal cells start to pop up and increase in numbers. Being different from the old caterpillar cells, the imaginal cells are first perceived as a foreign enemy or threat to the system. Behaving as if these new cells are viruses coming into the system and causing the breakdown, the old caterpillar cells attack the imaginal cells and try to kill them off. See Figure 31-2.

Figure: 31-2. *As imaginal cells unite within the Alchemical soup, they gain strength in numbers.*

These new imaginal cells hold a new pattern of DNA expression. Despite the attacks from the old cells, these new cells continue coming onto the scene, because the DNA of the transforming caterpillar is putting out the instruction to create them; they are part of the larger plan. As they continue to be created and their numbers increase, they soon find each other and, gathering together, gain strength in numbers. In terms of a Quantum field, they are heading the same direction. Through that strength, they become more able to withstand the attacks from the old system.

At some point the imaginal cells reach a certain critical mass in grouping together. Heading the same direction in Quantum Field terminology, they start to realize that they don't have to do everything on their own anymore. They are part of a larger group which can share duties and distribute tasks among the group. So, they start to build a new form of order, a new structure. Once the critical mass is achieved, the development gains momentum, and it starts to take on a life of its own. This new structure is guided by the clear and definite vision that is held within—a blueprint for the butterfly that the caterpillar is ultimately destined to become. This separating of the old from the new and of the various essential components, as well as coming to a clear vision of where to go from here is the **Separation** stage of Alchemy.

As the imaginal cells gain strength by uniting around a new common vision and pattern, the old caterpillar cells that were clinging to the old crumbling system must repurpose themselves by uniting with and adding to the cause of the imaginal cells. They bring with them certain functionality and experience that is a valuable contribution to the growth and development of the new system. For example, a digestive cell can still function as a digestive cell, an immunity cell can still function as an immunity cell, they just need to reorient to the new system. By doing so they free up the imaginal cells to specialize in new elements that did not exist in the caterpillar, such as wings, diverse colors, antennae, etc. This harmonization, re-balancing, and union of what were once opposing elements is what Alchemists call the fourth stage of **Conjunction**. Putting essential parts back together into one whole, this becomes an integrated system where the various parts can now effectively and harmoniously collaborate.

From a personal or organizational level, this stage brings a renewed sense of self and functionality that more closely matches our new vision, bringing with it increased confidence and knowledge of who we are, greater self-awareness, and expanded consciousness. However, this is not the stopping point. *There are three more stages to go.*

The final three stages take a lot more discipline, intention and proactive stepping-up to become conscious change agents working to *perfect* things. For example, Steve Jobs, Apple's co-Founder and former CEO, innately (albeit unknowingly) had a knack for driving innovation and cultural change through the alchemical process. The key to Jobs' success is that he looked beyond just the bottom-line approach of driving for the highest ROI (return-on-investment) from the least amount of effort. Instead, he constantly sought to push the envelope of creating great products and redefining the digital technology-based consumer market. Jobs almost single-handedly kicked off a revolution in our modern way of life by reaching way outside the box and brining new paradigm ideas into practical, easy-to-use products. He never allowed his teams to get too comfortable or stuck in a rut with one-track thinking. To Steve Jobs only excellence would do, everything else "is Shit!" and must be purified and refined further. Mediocrity is the enemy of truly transformative innovation.

<<<<<<<>>>>>>>

INSIGHT: **The final three stages take a lot more discipline, intention and proactive stepping-up to become conscious change agents working to** *perfect* **things.**

<<<<<<<>>>>>>>

Jobs left a legacy that launched many a person into a whole new way of life, providing tools for others to connect, individually and collectively advancing themselves, while simultaneously making Apple the most profitable corporation in the world by 2011. Applying unique methods into the business world, Jobs innately tuned-in to certain underlying alchemical principles that helped drive his genius. At the core of Jobs' success were his continuous effort to keep the pressure on and catalyze change, reaching beyond the ordinary to become extraordinary, striving towards perfection, and maintaining high ideals and personal values (Isaacson, 2011). He unleashed his creativity, not only connecting and empowering people through innovative technologies, but creating masterpieces of art, things of beauty.

In the **Fermentation** stage, those old cells that fail to re-purpose and align with the new structure continue to dissolve and die off. The Alchemical soup then provides the sustenance and raw material needed by the newly emerging system to continue its development until it reaches a stage of maturation. Fermentation is both a maturing of the new form and a final death of the old. Anything that is not of the purest essence or is still corruptible *must* go. This includes the last remnants of the old structure, with its impurities and limitations. This stage takes discipline, patience and dedication, asking that we face the darkness of what is not working and insist that *everything* be purified or let go, until all that remains is integral.

Without the conscious and consistent involvement of the Alchemist, the Fermentation stage can be a long process. In a religious context, as well as a spiritual healing context, this could be likened to *the long dark night of the soul*. The only way to speed it up is through initiatory and vision quest processes that come from the ancient mystery schools and shamanic traditions. These are rituals that are aimed at moving beyond the mundane, beyond the desires of the ego, with energy focused in service to others and the greater whole. And then in a flash of transformation, there is light and the new structure is there. There are no more impurities; everything that remains is essential, and the work moves on towards refinement and elevation.

Eventually the butterfly emerges from the Alchemical soup and breaks out of the chrysalis. As the struggle strengthens the butterfly's wings, he emerges wet and groggy and spends the first few hours of freedom drying his wings and resting a bit before taking flight. This is the Alchemical stage of **Distillation**, re-ordering and refinement. In personal or group Alchemy, Distillation is usually done through a series of meditative processes to clear the mind. This helps get past the chatter of the lower mind, and into accessing the true creativity of the intuitive. This is the stage where the power of Alchemy becomes evident, as the physical, emotional, and mental are fully employed to consciously engage the intuitive.

Having victoriously emerged from the chrysalis, and crystallized its new form into a thing of strength and beauty, the butterfly is ready to take flight and live a glorious existence—flying freely in the air, drinking the nectar of flowers, and bringing beauty to the world. Like the phoenix that rises from its own ashes, the butterfly has risen from the alchemical soup formed by the death of the caterpillar, completely transformed. This is the final Alchemical stage of **Coagulation**. All of the purified, elevated, consciousness-infused substance has crystallized into a final, perfected form. In this form, all the different elements are balanced and harmonized into one whole.

Sometimes we must go through the first six stages again, and again, before getting to the seventh stage of Coagulation, the final perfected product. Eventually we come to that perfect result. That is the promise of alchemy, the incorruptible, all-powerful, unstoppable *Philosopher's Stone* that has the power to turn anything it touches into gold.

Consider this process in terms of what is underway today in our social metamorphosis. There is a part of the population—and perhaps you are among them—that are playing the role of human imaginal cells. What are the demographics of people that are driving the change? Who are the one's holding a new vision for a new society that is going to be remarkably different from the old structure? Who has done the mental work, balancing the past, present and future to bring time and space together? Who has shed the ego enough and tapped into higher purpose and spiritual connection in order to truly serve the greater good? and Who will take the creative leap, guiding the way for others to take flight and be glorious?

Our Current Cycle of Change

In the Alchemy of Change model, while there are cycles within cycles, humanity's present cycle appears to be a little over midway through the process of dissolving the old systems and forming better ones. We entered into the current alchemical cycle around the turn of the new millennium. Looking from the Western viewpoint, the first death in the Calcination stage came with the Dot-com bubble burst in 1999, followed by the financial Modernization Act (signed by Bill Clinton into law) that deregulated the banking industry. Then in 2001 the world reeled from the shock of the infamous 9-11 tragedy, which instigated the George W. Bush administration to put into effect the Patriot Act and the Department of Homeland Security, as well as to declare war on terrorists. While this may have protected USA borders from some terrorist acts, it also stripped American citizens of many "unalienable rights" and privacy. The Calcination continued with the wars in the Middle East, which led to further death as well as sky-rocketing national debts. While most of these Calcinations were instigated by people and certain powers-that-be, they were not likely made with conscious intent for positive transformation, thereby creating forces that compounded the process. These events, while tragic, served as catalysts that kicked off a more conscious movement for change.

The Dissolution stages came as emotions were stirred from the various deaths, losses, and tragedies. The people protested, but to not much avail, for their voices were drowned out by mainstream media and political rhetoric, filled with propaganda that reversed causes and effects. The system continued to dissolve as the housing and credit bubbles burst in 2008 with the banks themselves facing bankruptcy. This debt, which had been unchecked since the Financial Modernization Act of 1999, was then transferred to the people of the United States as the banks were bailed out under the Bush administration. More anger, more sadness, more disillusionment rose up amidst the people. Other countries also suffered as a result of wars and the failing global financial system of central banking.

Fueled by emotion, disillusionment at the system, and dissatisfaction that comes from realizing the foundation upon which our system is built has become corrupted and is no longer supporting the whole, the people either rose up in anger or sunk into dismay and depression. Dissolution tends to be a more introspective stage, providing an opportunity to reflect and dig deeper into what is at the root of the issues. It is one thing to be angry about things that are not working, but it is another thing to start going deeper into what is really at the source of this. What is the cause and what is the effect? What is the truth? What actions can we take that will mitigate harm and help others help themselves?

With the introduction of social media platforms, such as *Facebook* in 2004, YouTube in 2005, and Twitter in 2006, the scene started to shift and the people found a tool they could use to self-organize, express their voice, and find power in numbers. As the social media revolution gained momentum, and self-organizing increased, we transitioned into the Separation stage. The first obvious result of the new movements that emerged from the power of social networking—cooperation and knowledge sharing—came with the sweeping victory of Barak Obama during the 2008 election and his emotional "Yes We Can" slogan, making history as the first African American to take office as President of the United States. This event was not just isolated to the USA; it was an event that captured the attention of people around the globe, mostly cheering at the hope it brought that change could happen. Regardless of Obama's actions in office since that time, the energies of hope, conscious change and the power-of-the people were fueled from this historic event.

Obama inherited, from the Bush administration, a country facing multiple crises with the Great Recession of 2009, over 800,000 domestic jobs per month being lost, war in Iraq, and a global environmental crisis on the verge of several tipping points. It was a very convoluted and complex situation, with so many issues to address. So, the Separation stage continued, as various groups of differing perspectives and agendas began to distinguish themselves from the rest with the emergence of the Tea Party Movement, the Libertarian Movement, the Occupy Movement, the Environmental and Green Movements, Sustainability and Alternative Energy Movements, and so forth. Documentary films abounded, revealing the once-hidden truth about how flawed these systems really are, from politics to computer hacking, privacy invasion, fraud, food labeling, auto industry disruptions, the health of the nation's water supply to the collapse of major U.S. cities and our economic infrastructure. These documentaries lifted the veil on what was really going on, pointing out the flaws and impurities that needed to be rooted out and eliminated. Big questions emerged: What do we really want our world to be? Who can we trust? What is our individual responsibility?

The challenges faced in the Separation stage have very much to do with discerning truth. Take for example, the dark side of social media that has emerged. With so much information available now at the click of a button, which can be easily spread with just another click, it has led to a growing lack of patience and discipline among people. We have become trained to expect almost instant response and many get caught in immediate reaction to anything we read online or anything we hear from our leaders, without the rigor of doing deeper research. Even after doing the research, it is difficult to discern truth from fiction, with both sides of any issue becoming abused by corrupt and special interests that work to virally spread false and misleading information like never before (see Chapter 24/Part IV). Discernment is critical.

Forces also continue to accumulate causing a separation of time and space, the inability to identify cause and effect, which ultimately brings us to a breaking point (see Chapter 3/Part I on Forces We Act Upon and Chapter 16/Part III on Time and Space). In laboratory Alchemy, this breaking point may lead to a shattering of the Alchemical vessel, which requires us to start over again. One such shattering came at the beginning of 2011 with yet another round of global Calcinations taking place during the Egyptian Revolution, followed by the domino effects of the Arab Spring and Occupy Movements. Millions of people from all ages, genders, races, educational backgrounds, financial brackets flooded into the streets to protest and occupy together. The domino effect rapidly spread to becoming a worldwide event from Egypt to the Middle East, to cities across America, to London, Madrid, Berlin, Athens, Mumbai, Tokyo, various cities in Australia and many Asian countries as well.

<<<<<<<<>>>>>>>>

INSIGHT: **Forces continue to accumulate, causing a separation of time and space, and the inability to identify cause and effect, which ultimately brings us to a breaking point.**

<<<<<<<<>>>>>>>>

Emotions were high, especially anger about a small group of the wealthy element (coined as *The 1%*) having grown increasingly richer while the other 99% were left behind. This had nothing to do with the leftist or rightist, or Democratic or Republican or Independent. People across the spectrum of political views agreed that the system had gotten out of hand, and that the divide of wealth had become very disproportionate. Citizens of the world in over fifteen hundred cities worldwide joined the movement for the voice of "The 99%" to be heard. The downfall of this movement was the lack of clear vision and viable alternative solutions that could lead us forward in a better way. **The Separation stage demands that we reach clarity and purification of our essential ingredients before we can move on.**

Nature may have added her own voice, pronouncing her discontent with our modern way of life. Could it be inferred that the 2010 Gulf of Mexico oil spill disaster, the massive March 2011 earthquake and tsunami that hit Japan, and the doubling[28-1] of large 7+ magnitude earthquakes around the Ring of Fire in 2014 were Nature's way of adding to the re-Calcination of modern man? These events triggered huge amounts of toxins such as crude oil and radiation from nuclear waste to be released into the environment that will cause problems for generations to come. This was a wakeup call to the fact that these energy sources are not environmentally safe, adding to the impurities that must be cleaned up.

While the vessel might have shattered at the international level, setting off another round of Calcinations and Dissolution, surprisingly, the Separation cycle in the United States quietly and slowly continued to progress under the Obama Administration, almost unnoticed. Whether you agreed with his changes or not, President Barack Obama managed to change the United States' trajectory with a few silent revolutions, accomplishing much of what he said he would in his 2008 and 2012 presidential campaigns. During Obama's presidency, not only did he help end the Great Recession and the Iraq war, he also reinvented America's foundering health care system, strengthened regulations of Wall Street and Big Banks, implemented a student loan debt-relief effort, reduced domestic energy use while increasing clean energy production, got the International Climate Change Agreement signed in 2015 that committed almost every nation in the world to reduce carbon emissions, and pushed for the victories of "equal pay for equal work", same-sex marriage equality, and LGBT (Lesbian, Gay, Bisexual, Transgender) rights in the military.[28-2] All together, this brought sweeping changes to how America did things, and by 2014 we had reached a form of Conjunction.

Beyond the Obama Administration's changes in the US, there are other influences that took place at the international level that also supported a Conjunction stage. Examples of such changes are the reforms that the first Jesuit, non-European Pope in over 1200 years, Pope Francis, brought to the Catholic Church and its image, bringing many of its edicts into a more modern context. This time also saw an increase of the number of women in positions of leadership in global politics, academia, and business. For example, while still low, the number of female world leaders and heads of governments doubled between 2005 and 2017.[28-3] At an even larger scale is the force of connectivity that has been the Internet and the virtual world of social media, allowing people everywhere to self-organize with others of like-mind, similar interests, and common-causes. So wide-spread have "smart" devices become that even people in 3rd world countries, with barely a penny to their name, are able to connect to the web and find information, resources, music and everything else the Internet has to offer, including others of like-mind.

While a sort of Conjunction stage was accomplished by 2015, it was by no means a perfect or stable system. But it did allow many westerners to get somewhat comfortable again, compared to the situation faced in 2008-2010. However, each change implemented to bring about this shift came with its own set of added complications, and plenty of impurities still abounded.

Beginning in 2015 and especially by 2016, the beginnings of the Fermentation stage started to show itself with further division, wars, systems breaking down, and a world in turmoil. Moving into 2017, corruption on all sides was being revealed on the right and the left, front and back, up and down and center. The old paradigm's gig is up! The impurities and corruption that were still lurking in the shadows can no longer hide, and sometimes are not even trying to hide anymore, and have thus commenced a full-tilt struggle with the emerging new paradigm.

<<<<<<<◇>>>>>>>

INSIGHT: **The impurities and corruption lurking in the shadows can no longer hide, and have thus commenced a full-tilt struggle with the emerging new paradigm.**

<<<<<<<◇>>>>>>>

From the strange and volatile U.S. Presidential election season, to the breakdown of both the Republican and Democratic parties, the shocking victory of Donald Trump as the 45th President of the United States convoluted by the Wikileaks scandals, the interference of Russia in the U.S. political scene, the leaking of fake news, and multiple versions of "truth" from world leaders, turbulence began to expand into chaos. There are so many truths and untruths mixed together regarding so many different subjects that it has become difficult to sense the difference. Recall from Chapter 24/Part IV that the greater our exposure to untruths, the lower our ability to sense those untruths. The continuous layering of untruths causes redundancy in the progression of thought, which leads to lessoning of the mental faculties and diminishing of consciousness. This pattern has continued—and expanded—throughout this presidency.

Paralleling the above was the Brexit vote in the UK to pull out of the European Union, which set off a panic throughout Europe … combined with growing fears and casualties from fanatical Islamic State terrorist attacks, the rampant cases of police brutality towards minorities, the increase of domestic terrorism, the DARK act related to GMO in foods, the controversy and violation of indigenous rights, the desecration of sacred land at Standing Rock, North Dakota, over building of the Dakota Access Pipeline, and other cases of corporate greed and disregard for environmental and human rights, and the list goes on and on. Adding salt to the wounds, we have also mourned the deaths of so many of our most beloved heroes, actors, music artists, and icons that stood for light, nobility, and/or the kind of creative genius that brought inspiration to many generations.

Recall that the Fermentation stage involves facing the Shadow Side and going through a Dark Night of the Soul, to further breakdown the hidden impurities and have the final death of the old structure. Consider it like a death match between our egos and our true selves. By 2016, humanity was coming face-to-face with its fears, judgments, racism, sexism, arrogance, deceit, violence, and evil doings. Without a doubt, we had entered the final "black" stage of dealing with the core issues that have plagued humanity, with the task of cleaning up our *karma*, both current and ancestral. The concept of karma in the Hindu and Buddhist traditions is considered the sum of a person's actions in all states of existence, which in turn decides their fate in the future (Merriam-Webster, 2016). In the Hermetic tradition, karma is the same as cause and effect, or the old saying "what goes around, comes around."

To move through the Fermentation stage, we must look inwards and enter a time of deep reflection and introspection. We must truly reconcile with the parts of ourselves and others that we reject, judge, fear, suppress, or deem as unacceptable. And rather than project them onto others, or onto an "invisible enemy", we must own our own shadow. Only when we do, can we succeed at transforming and integrating it. It is interesting to note that during the 2020 COVID-19 pandemic, the world was brought to a halt and everyone made to isolate for months in order to stop the spread of the virus. This global event catalyzed the progression of the Fermentation stage to move it further along. It's as if Nature was bidding us to take a time out, to withdraw inwards, and not only face our fears, but also face he reality of death and loss. As we re-emerged from the isolation, our way of life was transformed; the old ways are dying away, and a new way is being birthed. Fermentation is a long, slow process, and it will continue until the remaining corruptible parts are eliminated. The key for us is to continue to find he light in the darkness—to hold on to hope for a better future.

Humanity is standing at the precipice of a great abyss, in the final face-off with its dark side, searching for the way across into the new paradigm. The most critical element at this stage is that we pass through without giving up or getting dragged down into the bottomless pit of fear, separation, and negativity. Since we have learned from neuroscience that our thoughts and feelings directly impact the creation of our reality, it behooves us to stay in a positive mode, to chose hope and keep moving forward, no matter how bad and dark it might seem! As the saying goes, *the darkest hour comes just before the dawn.*

These events—and so many more underway—have created an intense and exponentially accelerated ride since the turn of the new millennium. The purification stages are always intense. Egos get burned, people get enflamed, systems break down, death occurs. Perhaps these forces are serving as catalysts to shift us away from a crash course toward extinction, driving our world out of balance from selfish lifestyles and a continuous need for power and control. If we can properly harness the dynamics of change, we may yet be able to steer the evolution onwards, beyond the struggle with our darkness, and into the glory of our more essential goodness and potential.

Where Can We Go from Here as We Live the Future?

One thing is for certain, now that the metamorphosis has begun, we can't cling to the old structures or ways of life. They are no longer there. **The current unrest will not go away on its own, as it is fueled by an inner fire driven by the need for change**. We are faced with the same dilemma that the dying caterpillar cells face.

We can either give up and dissolve into the chaos or take one of two roads: (1) Cling to the old and fight a losing battle, or (2) make a shift to an alternative way of being by together, as a humanity, re-purposing and aligning with the new paradigm systems that are developing at increased momentum. The shift comes as we more skillfully and intentionally push onwards through the remaining stages of the alchemical process, freeing our creativity to create a world of beauty. It is time to re-invent ourselves, individually and collectively.

<<<<<<<>>>>>>>

INSIGHT: **Now is the time for us to make the leap to an alternate way of being by collectively re-purposing and aligning with the new paradigm systems that are developing at increased momentum.**

<<<<<<<>>>>>>>

It might be easy to claim that these national and global problems are beyond our control as individuals or even as organizations. But in Alchemy there is a famous **Principle of Correspondence**, "As Above, So Below. As Below, So Above." This gives a whole new context to the inscription located in the ancient Luxor Temple in Egypt in the innermost chamber: "Man, know thyself and thou shalt know the gods."

As described in The Kybalion (1940, p. 28), this can also be extrapolated to mean, "As the Outer, So the Inner. As the Inner, So the Outer." Meaning the answers *do* reside within each of us, and the outer world is a reflection or manifestation of what is going on inside the collective unconscious of humanity. In other words, our world reflects our thought forms, as described more fully in Chapters 22/Part IV and 26/Part IV. If we wish to change our world, **we must change our inner landscape of emotions and thoughts first**. With this approach, we *can be the change*, as Gandhi advised.

The Fermentation stage, in particular, forces us to look inside and to see where the roots of corruption and imbalances lie within. Whatever old ways we still cling to, whether individually or collectively, they will have to die in order for us to make the transformation needed. Successfully making it through the Fermentation and higher stages requires discipline, patience and devotion to a higher purpose. Here, we are asked to face the darkness of what is not working and insist that *everything* be purified or let go, until all that remains is integral. Wherever there is anger, fear, judgment, violence, greed, deceit, segregation or labeling of "worthy" and "unworthy", etc., these shadows in us need to be healed, individually and collectively. To Ferment involves both a death of the old and a maturing of the new. It can only be driven by an internal fire, flamed by a higher vision of purpose and spirit. The impurities that have made it to this stage are more deeply rooted and thus take much soul-searching to root out.

Through the conscious and consistent involvement of the Alchemist the Fermentation stage can be successfully traversed. The only way to speed it up is through deep meditation, vision questing, or undergoing ancient initiatory processes that come from the mystery schools and shamanic traditions of old. These methods aim at moving us beyond the mundane, beyond the desires of the ego, with *energy focused in service to others and the greater whole*. Here, we must face and slay our own inner demons. **Rather than staying focused on or distracted by outer circumstances, this battle can only be won on the inside. The power to change is found within!** Only after the inner battle is won and the Fermentation stage reaches completion, does the light enter back in, bringing with it the power to create outer change.

In the world of 2020, we have been given an opportunity to go within and understand ourselves. Now is a great time to ask ourselves how we can contribute in a positive way to a solution, or what can we do to have a greater impact on the whole. There are many positive things awakening in humanity as a result of the current world happenings. Examples include a greater recognition of how individual actions and choices impact everyone. Awareness of our interconnection and that "no man is an island", nor do we want to be. We are realizing that the increasing trend of virtual and online connection isn't enough, that we need human connection and value interacting with each other *in person*. There is a greater willingness to take personal responsibility for doing our part, for example, to practice cleanliness and good hygiene. The majority are realizing that they want to be part of the solution, not part of the problem, and that it is time for change. These are all silver linings from the tumultuous time of 2020.

Finally, in a flash of transformation, innovation, and light, a new structure emerges, marking the end of Fermentation. New life is born out of the ferment. Something innovative emerges and a whole new epiphany or revelation comes through. The impurities have been rooted out; the dark stages are done, and everything that remains is essential. As we move out of the Fermentation stage, we come into greater clarity of the vision of light. Transformation has occurred, and the work can move on towards refinement and elevation as it progresses into the stage of Distillation. The next steps are to distill the positive lessons and new ways of life that have been learned from the previous stages, and continue integrating them into our lives in a good way, in order to elevate our way of life to a more pure expression. From where we stand now, there is much work to be done to complete the transformational process, and it will take many rounds of Distillation and implementing new positive solutions until they become integrated into our new collective way of life. Ultimately, if all goes well, we will achieve Coagulation, an enlightened, balanced and integral world.

[For ideas on how to move forward as an Alchemical Change Agent, see Bullard, Theresa (2012). **The Game Changers: Social Alchemists in the 21st Century***. Self published.]*

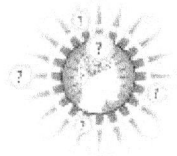

Questions for Reflection:

How do you feel about operating in a state where transformation is a constant?

What levers do you have to influence the Alchemy process?

How does reflecting on the current world events through the Alchemy lens aid your understanding? What are the implications for you?

Where and what is the shadow in you that needs to be healed?

Chapter 32
Balancing and Sensing

SUBPARTS: THE SENSE OF BALANCE ... SELF-BALANCING ... BALANCING THE SENSES ... DYNAMIC BALANCING ... FINAL THOUGHTS

FIGURES: 32-1. IN THE WORDS SUNG BY JANIS JOPLIN: "FREEDOM IS ANOTHER WORD FOR NOTHIN' LEFT TO LOSE" ... **32-2.** THE BALANCING OF THE PLANES, THE SENSES AND TIME.

TOOLS: 32-1. THE LOKAHI TRIANGLE AND THE LIFE TRIANGLE ... **32-2.** HOLDING NEUROVASCULAR REFLECT POINTS

Balance is one of the most important concepts for us to understand at this point in human history, because there are choices to make and, in many ways, we are *out of balance*. For example, in the discussion of self in Chapter 4/Part I, we recognized that our accelerated mental development and a focus on hard competition void of a spiritual counterbalance has led to expansion of the ego into arrogance, plaguing both individuals and the organizations from which we operate. While spiritual energy weaves throughout all of our planes, its balancing effects may be embraced or rejected through conscious choice. As a counterbalance of arrogance, we introduced the tool of humility, which supports openness, learning and the expansion of consciousness.

In Chapter 28/Part IV we again brought up the imbalance among our physical, emotional and mental planes. While humanity has been on the track of, and focused on, accelerating mental development for as long as we can remember in recent history, today we recognize that *a balancing of our outer and inner worlds is necessary*. As Harvey (2013) contends, we are "in a period of evolution where the world has expanded and developed outwardly and left the inner world behind. Our inner selves must catch up and restore the balance." If we pause for a moment and reflect within, we can recognize the truth in this statement.

The continuous expansion of information and knowledge is viewed as a positive reinforcing feedback loop. In his introduction to systems, Kauffman (1980) uses the knowledge explosion as an example of a positive reinforcing feedback loop. The continuous expansion looks something like this: there is a lightning strike that starts a fire, which is then used to cook food, which then provides light as a torch, which then is utilized in science experiments, which then turns into modern day appliances, and so forth. As Kauffman (1980, p. 23) says, "The more knowledge you have, the better off your society is, and the more people it can support to spend their time looking for more knowledge"... AND, the more time that can be spent creating the systems that will help manage an ever-increasing information explosion! In regards to knowledge expansion, there are no visible limits to growth.

Yet balancing loops ARE needed in terms of the physical and emotional planes. The mind/brain does not operate in isolation. For example, we now know from neuroscience that physical health plays a significant role in the mental and physical operation of the mind/brain. Exercise increases blood flow, burning glucose as an energy source for neuron operation, and also provides oxygen to take up the toxic electrons (Medina, 2008). Exercise stimulates neurogenesis, the creation of new neurons in certain locations in the brain, and exerts a protective effect on hippocampal neurons, thus heightening brain activity. The hippocampus is part of the limbic system and plays a strong role in consolidating learning and moving information from working memory to long-term memory (Amen, 2005). Exercise boosts brainpower, stimulating the proteins that keep neurons connecting with each other (Medina, 2008). This is the *use it or lose it* concept that applies both to the mind and the body, both of which need to be regularly exercised. Thus, from the viewpoint of the mind/brain in terms of interaction with the health of our physical body, we now know that: (1) Physical activity increases the number (and health) of neurons; (2) Exercise increases brainpower; and (3) Choice is necessary for benefit. Forced exercise does not promote neurogenesis (Begley, 2007).

Further, as we've forwarded throughout this text, the material brain can influence the creation, association, and exercise of the brain patterns, while at the same time these patterns can influence the architecture of the brain. What patterns are created, how many, and how often they are utilized is influenced by the physical and mental environment within which an individual lives and the decisions and actions that individual makes and takes. As can be seen, **there is continuous interplay between the physical and mental planes**.

And we haven't brought in the emotions. When exploring emotions as a guidance system in Chapter 19/Part III, we introduced several key points from neuroscience in support of that discussion, specifically, that: (1) emotions influence all incoming information; (2) emotions can increase or decrease neuronal activity; (3) the brain can generate molecules of emotion to reinforce what is learned; (4) emotional tags influence memory recall; (5) emotions miss details but are sensitive to meaning; and (6) unconscious interpretation of a situation can influence the emotional experience.

Reiterating, as Pert (1997) details,

> Emotional states or moods are produced by the various molecules known as neuropeptide ligands, [molecules] and what we experience as an emotion or a feeling is also a mechanism for activating a particular neuronal circuit—simultaneously throughout the brain and body—which generates a behavior involving the whole creature, with all the necessary physiological changes that behavior would require. (Pert, 1997, p. 145)

Thus, there is continuous communication among the brain and the body in terms of thoughts, and the emotions connected to those thoughts. The entire body is involved in emotions, and the body drives our emotions. Thought can *directly trigger* emotions at the same time it is being *directly impacted* by our emotions!

From this short treatment, it may be clear how important it is to achieve a balance among the mental, emotional and physical planes through which we *live our lives*, and the spiritual energy which *gives us life*. While imbalances can be useful for accelerating learning and experiencing, over a period of time imbalance can cause collapse of the system, that is, reduction of consciousness and the inability to sustain the system. Thus, **there is a finite period of time to achieve the rebalancing necessary for human sustainability**.

The Sense of Balance

Every structure we see in the Universe is a result of the balancing between opposing forces of Nature. For example, spiral galaxies and clusters of galaxies result from a balancing between gravity and the rotation of stars as they orbit the center of the galaxy or cluster. Individual stars sustain a balance between the hydrogen gas or radiation in the center of the star pushing outwards and gravity pulling inwards. A balance occurs between gravitational and atomic forces when matter has a density close to the density of single atoms. Planets, mountains, trees, people, insects, cells, and molecules are all composed of closely packed arrays of atoms. The density of these collections of atoms is therefore similar to the density of a single one of the atoms of which they are made. Despite their superficial diversity, they are linked by a single thread—the similarity of their densities—that issues from the fact that they represent states that can withstand the crushing inward force of gravity.

The yin and yang, ancient Chinese symbols of male and female, represent the eternally shifting balance between energies that are inseparable and contradictory opposites. This is a *Great Idea*, a timeless insight that reflects an understanding of human nature (Haidt, 2006). For example, take science and spirituality, once thought to be opposites but coming closer to being recognized as two different frames of reference for considering the same Universe, perhaps serving as steps toward understanding a Quantum reality.

From the balancing of opposites, wisdom can emerge. For example, Haidt (2007) says that a good place to look for wisdom is in the minds of your opponents, the last place you expect to find it. He reasons that you already understand the ideas common to your own side. So, if you can remove your blinders and look closely at your opponent's point of view, you may see some good ideas for the first time. This is the concept behind the Humility Tool in Chapter 4/Part I. You already know that which you know, through the richness of the diversity of others there is much more to learn! As Haidt explains:

> By drawing on wisdom that is balanced—ancient and new, Eastern and Western, even liberal and conservative—we can choose directions in life that will lead to satisfaction, happiness, and a sense of meaning. We can't simply select a destination and then walk there directly—the rider does not have that much authority. But by drawing on humanity's greatest ideas and best science, we can train the elephant, know our possibilities as well as our limits, and live wisely. (Haidt, 2007, p. 243)

The equilateral triangle is often used as the basis of balancing tools. For example, two such tools are the Lokahi Triangle and the Life Triangle. We briefly share these below.

****

TOOL 32-1: The Lokahi Triangle and the Life Triangle

*Lokahi i*s a Native Hawaiian word reflecting balance and harmony, representing the seamless unity and interconnectedness of all things. A life of harmony is one that is ordered. The *Lokahi Triangle* is an equilateral triangle with the three points representing the physical, mental and spiritual parts of a person, embedded in the environment in which they exist and entangled with a myriad of relationships, family members in the present and the past, ancestors and gods (Stanford, 2016). The triangle is central to the Native Hawaiian understanding of health, that the physical body cannot be healed when the triangle is out of balance, with the points working together to harmoniously participate in life.

According to Levey and Levey (2014), these points represent nature, community and Spirit. From this viewpoint, the triangle can be used as a navigational tool, an inner compass for the journey through life. As they say,

> Taking this practice to heart as a way of life cultivates a quality of continuous mindfulness regarding the vital resources that sustain your life, and encourages you to closely monitor and carefully manage the quality of relationship you have to each of these dimensions of experience. (p. 18)

The simple wisdom of the triangle is reflected in three questions upon which the practitioner frequently pauses and reflects, assessing the truth of the responses:

REFLECTION (1): "What is the quality of my relationship to my natural world, the biosphere, and the land that sustains me?"

REFLECTION (2): "What is the quality of my relationship to my community—friends, family, colleagues—with whom I share my life?"

REFLECTION (3): "What is the quality of my relationship with Spirit, Mystery, the ground of all being, the powerful, subtle, essential dimension of all that is true and sacred?" (Levey & Levey, 2014, pp. 18-19)

After each question is asked, take time to reflect upon whether you are in balance with nature, community and Spirit. If the answer is yes, then reflect upon how you can deepen that relationship with balance. If the answer is no, then reflect upon how to skillfully return to a state of balance.

THE LIFE TRIANGLE: Similarly, one of the authors has used the equilateral triangle—the *Life Triangle*—as a simple balancing tool in everyday life. The three points represent (1) physical needs, (2) relationships, and (3) personal aspirations and accomplishments. When any of the three points sinks inward and is out of balance there is discomfort, irritation and worry, and that point must become the focus of attention until balance is regained. With focus and effort, balance can be regained by the individual. Two points sinking inward are followed by deep depression, calling for immediate help and the assistance of a trusted other. With this simple understanding, the Life Triangle can be used as an assessment instrument, helping an individual pull away from the immediate issues, take a systems viewpoint of the current state of life and, when indicated, reach out for assistance.

****

Self Balancing

In our search for balance, we need to first understand that **balanced does not mean equal!** Because each of us is unique with different thoughts, beliefs, feelings, etc., *the balance of elements in which you best experience life is unique*. For example, in Chapter 3/Part I we introduced forces. There are times in your life when you *choose* to engage forces, and times when you choose to disengage. Eventually, you discover a comfortable balance that provides the right amount of stimulation and the right amount of peace in your personal learning journey, and you vacillate back and forth to experience the fullness of life! Yet, from a higher systems viewpoint, you are achieving balance as by choice you weigh in and out of learning experiences. An example of this is the optimum level of stress for learning (discussed in Chapter 13/Part III) and the optimum level of complexity for an organization operating as an intelligent complex adaptive system (introduced in Chapter 14/Part III) (Bennet & Bennet, 2004).

<<<<<<<>>>>>>>

INSIGHT: **Balanced does not mean equal! Because you are unique with different thoughts, beliefs, feelings, etc.,** *the balance of elements in which you best experience life is unique.*

<<<<<<<>>>>>>>

The movie *Inner World, Outer World* (2012) contends that the balance of the inner and outer worlds is the birthright of every human being. This balance was introduced in the opening paragraphs of this chapter. Balancing our inner and outer worlds is the middle way of the Buddha and the golden mean of Aristotle. If we can keep our life balanced, we are assisting everyone else to take a forward step. When we are able to manage our own challenges, we become more free and independent to enjoy life, both alone and with others, and we learn to allow others the freedom to manage their challenges. When we have an inner balance, the outer world can be firing away and we are still able to function coherently. Further, there is less of an impulse to achieve balance in the exterior world when we are experiencing an inner state of balance.

<<<<<<<>>>>>>>

INSIGHT: **If we can keep our life balanced, we are assisting everyone else to take a forward step.**

<<<<<<<>>>>>>>

One approach to inner balancing is meditation (for example, see Kornfield, 2008; and Chodron, 2002). Another similar approach is hemispheric synchronization, the use of sound coupled with a binaural beat to bring both hemispheres of the brain into coherence. Binaural beats were identified in 1839 by H.W. Dove, a German experimenter. In the human mind, binaural beats are detected with carrier tones (audio tones of slightly different frequencies, one to each ear) below approximately 1500 Hz (Oster, 1973). The mind perceives the frequency differences of the sound coming into each ear, mixing the two sounds to produce a fluctuating rhythm and thereby creating a beat or difference frequency. Because each side of the body sends signals to the opposite hemisphere of the brain, both hemispheres must work together to "hear" the difference frequency. This perceived rhythm originates in the brainstem (Oster, 1973) and is neurologically routed to the reticular formation (Swann et al., 1982), then moving to the cortex where it can be measured as a frequency-following response (Hink et al., 1980) This inter-hemispheric communication is the setting for brain-wave coherence, which facilitates whole-brain cognition (Ritchey, 2003), that is, an integration of left- and right-brain functioning (Carroll, 1986). What can occur during hemispheric synchronization is a physiologically reduced state of arousal while maintaining conscious awareness (Atwater, 2004; Fischer, 1971; Delmonte, 1984; Goleman, 1988; Jevning et al., 1992; Mavromatis, 1991; West, 1980), and, from this balanced state with both hemispheres of the brain engaged, the capacity to reach the unconscious creative state through the window of consciousness.

A version of brainwave entrainment is Field Effect Audio Technology (FEAT), a trademarked product of Byron Metcalf (2016) that is a complex and unique integrated system of isochronic and binaural beats with specific drum and percussion rhythms and patterns. The combined harmonics, spatial audio processing and auditory driving support a natural state of coherence and balance within us and our immediate surroundings—a phenomenon that Metcalf calls field Effect resonance. What is fascinating about this particular product is that it builds on the drum and rattle resonances created by early man to achieve this same state. In other words, while the use of technology to assist brainwave entrainment is relatively new, the idea of creating isochronic and binaural beats for inner work has been around for thousands of years!

Balancing our outer world can be assisted by how we manage stress. We use the example of stress repeatedly because this is a state to which almost every individual can relate as a personal example. Recall in Chapter 13/Part III the discussion around optimum arousal. We forwarded that learning is highly dependent on the level of arousal of the learner. Too little arousal and there is no motivation, too much and stress takes over and reduces learning. Thus, maximum learning occurs at the balance point where there is a moderate level of arousal. (See Figure 12-1.)

When under stress, up to 80 percent of the blood rushes from your forebrain (the primitive brain) to your extremities and chest to support the flight-or-flight response. We lose our ability to think clearly and, instead, begin to totally "lose it". We as humans did not evolve to *think* our way out of danger. These primal behaviors were programmed into us millions of years ago when we were cave dwellers living with constant mortal danger. Thanks to the autonomic nervous system, we have automatic, rapid responses (fight, flight or freeze) that help sustain life.

As can be perceived, the body's fight-or-flight response is not intended to effectively handle the plethora of stressors that bombard us in today's modern society. For example, someone may cut you off in traffic or you may have an argument with your spouse—both of which throw you into a clear autonomic explosion of caustic stress chemicals when there is no true physical threat. Hence, our bodies react to the daily stressors of civilized life as if they were the perils of life in the Ice Age.

How can we slow or interrupt this cyclic procession of thinking, feeling and acting/behaving to allow for balance and harmony. Balancing the physiological body's stress response can serve as a key. As practiced for thousands of years, the ancient arts of yoga and Qigong accomplish energy balancing for optimal health and vitality. More recently, after studying the masters of these and other ancient arts, Eden (2008) established a method of self-care that consistently balanced these intermingled systems. She determined that you can effectively balance your energetic body by keeping the energies flowing in vibrant harmony utilizing postures, movements, tapping, massaging, and holds on specific points on the skin. Below is a simple tool that can help. (See Chapter 18/Part III on Flow and Chapter 20/Part III on stuck energy.)

****

TOOL 32-2: Holding Neurovascular Reflect Points

Ideally, we would benefit from optimal functioning of the forebrain-the thinking part of our brain-to make prudent/wise choices under stressful circumstances. This simple yet invaluable energy technique can interrupt the stress response, as well as reprogram the way your body responds to stress.

STEP (1): Find a quiet place where you will not be caught up in the everyday sounds and movement of life for a few minutes. Close your eyes and take a few deep breaths.

STEP (2): Using your palm or fingertips, hold or touch the main Neurovascular reflect points above your eyes, with your thumbs on your temples. The Neurovascular points or frontal eminences are the raised areas on the forehead directly above the eyes. The main Neurovascular Reflex Points allow us to shift our physical body's autonomic response and assist us to meet stress with a high functioning thinking brain. They are often referred to as the "Oh my God" points which you often intuitively hold when shocked by an alarming event. By simply holding or touching the main Neurovascular reflex points with your palm or fingertips, you boost blood and oxygen flow back up into the forebrain, allowing for clear thinking while shifting energetic patterns to calm and re-center emotionally.

STEP (3): Remaining in this position, breathe deeply for 1-5 minutes. This simple and gentle pressure instructs the primitive brain that the crisis is not a real physical threat that needs to be met with a fight-or-flight response flooding toxic stress hormones into the bloodstream. Considering that stress reactions are physical, mental and emotional responses, this process is the foundation for reprogramming what becomes an emergency response loop. By placing fingertips over the "Oh my God" points, thumbs on your temples and breathing deeply for 1-5 minutes while feeling stressed or focusing on a stressful memory, your mind will clear and your emotions will calm as you free yourself from your memory's emotional grip.

STEP (4): When you reach completion, thank your body for its response, take several cleansing breaths, on the out-breath releasing any tension still remaining, and open your eyes.

****

Let's briefly explore other areas of self balancing. Self balancing concerns important choices. For example, understanding that thoughts induce emotions and emotions affect thought, in this continuum there is a propensity to get caught up in a cycle of repetitive thinking. This is where beliefs come into play. A belief is a thought that you continue to think for an extended period of time. The longer you think the thought, the stronger the belief, with the belief potentially influencing you to behave in a delimited manner. This paradigm explains the prejudices and opinions that limit our creativity and slow expansion of our consciousness. As a reminder, *remember* that humans have the ability to balance their emotions. Our emotions are just that, *ours* (see Chapter 19/Part III). Thus, once emotions are acknowledged and embraced, meeting their purpose and responsibility as a guidance system, it is our choice whether or not we continue to "feel" them.

<<<<<<<>>>>>>>

INSIGHT: **Self balancing concerns important choices. It starts with awareness of what is out of balance.**

<<<<<<<>>>>>>>

The self also has the opportunity to balance the past, present and future through the expansion of truth (see Chapter 24/Part IV). From the viewpoint of the present, the higher the level of truth of a concept the more we can understand the relationship of that concept to the past and the future. This is why the saying, "it's easier to know what you should have done after the fact" came into being. Indeed, looking back from the present and recognizing patterns of the past can provide healthy fodder for future decisions, as long as we're not stuck into patterns of repeating past mistakes! Truth creates visibility and expands consciousness and, as MacFlouer (2004-16) says, *When truth becomes foundational in life then magic happens.* The result is more balance, and we are more joyful and playful. Self truth comes into play here. As Willis (2012, p. 20) explains quite simply, "To achieve balance adjust your behavior and actions to always be true to who you are and be clear and consistent about your values." MacFlouer (2004-16) also forwards that *virtue equals balance.* Virtue is addressed in relation to its ability to expand our consciousness in Chapter 34.

A balance important to our learning and growth is that of balancing our freedom, purpose and creativity with a consistency of choices (direction) and the actions we take. The U.S. Department of the Navy used the term *connected of choices,* acknowledging that decisions made at different parts or levels of the organization may appear conflictive and still be heading the organization in the same direction. This was based on an understanding of the wide diversity of people and knowledge, and the specific needs and contribution to the whole of each part of the organization. Understanding and embracing the idea of a connectedness of choices, and allowing the freedom and creativity at the point of action to achieve local goals while supporting the larger organizational purpose, represents movement toward intelligent activity. Recall that intelligent activity is defined as *a perfect state of interaction where intent, purpose, direction, values and expected outcomes are clearly understood and communicated among all parties, reflecting wisdom and achieving a higher truth.*

At the societal level, there is a balancing of freedom with the human need for security, and how much control we are willing to relinquish to the government in order to ensure that security. Examples would include the control of borders and the policing of civilians to ensure obedience in terms of laws and regulations. As musical entertainer Janis Joplin sang many decades ago in a best-selling hit titled *Me and Bobby McGee,* "Freedom is another word for nothin' left to lose ..." (See Figure 32-1, a Conversation Starter graphic.) Unfortunately, it is easy to push this too far. There is a balance, and choices, that come along with advancement of society. When this balancing of freedom, purpose and creativity does *not* happen, energy is manifested as a substitute for intelligent activity (MacFlouer, 2004-12), which then produces forces. It is then up to us to take this energy and develop higher and higher levels of intelligence.

Balancing our potential and our actions is critical to a successful life. Willis (2012, p. 76) says that each individual has two main areas of potential (1) the ability to perform specific tasks, which is comparative to others, and (2) "the degree to which you have found balance and inner peace," which is the same for each individual. He contends that fulfilling your potential runs

Balance

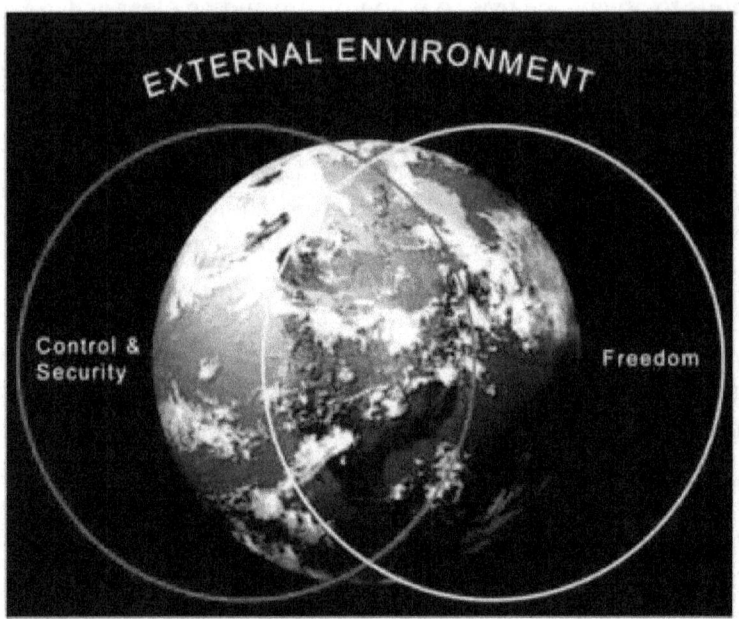

Figure 32-1. *In the words sung by Janis Joplin: "Freedom is another word for nothin' left to lose."*

hand-in-hand with your ability to think positively and always give your best. This, of course, refers to the power of intent (Chapter 25/Part IV) and the power of thought (Chapter 26/Part IV). (Positive thinking is also addressed in Chapter 9/Part II.) *When we are less than we can be, and aware of this, we live in a mix of failure and regret punctuated by fear.* If we do not try, we cannot fail. If we do not share our capabilities, our limits will never be tested, or visible. Nor will we ever know the fullness of life that is our potential, our birthright.

<<<<<<<<>>>>>>>>

INSIGHT: **If we do not try, we cannot fail. If we do not share our capabilities, our limits will never be tested, or known.**

<<<<<<<<>>>>>>>>

From the physical perspective, the great balancer of the human body is the rhythm of rest. We all know that sleep is essential to life. This is the time when the body and mind cleanses and repairs itself, letting go of the tensions of the day. As

Levey and Levey (2014, p. 125) describe, in deep sleep "our brain slows way down, and all the 'mental programs' that we run cease to operate, allowing us to rest in a state of pure being." In our wake state, we have the choice of balance in terms of what we eat, the exercise we get and the thoughts and feelings that permeate our experiences.

Balancing the Senses

Without balance or senses we cannot be aware of our own consciousness. Remember that we have seven senses, the five senses of form and the additional two inner senses, which develop as we mature, emanating from the heart energy center and the crown energy center. From the heart we have a sense of connectedness with a larger ecosystem, a sense of Oneness. When this is coupled with feelings, it produces empathy (a Phase 2 attribute) that can lead toward compassion (a Phase 3 attribute). This balance refers to how your learning is acted upon in service to others, the larger ecosystem of humanity, and the world at large. From the crown energy center, we have a sense of co-creating our reality. When coupled with higher mental thought, we seek truth. This balance refers to the consistency of thought and feelings as we create the physical and interact with and in our creation.

We always associate seeing, hearing, smelling, tasting and touching with specific sense organs, that is, the eyes, ears, nose, mouth and hands. These senses are also connected to various energy centers within the body. (See Chapter 18/Part III on Flow.) Development of lower mental thinking is stimulated by development of the senses. Intelligent interaction requires senses. For example, as you co-evolve with your environment, you get information from others and give information to others, and that information comes through your senses. If your senses are not open or well connected, then you get and give bad information. When your senses are well developed you increase the flow of information that is, in turn, used to create knowledge. In this way a balance is sustained between incoming information and action based on knowledge. This is the concept of co-evolving.

Information that leads to applied knowledge has the potential to become part of all other human beings through their senses. When this occurs, the construction of concepts (higher mental thinking) increases, and with it the level of truth increases (see Chapter 24/Part IV). This process is a *beautification of the mind*. (See Chapter 33 on the Harmony of Beauty.)

As an individual, you can lighten and balance your senses. For example, beauty has the unique capability of unifying the senses with thought, that is, capturing the attention of all of your senses with thought and feelings heading the same direction. The unification of senses with thought leads to greater levels of knowledge and creative energy, *and* expanded consciousness. Another example is the use of yoga, which is the process of joining thought and the senses of the body together, thus bringing greater balance to the senses.

Figure 32-2 represents the balancing of the physical, mental and emotional planes; the balancing of past, present and future; and the balancing of the seven senses across those planes.

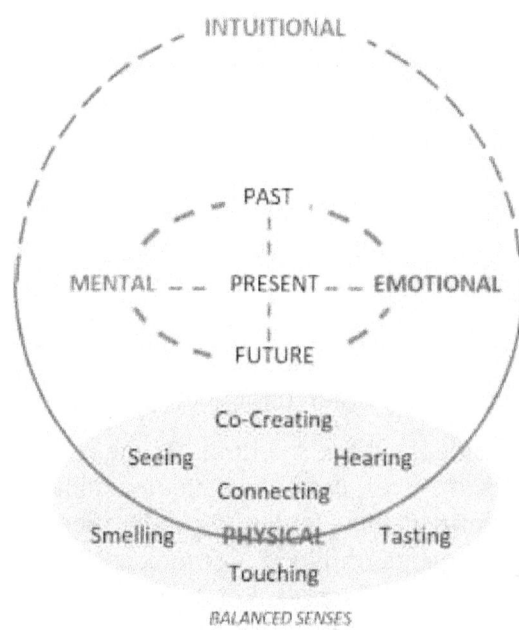

Figure 32-2. *The balancing of the planes, the senses and time.*

Dynamic Balancing

Dynamic balancing is the necessary real-time balancing—symmetrization, harmonization, equalization, co-ordination and integration—of forces or demands. While symmetrization is used to denote a mathematical process, in a larger sense it refers to the process of making something symmetrical, a quality of having mirror images opposite each other emerging from a common center line. (Symmetry is a learning point along the path in Chapter 22/Part IV.) Harmonization is bringing into harmony, bringing into agreement, adjusting differences and inconsistencies. In music it is the mixing of melodies and chords to create pleasing sounds. Equalization is the act of making equal or uniform. Co-ordination is having two or more elements work together effectively, efficiently and smoothly. Integration is the bringing together of parts combining them to create a whole. All of these are elements of dynamic balancing.

Since everything is subject to change, balance in a CUCA environment[32-1] will rarely remain constant for very long. Thus, our need in organizations for continuous learning is actually a need for continuous learning and rebalancing, which means (1) huge amounts of creation; and (2) a huge amount of conscious balance among these creations (MacFlouer, 2004-16).

Final Thoughts

Balance is not a state of being, but rather continuing, profound choices of how we interact with the world. Balancing and sensing are entangled in an interdependent relationship that actively engages us in our social environment and, if we allow it, leads to conscious compassion.

As a humanity, we are bringing our consciousness back into balance as we engage in the Intelligent Social Change Journey. In our acceleration of development of the mental faculties, we have focused on the material world and suppressed our inner spiritual senses. Humanity is maturing, and it is time for us to bring all that we are to the table, to reach the full potential of who we are—physical, mental, emotional and spiritual—and bring ourselves and our world into balance.

Questions for Reflection:

When you sense changes in your environment, how do you adjust to maintain balance?

Do you fully engage all seven of your senses in decision-making?

Do you engage in physical and mental exercise to maintain balance of body, mind and emotions?

Chapter 33
The Harmony of Beauty

SUBPARTS: SENSING BEAUTY ... BEAUTY IN OUR THINKING ... BEAUTY IN ART ... HEALTH AS A WORK OF ART ... SHARING BEAUTY ... BEAUTY AS TRANSCENDENCE ... FINAL THOUGHTS

FIGURES: 33-1. THE ART OF REEFKA SCHNEIDER ... **33-2**. THE ART OF CINDY TAYLOR ... **33-3**. THE ART OF CORBIE CROUSE ... **33-4**. THE ART OF JACKIE URBANOVIC ... **33-5**. SHARING THE BEAUTY OF LIFE AT MOUNTAIN QUEST ... **33-6**. A *MYST* PICTURE ENTITLED: "CROWNED WITH LIGHT." *THE MAJESTY OF COMMUNING IN THE MYST: ONE VOICE, ONE SONG, ONE HEART.*

TOOL: 33-1. CHOOSING BEAUTY

We've heard the old adage that *Beauty is in the eye of the beholder*. We expand that to say, *Beauty is in the **senses** of the beholder*. And add, *Beauty is in the **thoughts** of the beholder*. And, *Beauty is in the **feelings** of the beholder*. And, as visible to others, *Beauty is in the **actions** of the beholder*.

In the movie *Next* (2007) starring Nicholas Gage, the hero says: "There's an Italian painter named Carlotti, and he defined beauty. He said it was the summation of the parts working together in such a way that nothing needed to be added, taken away or altered." While to our knowledge this represents an imaginary painter, nonetheless the description captures the essence of the word: a perfection, a truth. Consistent with this description, in *The Courage to Create*, Rollo May (1975) says, "Suppose the apprehension of beauty is itself a way to truth? Suppose that 'elegance'—as the word is used by physicists to describe their discoveries—is a key to ultimate reality?" Let us explore *why this may be true*.

Harmony is the beginning of beauty, a consistency or pleasing arrangement of parts, harmonious relations (*Dictionary.com*, 2016). Beauty comes from the overall harmony that has been created. The recognition of beauty begins with the freedom—and desire—to choose that which is beautiful. *Life is what it chooses to be*. When we choose beauty as our expression in life or sense beauty around us, we are simultaneously exercising our individual choice and connection to larger concepts of truth.

Humans have long associated beauty with fractal patterns, that is, infinitely complex repeating patterns with each part of the pattern including seeds for the whole. Inherently chaotic, fractals are full of noise AND order (*Inner World, Outer*

World, 2012). We are reminded that to focus on a specific pattern and hold it in our mind, we have to drop away the surrounding "noise." This is the power of limits that helps us comprehend our world, one piece at a time. "By naming and labeling we limit things, lock it into a thing, at the same time creating it, defining it to exist" (*Inner World, Outer World*, 2012).

<<<<<<<<>>>>>>>

INSIGHT: **Life is what it chooses to be.**

<<<<<<<<>>>>>>>

Gardner (2011) says that beauty is the property of experiences, because any experience could be considered by the individual experiencing it as beautiful. He says that in order for an experience to be beautiful, "It must be interesting enough to behold, it must have a form that is memorable, and it must invite revisiting" (Gardner, 2011a, p. xi). Gardner goes on to remind us that many things initially found interesting tend to quickly fade from memory, interesting things can be quickly stored away and forgotten, and "some experiences that are both interesting and memorable do not invite revisiting—either because they are too awe-ful or because their content has been exhausted" (Gardner, 2011a, p. xii). When what we experience is truly beautiful—meeting all three of these criteria—our emotional guidance system provides a signal, a *pleasurable tingle*.

MacFlouer (2004-16) says that in order to achieve beauty in the physical world, you need to reduce conflict. Forces destroy beauty. Reflecting on our experiences as individuals and as a humanity, this certainly makes sense. For example, consider the great works of art (architectural, books, paintings, sculptures) destroyed during World War II. Going on today, MacFlouer uses the Israeli's use of force in an attempt to counter forces being used on them, and vice versa, as an example. This, of course, is called war, and the reason it is unlikely to resolve any issues is because war has the immediate effect of destroying the senses and uglifying the environment that you are enacting force against. Not only is art destroyed during war, but artists, creatives and intellectuals are murdered and imprisoned. They are considered dangerous since art and beauty have the power to inspire revolutions!

Artist Urbanovic (2017) reminds us that there are times when under the duress of destruction, worry and loss that our sense of beauty is heightened. For example, the sight of a single flower in the debris or the helping hand of a stranger can lift our spirits. Nowhere is this clearer than in the work of Viktor Frankl, who discovered moments of love and beauty of thought in the midst of the horrors of Auschwitz (Frankl, 1939/1963). Urbanovic thinks the desire for beauty is heightened during difficult times, and that it becomes more important because it reinstates hope, and that the memories of intense, negative experiences can also lead to the creation of art as a way to understand and transform those experiences from destructive to meaningful, and even beautiful. (See Figure 20-1 in Part IV on the learning cycle from threatening events.) When reflecting on the human as part of a larger ecosystem, Urbanovic (2017) struggles with this concept.

> There is exceptional pain and beauty at the heart of our entire ecosystem: we must all destroy other lives in order to survive, but the resulting web of life works together in a way that is beautiful. This is a fact that I've struggled with all of my life. Destruction lives side-by-side with beauty. I also wonder if there would be creativity if there were no problems, no sadness, no complex situations to solve? Without pain, how would the meaning and importance of beauty change for us?

This, of course, is the experiential nature of learning in the realms of duality. In Chapter 38 we take a closer look at the role duality has served in the past, and ask if, once our lessons have been learned, this contrast is still necessary for co-creating the future.

While discovering great peace does not always equate to finding beauty or creating great art—and noting that it can be difficult for an individual to move beyond emotionally-involved negative experiences—we do know that when forces are reduced, it becomes easier to focus on the beauty around us. However, when people *choose to work together* to produce beauty, with their energy focused in the same direction, there can be amazing results! And, the more you are aware of the reality of what you are doing, the more positive the results. That brings us to a discussion of sensing beauty.

Sensing Beauty

From the viewpoint of our senses, beauty is something good, pleasing, attractive and satisfying, specifically, a combination of qualities, impressive to touch, feel, look at, taste, smell, listen to and think about.

Beauty enhances and unifies the senses in our body and in others. This may begin with a single sense recognizing beauty and then spreading to other senses, that is, if we "see" something that resonates with the beauty—perhaps a painting that engages us with color and triggers memories and inspires our thinking—it is connecting to thought patterns developed in the past, with the potential of engaging additional senses. As we reflect, our thought becomes more beautiful and we express this to others, helping others to see the beauty in relationship to their own mental and emotional experiences, thus lightening the field of thought around us.

Dave Austin (a motivational speaker, former professional athlete, and sports coach of a U.S. Olympic team) tells the story that he was swindled by a business partner. It took quite a long time for him to forgive his partner. Then, one day when he was in China, a place of great beauty, and in the midst of that beauty he all of a sudden had an experience of complete forgiveness.

Feng Shui, developed in China about 4,000 years ago was originally linked to the land and rivers (*feng* is wind, and *shui* is water) Today, millions of people use it to live in harmony with their environment and create abundance and prosperity. In Feng Shui, beauty is created via balance which reflects the trade off or a balanced integration of the five elements (fire, water, metal, wood, and earth). This concept of balancing the five elements is what Japanese or Zen gardens are based upon.

Beauty in our Thinking

What does beauty in our thinking mean? Besant and Leadbeater (1999) focus on the thinker as clothed by subtle matter of the mental plane. As they describe this:

> The mental body is an object of great beauty, the delicacy and rapid motion of its particles giving it an aspect of living iridescent light, and this beauty becomes an extraordinarily radiant and entrancing loveliness as the intellect becomes more highly evolved and is employed chiefly on pure and sublime topics. Every thought gives rise to a set of correlated vibrations in the matter of this body, accompanied with a marvelous play of color, like that in the spray of a waterfall as the sunlight strikes it, raised to the nth degree of color and vivid delicacy. The body under this impulse throws off a vibrating portion of itself, shaped by the nature of the vibrations—as figures are made by sand on a disk vibrating to a musical note—and this gathers from the surrounding atmosphere matter like itself in fineness from the elemental essence of the mental world. (Besant & Leadbeater, 1999, p. 8)

This is, then, looking from the outside of the thinker at the thought being manifested, a subjective view through the eyes of an artist. This is a thought form pure and simple, "and it is a living entity of intense activity animated by the one idea that generated it. If made of the finer kinds of matter, it will be of great power and energy, and may be used as a most potent agent when directed by a strong and steady will" (Besant & Leadbeater, 1999, p. 8). There was a movie entitled *A Beautiful Mind* (2001) staring Russell Crowe, which was based on the life of John Nash, a Nobel Laureate in Economics. His revolutionary work on game theory, his beauty of thought, is juxtaposed with psychotic episodes, which eventually he learns to ignore. Thus, while having great power and energy, the intense activity of the mind that generates the beauty of thought must be directed by a strong and steady will. There is also the issue of balance (see Chapter 32).

MacFlouer (2004-16) forwards that the mental mind works better when someone is thinking intuitively; this is not really "working" as we define the term today, rather, it just happens, instantly creating in the moment. The intuitive makes thinking and listening and expression of thought beautiful. We all have this capability. Beauty goes beyond mental thinking by creating a condition in which the thought itself causes our mental senses to become unified and thus beautiful, joining them over time. For example, truth balances the senses, getting rid of forces (interference) and allowing us to be open to new thoughts. However, truth only does this for a limited time and a limited number of people by their expression of integrity. Beauty balances the senses in all four bodies and in infinite ways.

While the thought form is clearly a product of the thought, with the energy of the thought form animated by the idea that generated it, there is more beauty of thought to be recognized as we begin to understand the thought, connecting and integrating it through our own senses.

Nobel physicist Paul Dirac (1964) recognized the role of beauty in the advancement of humanity.

> It is more important to have beauty in one's equations than to have them fit the experiment. It seems that if one is working from the point of view of getting beauty into one's equations, and if one has really a sound insight, one is on a sure line of progress. (Davis, 1996, p. 231)

Dirac spent his life in search of beautiful equations, with the essence of this beauty lying in the economy and elegance that brings to the surface the mathematical property of being deep. He felt that it was more important to have beauty in an equation than to have it fit the experiment. As Polkinghorne (1996, p. 80) explains, "Time and again we have found that it is equations with that indispensable character of mathematical beauty which describe the nature of the physical world."

Plato believed that the love between two people was a stepping stone to love between souls, and then in *ideas and philosophy*. Through this route, ultimately the individual can come to know the form of beauty itself. Thus love as an attachment between two people is dignified when "it is converted into an appreciation of beauty in general" (Haidt, 2006). In *Symposium* at 210d (Nehamas & Woodruff translation), Plato says:

> The result is that he will see the beauty of knowledge and be looking mainly not at beauty in a single example—as a servant would who favored the beauty of a little boy or a man or a single custom ... but the lover is turned to the great sea of beauty, and, gazing upon this, he gives birth to many gloriously beautiful ideas and theories, in unstinting love of wisdom .... (Cooper, 1997).

Beauty in Art

As a global world, we've made enormous technological, economic and genetic advances that have both elevated and troubled our minds. In the midst of this expansion the aesthetic has taken a back seat. Yet the aesthetic has the power to mold our thoughts and alter our perceptions, fully engaging all of our senses and bringing our bodies, emotions and thought into balance (MacFlouer, 2004-16).

<<<<<<<<>>>>>>>>

INSIGHT: **The aesthetic has the power to mold our thoughts and alter our perceptions, fully engaging our senses and bringing our bodies, emotions and thought into balance.**

<<<<<<<<>>>>>>>>

Reflect for a moment on the art of today, much of it projecting ugliness and dissonance in a search for difference or expanded repetitiveness. Concerts featuring repeats of the great works of music. Remakes of movies, failing to capture the beauty of the original, with added elements of violence to grab attention. Reruns of reruns. When we interact with these, we are pulled into a frame of reference that focuses our attention away from the meaning and purpose of our own lives. However, we do have choice. Since the arts are dependent on stimulation of the senses, if people refuse to sense it the art goes away. As a discipline, we can simply turn our senses off to this media, and turn our attention to something better.

Art has the potential to enrich human life in so many ways. Patterns are essential to art. The arts thrive on the recognition and exploitation of patterns of association and regularity, patterns often unrecognized by science (Gell-Mann, 1994). For example, similes and metaphors embedded throughout poetry are patterns largely ignored by science.

Beliefs have inspired glorious works of art across the span of music, architecture, sculpture, painting, literature and dance. For example, the powerful influence of mythology on human intellect and emotions has led to the creation of magnificent art. Gell-Mann (1994) suggests that archaic Greek black figure vases bear witness to the creative energies released by myth. As literature, Gell-Mann describes the powerful influence of myths:

> They encapsulate experience gained through centuries and millennia of interaction with nature and with human culture. They contain not only lessons but also, at least by implication, prescriptions for behavior. they are vital parts of the cultural schemata of societies functioning as complex adaptive systems. (Gell-Mann, 1994, p. 278)

Of course, belief in myths is just one source of inspiration. And then, that which is inspired serves as inspiration for those who connect with it. A glorious work of art can surface a deep emotive response, connecting with inner memories and feelings. For example, a great work in the visual arts can lead the viewer to new ways of seeing. Art is symbolic, conveying so much more than what is seen on a canvas. As poet William J. Stewart (1985) said so many years ago in *The Runkels—A Manual of Wisdom and Wit for All Ages*, and as shared by his daughter, Heidi Lannert,

> There are symbols of grace and beauty,
> which help lift us to levels of height.
> Taking us beyond our "wounded humanity",
> restoring love and compassion to might.

Although we don't generally consider it as such, even our written language is comprised of symbols, which now flow around the world in unfathomable numbers. When eBooks and hand-held devices became the norm, it was predicted that hard-back books would disappear. Indeed, several large and well-known bookstores closed their doors. However, according to the U.S. Census Bureau 2016 figures for book sales increased. In the January-June 2016 time-span, sales totaled $5.44 billion up from $5.13 billion in the same time period in 2015, a 6.1 percent increase. Further, in 2015 self-published eBooks made up 22% of eBook sales. As one self-published author touts, "By eliminating the middle-man, you can get your work out there faster and at a lower cost. Ultimately, it's all about knowledge sharing. Knowledge is expanding so quickly, and you want people to have the advantage of your work so they can push it even farther."

The renaissance underway in literature appears to expand to all the arts. In major cities there is an increase in theater attendance and sports events, and more people going to museums. In the U.S., the number of live theater visitors has steadily increased since a low in 2012. Spring 2015 figures show 47.42 million visitors, up from 46 million in Autumn 2014 (Statista, 2016).

The *Art Newspaper*, which does an annual survey on exhibition and museum attendance, consistently touted large numbers of daily visitors to special exhibitions held around the world. Nine exhibitions held at Taipei's National Palace drew in over 12,000 people a day. A Monet exhibition held at Tokyo's Metropolitan Art Museum drew in over 10,000 people a day. While some museums surveyed had lower regular attendance due to reported local difficulties, London's British Museum, which is free, pulled in 6.8 million visitors in 2015, over 100,00 more than in 2014. Even the Louvre in Paris, despite November terrorist attacks on the French capital, pulled in 8.6 million visitors, only 600,000 less than in 2014.

A number of artists periodically dance with their art in the middle of the Allegheny Mountains of Mountain Quest. For example, Reefka Schneider is one of the foremost artists of "la frontera," the binational region of the Rio Grande Valley in South Texas. Her work was featured in the book borderlines: *Drawing Border Lives / Fronteras: Dibujando las vidas fronterizas*. In collaboration with her husband, poet Steven P. Schneider, they recently published their second book together, *The Magic of Mariachi / La Magia del Mariachi*.

Reefka, who suffers from electromagnetic sensitivity, found relief in nature in so many ways. She came to the area around Greenbank, West Virginia, to get away from cell phone towers. During this time, she spent the summer roaming and painting the hills of Mountain Quest. Here's what she wrote about her experience.

> ***Beauty is love made visible****. Inherent faculties of the soul, such as faith, intuition, creativity and love need cultivation, just as such mental faculties as critical thinking do. Painting is a process that opens my heart to intuitive thinking and creative functioning.*
>
> *We are all caught in the crossfire now, as I was when I arrived at Mountain Quest Institute, a sanctuary in time and space for me. I would arise before the sun did so I could paint the silence and color of early morning. Later I would climb the mountain and paint, perhaps observed by a red fox or young bear. I worked small, painting in watercolor with the brushes and paints and paper I could fit in my waistpack. Formerly, I had always worked much larger in my studio, where I drew and painted the people of the U.S./Mexico border where I lived. At Mountain Quest I experienced the singular beauty of the spontaneous statement that small watercolor work provided me as I attempted to capture the feeling of the soul of the place, that transcendent connection to the inner life that is both silent and beautiful.* (Reefka)

See Figure 33-1. Reefka's books are available on amazon.com, Barnes and Noble and through their publisher, Wings Press.

Figure 33-1. *The Art of Reefka Schneider (with permission).*

Cindy Taylor is the resident artist at Mountain Quest. Growing up on a farm, Cindy has spent her life feeling a deep kinship with the beauty of the land and its animals, both domestic and wild. Self-taught, and working primarily in oils and acrylics, she re-purposes cast-off objects, painting vivid scenes on saw blades, wood pallets, tin tea cans and ironing boards. As the resident artist, Cindy's colorful representations, executed with delicate precision, accent the walls and ceilings of MQI, and are available on greeting cards in the MQI shop. See Figure 33-2.

Figure 33-2. *The Art of Cindy Taylor (with permission).*

Corbie Crouse—a former Walt Disney World artist who taught guests how to draw Mickey, Donald and Rapunzel—lives in Orlando, Florida, what she describes as "a populated environment with many distractions." Every year she and her husband come to West Virginia and stay at the Inn. As she shares:

> *The atmosphere is beautiful and quiet. The environment brings us great peace, allowing my creativity to expand in ways that are new to me. The watercolor paintings I create at Mountain Quest have a boldness and surety to them that is rare for me. These new creative experiences help me to grow as an artist and a person.*

See Figure 33-3.

Figure 33-3. *The Art of Corbie Crouse (with permission)*.

As a final example, Jackie Urbanovic is an award-winning illustrator of children's books, best known for her *New York Times* Bestselling Max books, *Duck at the Door and Duck Soup*, *No Sleep for the Sheep*, and *Grandma Lena's Big 'Ol Turnip*. As she moves through life, Jackie picks up inspiration from her surroundings. As she describes,

Being in the meadows and hills of Mountain Quest, I found that my mind had room to roam. While my feet trod across unknown fields, my mind floated to new places, storing up ideas for later creations. Then, at night, in a place without streetlights, neon signs or other homes: the sky! Oh, the experience of a sky filled with that many stars—thousands more than I'd ever seen in my life—such awe-inspiring beauty. Add to that the thrilling experience of being in the presence of the Myst—seeing it show up on even my photographs, and knowing that this presence was beside me, was thrilling. I also visited with the llamas, the goats, the horses, the bluejays, the sparrows and the goldfinches. The experience there confirmed to me that we are not alone. Add to all this the lively conversations in the library, and my mind left there happy and on fire.

A print of the dragon pictured in Figure 33-4 is a treasured part of The Fantasy Room at Mountain Quest.

Figure 33-4. *The Art of Jackie Urbanovic (with permission).*

Health as a Work of Art

Your physical body—along with your emotional and mental bodies—is your creation. In order to be beautiful, we must become healthy. We all understand that what we put in our bodies is important, that is, what we eat and the air we breathe. We also understand how important it is to exercise our bodies, and that how we use our bodies impacts our wellness. What many of us do *not* realize is that what we think and how we feel also directly impacts our bodies. For example, when you are under stress how does your body feel? You may suffer headaches or an upset stomach or even have a stroke or heart attack. As Mulford (2007, p.66) describes,

> Your thoughts shape your face, and give it its peculiar expression. Your thoughts determine the attitude, carriage, and shape of your whole body ... **The law for beauty and the law for perfect health is the same. Both depend entirely on the state of your mind**; or, in other words, on the kind of thoughts you most put out and receive [emphasis added].

Note the relationship between beauty and perfect health. Mulford contends that the prevailing mood of mind affects both the health *and* looks of the body. That which you think most you will become. If your thought is determined and decided, your carriage and movement show it. If you are cheerful, your face will show it. So, "Persistency in thinking health, in imagining or idealizing yourself as healthy, vigorous, and symmetrical, is the cornerstone of health and beauty" (Mulford, 2007, p.73).

Health is a relative concept denoting a physical, mental and emotional state of being. It has to do with the level of functioning and metabolic efficiency of living organisms. While we must be healthy to be beautiful, *health is a state internally created through the creation of beauty.*

<<<<<<<<>>>>>>>

INSIGHT: **While we must be healthy to be beautiful, heath is a state internally created through the creation of beauty.**

<<<<<<<<>>>>>>>

You can't create beauty by periodically going to a gym or eating well. Developing a foundation for health requires a *consistency of choices*. There are internal drivers that manifest in the physical that drive our choices. When you get down to it, your choices in food and who you consult for your health care require mental development, unusual fortitude and great wisdom (MacFlouer, 2004-16). A negative example that impacts choices is the stress discussed in Chapter 20/Part III. A positive example that impacts choices is the use of positive thinking discussed in Chapter 9/Part II.

The concept of aging is one that has been culturally and globally adopted. However, aging as a yardstick is an illusion. As MacFlouer (2004-16) says, beauty in body is not aging by the standards of today. If you use that standard, aging means that everything is breaking down. MacFlouer's definition of health is the ability to develop an on-going state of wisdom while *living longer and longer without the signs of aging*. Whatever your age, if you live a "healthy" lifestyle (physical, mental and emotional), aging will slow down. The more beauty created, the slower the aging process.

Of course, beauty of the self is in producing health in *all* of our bodies (planes). From this frame of reference, there is beauty in aging; for example, often the mind is more content, focused and calm than in youth. Urbanovic (2017) describes it this way,

> I am focused on different priorities and I've come to enjoy the difference between the beauty of youth and its intense sexual passions, its desire to be everywhere at once, the joy of beginnings and, with older age, the increased focus, gained wisdom, and greater sense of security and self. *Like art, aging is difficult, revelatory and beautiful, all at once.*

While health is intended as the natural state for the human, for most of us this is not the case today. To a large extent, being unhealthy is a product of today's life style, as evidenced by the propensity for people to be overweight, eat things that are bad for our bodies because of accepted food processes or because we are in a hurry. Ultimately, it all comes down to the choice of what we *think, feel and do*. Beauty is a choice.

****

TOOL 33-1: Choosing Beauty

STEP 1: If you have one of those watches that has an alarm on it, set it to go off on the hour every hour. If you don't, go about your day checking your watch regularly. When the alarm goes off, or when it is close to the hour, turn the alarm off, stop whatever you are doing and go to Step 2.

STEP 2: Slowly turn completely around, scanning those things that are close to you, say within five or six feet. Spend a moment thinking about each of the things that come into your view. About each, **consider:** How is this useful? Who created this? Does it serve a purpose? Do the pieces all fit together well? Are the colors pleasing? Allow yourself to be fully in the NOW; FEEL into the item upon which you are focusing. Allow each item their moment of importance.

STEP 3: Slowly take a second complete turn, this time focusing further out into the distance, reflecting on all that comes into your view. If you are outside, you may wish to take a third turn to reflect on the far distance. Give every item its special moment in time.

STEP 4: Closing your eyes, consider all of the things you have brought into your focus and how they all fit together. Imagine yourself as the model in a famous artist's painting, with all of the things around you of significance to the painting. What story do they tell? What is your relationship to these items? What do these things that surround you tell you about the figure in the painting, that is, YOU.

STEP 5: Take a leap into the future, say 100 years forward. Using your creative imagination, picture yourself in the middle of an art auction, and there in front of you is the picture of YOU and all those things surrounding you. Many people are bidding, and the price gets higher and higher. As people keep bidding, you look closely at the painting, and you begin to see *why* they are bidding. There is a relationship between the person that is YOU and all those things that surround you. They look REAL and yet there is an invisible energy that says more than the picture. You look closely at your face, captured with the eyes closed, and see a wonder expressed there. You note that the artist has captured the knowing that is occurring in the moment at hand, that even with the eyes closed this figure has *full awareness of who they are and where they are*. The bids continue to get higher and higher.

STEP 6: Still in that place, you hear the auctioneer pause and say: Is there another bid? This is a *Carlotti*, a special picture. The summation of the parts work together in such a way that nothing needs to be added, taken away or altered. He has captured a perfect life moment.

STEP 7: Still in that future place, push your hand into your pocket and pull out a credit card with no limits, recognizing that in this place you are wealthy and have the means to purchase this painting if you choose. Do you choose to do so?

****

Sharing Beauty

We now understand that when focused outward and shared, creative energy multiplies. This extends to the creation of beauty, whether a book, a painting or sculpture, or even creation of our self. And when we create with others, there is an expansion of our "creation juices."

Admittedly, as noted above, the creation of beauty has become harder through the past century as we embrace an artistic cycle of repetition and, in an attempt to grab attention, extremes are tapped over and over again, often resulting in negative experiences. It *is* difficult to take a play from the past and come up with a new creative approach that grabs the minds and hearts of today's audience while staying true to the message and intent of the work. One of the complaints we often hear is: "Everything's been done, and different is not always a thing of beauty!" However, there is always something new in the experience of living. We defer back to Chapter 29/Part IV on creativity. There are two types of creativity, P-creativity (personal) and H-creativity (historical). P-creativity unfolds for everyone throughout life.

We don't have to be a great artist to create and share beauty. We *do* each have the opportunity to beautify our environment, and if we have a stream of people moving through that environment, we are sharing that beauty and helping others to improve their senses. This may begin with members of our family, then extended family and friends, and even a larger segment of humanity. If people's values are similar, then the beauty they discover in your shared environment moves on to others, that is, they are creating beauty in their thought as they immerse themselves in the beauty of the environment, and have the opportunity to share that with others. Beauty is a multiplier and, as MacFlouer (2004-16) explains, we are each an example for everyone else. By creating a beautiful environment and sharing it, we are advocating beauty in the senses of others. Beauty supports the growth of all parts of life. Thus, it is our job to create environments that affect more others, so they can experience beauty in those environments. Sharing the beauty of our environment is one way that we can on a daily basis directly see the results of our actions.

<<<<<<<>>>>>>>

INSIGHT: **Beauty is a multiplier. By creating a beautiful environment and sharing it, we are advocating beauty in the senses of others, supporting the growth of all parts of life.**

<<<<<<<>>>>>>>

An example of sharing beauty is the creation of the Mountain Quest Retreat Center. See Figure 33-5. Some 20 plus years ago author David Bennet had a dream of building a research and retreat center, so as partners Alex and David set about doing just that, and today others are becoming part of this amazing dream! The intent was to create a place of **beauty in a natural setting**, designed with the thought in mind of elegant simplicity or simple elegance. Yes, there is beauty in the setting, with vibrant green fields set in a high valley of the Allegheny Mountains punctuated with trees, streams and wildlife.

Beauty in the experience is supported through themed rooms, bringing in a taste of international diversity and areas of interest and passion. For example, there is a Play House, with the heavy rich red and gold brocades of the turn of the century, a golden punched tin ceiling, carved poster mahogany beds, souvenirs from plays and musicals, a three-story "playhouse" with doll furniture from around the world and crocheted rugs from three generations of needle workers. Next door is the Inn Ovation Room, all black and white on the inside, with colors around the walls, tiled floor, a heat-vibrator chair, a red bathroom with black toilet, and various innovative toys. Down the way is the Nautical Cove, with a full-wall mural of a dock in Southeast Asia, with the two beds tied up to the dock (one a water bed). Large waves are embedded in the opposite wall and ropes and knots provide a ceiling band, all accented by a rose compass in the floor and a night sky for navigation in the bathroom. Then, a Safari Hut upstairs boasts a carbonized bamboo floor, a woven bamboo ceiling held up by tiger bamboo, and netted beds against a full-wall mural of sunset on the Mara in Kenya, Africa. And so on ...

Beauty of thought is honored and encouraged, with a two-story, 27,000 volume library sharing the thoughts of well over a hundred thousand authors. MQIPress publishes eBooks, of which this work is a part, to share the research resulting from Institute research programs in the never-ending quest for knowledge, consciousness and meaning. And for those with open minds and hearts, the energy of the *Myst*—shared through the concept of *Myst-Art*—can be experienced and explored. The *Myst* phenomenon could be described as **specks of dust, waves of water mist and bursts of light, all part of the Earth's natural ecosystem, which combine with the electromagnetic energies of orbs to produce** *Myst-Art*, an always intriguing, and

Figure 33-5. *Sharing the beauty of life at Mountain Quest.*

often mystical, phenomenon. The *Myst* represents a deeper look into the natural energies surrounding each and every one of us, energies that are often invisible and rarely capture our conscious attention. Today's technologies enable us to photograph these energies and produce pictures that are truly beautiful, engaging and unique. See Figure 33-5.

Exploring the patterns of *Myst-Art* encourages our search for understanding and meaning, starting "Conversations that Matter" in the two-story library and challenging us to revisit our beliefs and our place in the larger Universe. *What we see depends on what the camera captures, what we perceive, and what reality is trying to tell us.* Appendix A, introduced in Part I and shared here as well, is a prose treatment with pictures of this phenomenon.

Figure 33-6. *A Myst picture entitled: "Crowned with Light." The description reads: "The majesty of communing in the Myst: One voice, one song, one heart".*

There is also a **beauty of gifting for others to enjoy**. Visitors, colleagues and guests bring a piece of themselves into the rooms and common spaces. For example, a family picture of a bomber during the 1940's from a state employee (for the Hangar Room), five older goats raised by 4-Hers for visitors to enjoy, books from a naturalist whose sight was weaning, a book on playhouses (for the Play House), contributed by several young ladies on the volleyball team during their annual spaghetti dinner, and so much more. See www.mountainquestinn.com

Then, the **beauty of the sharing and learning from each other** occurs while reading in the library, sharing the breakfast table, or rocking on the front porch, feeling the soft breeze off the mountains and watching the gentle grazing of horses. Children in water shoes laughing and splashing, searching the creek for, and finding, rocks with the imprint of life forms long past.

As can be seen in our example, beauty has an immediate effect that involves all the senses; it is seen and felt inside and outside. By taking the time to separate from a busy and often overwhelming life to experience new places, join in new conversations and connect with nature, life can take on an entirely different meaning, or bring back purposes and directions that have been pushed to the periphery of our thought.

Beauty as Transcendence

In *Symposium* (211) Plato suggests that there is an ordering, that the beauties of the earth were to be used as stepping stones moving humanity upwards through fair forms to fair practices to fair notes and, ultimately, to absolute beauty, which he described as fair living.

How do *you* feel when you are surrounded by beauty, something you personally think is beautiful? This could be a place, perhaps the country or a historic building, your favorite piece of art, or a person you love. How do *you* feel when you understand a concept that is simple and elegant and excites all of your senses?

Close your eyes and create a picture of the beauty you have experienced in your mind's eye or an echo of that beauty in your heart. How does this remembering make you feel? When we bring beauty to mind all of our senses of form—and our additional two inner senses—come into balance (see Chapter 32). There is no room left for lower vibrational energy. Similar to what was accomplished during the period we describe as the Renaissance, the creation and sharing of beauty is a way of circumventing the long and often arduous development of the mental faculties to facilitate a leap forward in the advancement of civilization and consciousness. Much like the potential effects of a butterfly flapping its wings on the other side of the world, beauty shared can multiply exponentially with wide-spread impact.

<<<<<<<>>>>>>>

INSIGHT: **Beauty is a short circuit to thinking, enabling us to circumvent the tedium of everyday life in an instant, and inject a feeling of appreciation, love and joy into the essence of our lives.**

<<<<<<<>>>>>>>

As MacFlouer (2004-16) shares, beauty can leapfrog over clogged senses, can break through a log jam, and can overcome force and allow light to enter. When intentional thought perceives beauty through all of the senses, the senses are unified during the time that thought is occurring. Recall that intention is *the power to focus the knowledge and maintain direction toward a sense of the anticipated future* (see

Chapter 25/Part IV). Thus, unlike an intuitional flash, the intentional focus on beauty is sustainable for a period of time, based on the choice and focus of the perceiver. Yet, **the experience of beauty is similar to the experience of an intuitive flash, with all the senses involved, an awareness of connectedness, and** *an unexpressed knowing needing no expression.* Once we have experienced beauty—and as we continue to have experiences of beauty—life is never the same. We expand; everything is different from that point forward. When beauty is shared with others, they have the opportunity to share that same expansion.

Final Thoughts

Beauty is a transcendent state which can bring all of our senses into harmony. Plato suggests that there is an ordering, that the beauties of the earth were to be used as stepping stones moving humanity upwards through fair forms to fair practices to fair notes and, ultimately, to the absolute beauty of fair living. Thank you, Plato, for enriching our lives with this beautiful possibility for humanity to which we all can contribute. Are we ready to step upwards?

Questions for Reflection:

How can you bring beauty into your life?

How do you respond when you experience beauty?

What are the ways to engage beauty more fully in support of your Intelligent Social Change Journey?

How can we share beauty with others?

Chapter 34
Virtues for Living the Future

SUBPARTS: BEAUTY, GOODNESS AND TRUTH ... GOOD CHARACTER ... GOOD CHARACTER IS ACTIONABLE ... EXPLORING GOOD CHARACTER THROUGH CORE VALUES ... ALL PEOPLE ARE NOT CREATED EQUAL ... FINAL THOUGHTS

TOOL: 34-1. DEVELOPING A GOOD CHARACTER ACTION SET

MacFlouer (2004-16) refers to virtue as *spirit in form*. We have previously introduced cooperation and collaboration as the highest virtues on the physical plane, truth as the highest virtue on the mental plane, unconditional love as the highest virtue on the emotional plane, and beauty as the highest virtue on the intuitional plane. Consistent with this usage, virtue is considered morally good behavior or character; a good and moral quality; the good result that comes from something (Merriam-Webster, 2016). Thus, virtue and morality are synonymous, with other synonyms including: goodness, righteousness, integrity, dignity, rectitude, honor, decency, respectability, nobility, worthiness, purity, principles and ethics (Google, 2016).

In this chapter, we first take a brief look at the virtues of beauty, goodness and truth, beginning with their introduction by the great philosophers. We then delve into the concept of good character. As we focus on living the future, *never has it been more important to develop the virtue of good character*, which directly affects the growth of self and expansion of consciousness.

Beauty, Goodness and Truth

Much, much earlier in human history, philosophers such as Socrates, Plato and Aristotle were exploring and reflecting upon those things which were a crucial part of living a good life. From their great body of thought and feeling, we as a humanity began to expand our understanding of virtue in terms of beauty, goodness and truth. Beauty is the focus of Chapter 33; goodness is addressed below in terms of good character; and truth is the focus of Chapter 24/Part IV.

Virtues, qualities of being morally good, are concepts that when thought about expand consciousness and when acted upon increase intelligent activity. Recall that intelligent activity represents a *state of interaction* where intent, purpose, direction, values and expected outcomes are clearly understood and communicated among all parties, reflecting wisdom and achieving a higher truth.

<<<<<<<>>>>>>>

INSIGHT: **Virtues are concepts that when thought about expand consciousness, and when acted upon increase intelligent activity**.

<<<<<<<>>>>>>>

How did those early philosophers get it right so long ago? The concepts of beauty, goodness and truth are transcendental; in Latin that's *transcendentalia*, meaning having properties of being or Oneness. It is not surprising that these critical human concepts are emerging again into our awareness as we journey toward becoming a global community!

Perhaps the first mention of these virtues in written form can be credited to the Bhagavad Gita (Ch. 17 v. 15), describing in an example, "words which are good and beautiful and true." Nonetheless, it is Plato's well-known *Dialogues* where the concepts appear amidst those high ideals of wisdom and justice, that is most often remembered as introducing beauty, goodness and truth as virtues. For example, in *Phaedrus* (24) Plato talks about the "ability of the soul to soar up to heaven to behold beauty, wisdom, goodness and the like."

In the world of today, Howard Gardner, a Professor of Cognition and Education at the Harvard Graduate School of Education and author of the groundbreaking work on multiple intelligences, has embraced these three virtues as crucial to our existence as a humanity (Gardner, 2011, *Truth, Beauty and Goodness Reframed*). Through a networked humanity, a diversity of information is readily available such that a thinker can more easily discern truth, an explorer can more widely experience beauty, and a seeker can more readily discover goodness. In a global world, there are a lot more choices.

<<<<<<<>>>>>>>

INSIGHT: **Through a linked humanity, a diversity of information is readily available such that a thinker can more easily discern truth, an explorer can more widely experience beauty, and a seeker can more readily discover goodness.**

<<<<<<<>>>>>>>

These virtues—identified by our early philosophers as transcendental and reaffirmed by our thinkers of today as crucial to the existence of humanity—are directly linked to the Intelligent Social Change Journey. For example, we learned in Chapter 24/Part IV that knowledge and truth are irrevocably connected. As we develop our higher mental faculties, we hone our discretion and discernment (D^2), balancing our understanding of the past, present and future. In this balance, we move beyond relativity (context sensitivity and situation dependence) and bring time and space closer together (Chapter 16/Part III) to more clearly see truth, which is the highest virtue of the mental plane.

We forward that the continuous search for beauty, goodness and truth serves as the foundation of developing good character.

Good Character

In the book *The Death of Character*, Hunter (2000) provides a detailed account of how America has lost its older ideals about virtue and character. For example, prior to the Industrial Revolution, Americans honored hard work, self-restraint, and sacrifice for the future and the common good. As we entered the 20th century and people became wealthier, the idea of a self that was centered around preferences and personal fulfillment came to the fore, and the *moral* term "character" was replaced by the *amoral* term "personality" (Haidt, 2007) (not to be confused with our treatment of personality in Chapter 4/Part I). Hunter also forwards that this shift is a side effect of inclusiveness. For example, as Americans experienced increasing diversity, educators struggled to identify an ever-shrinking set of moral ideas that could be agreed upon. As Haidt (2007, p. 176) explains:

> [Inclusiveness] cut children off from the soil of tradition, history, and religion that nourished older concepts of virtue. You can grow vegetables hydroponically, but even then you have to add nutrients to the water. Asking children to grow virtues hydroponically, looking only within themselves for guidance, is like asking each one to invent a personal language—a pointless and isolating task if there is no community with whom to speak.

However, while certainly a price was paid for inclusiveness, Haidt acknowledges that we have "bought ourselves a more humane society, with greater opportunity ... for most people" (p. 177). This quote refers to demographic diversity, that is, diversity about sociodemographic categories such as race, ethnicity, cultural history, sex, sexual orientation, age and handicapped status, the inclusion of previously excluded groups. Conversely, *moral diversity* is what Durkheim (1965/1915) describes as anomic, which means a lack of agreement regarding moral norms and values. Haidt (2007) says that once this distinction is made, nobody would coherently *want* moral diversity. Nowhere is this more dramatically demonstrated than in the machinations of the U.S. government following the 2016 elections.

A positive example is what Damon (1997) calls the youth charter movement. This movement calls for cooperation between parents, teachers, religious leaders and coaches in child rearing. Together with the children, these groups come to a shared understanding on obligations and values, with all parties expected to uphold the same high standards of behavior, good character, in all situations. Note the similarities of this definition with intelligent activity. Recognizing the need for achieving a shared understanding of moral behavior, in Chapter 35 we forward the need for a Universal spirituality and introduce the Global Ethic, *a call for humanity to live a more mature expression of moral life through the transformation of consciousness*.

The concept of character is directly related to growth of the self—individuals and their choices and actions—and represents a quality of goodness. Good character is defined as "the self-created ability to give to others in thought according to what they need, with the thought containing knowledge as applied to the three lower bodies [the physical, emotional and mental planes] that has been synthesized from information" (MacFlouer, 1999, p. 164). What is clear from this definition is that character is created.

<<<<<<<<>>>>>>>

INSIGHT: **Character is created**.

<<<<<<<<>>>>>>>

MacFlouer (1999) forwards that there are *three senses of self created* as the self grows and expands. The first sense is of discriminating thought, the ability to recognize in form and sense their own self, who/what it is and who/what it is not. The second sense is of discerning thought, the ability to recognize in form and sense who/what others are and who/what others are not. This is in preparation for the sharing of knowledge. As MacFlouer (1999, p. 172) describes: "Because the self increases its understanding and prepares to give what is needed for others to give selflessly, it sees some shared Oneness, or similarity, between itself and the others—it develops discernment and good character." The third sense is the expansion of Oneness, the ability to recognize the connectedness of all things, thus openly and fully sharing with others *all* the sense, form, knowledge and consciousness it has created.

Enter the Quantum field. Continuing with MacFlouer's thought (1999, p. 172):

Through a group of selves all creating more of themselves and then giving to each other and to others, a commonality of direction to their thought develops as their choices are synergistically supportive of each other. The result is that the collective selves eventually limit over half of the larger field they think within, in similar or sometimes even the same ways, and thus use the senses of their lifeforms in similar ways to create knowledge and consciousness that is common to all of them.

Thus, the creation of good character in the individual is a critical step to expanding the consciousness of humanity.

<<<<<<<<>>>>>>>>

INSIGHT: **The creation of good character in the individual is a critical step to expanding the consciousness of humanity.**

<<<<<<<<>>>>>>>>

This is consistent with Aristotle, to whom the virtue of character is a central phenomenon for ethics. Aristotle argues that a virtuous person, just in so far as he is morally virtuous, "takes pleasure in and is distressed about the right things in the right ways; a vicious person takes pleasure in and is distressed about the wrong things and in the wrong ways" (Cooper, 1999, p. 264). Aristotle describes this in terms of the noble, fine and beautiful, versus the base, shameful and ugly. In his words,

> There are three objects of choice (*ta eis tas haireseis*) and three of avoidance: the *kalon* (the noble, fine, beautiful), the advantageous, and the pleasant, and their opposites, the *aischron* (the base, shameful, ugly), the harmful, and the painful. In relation to all these the good person gets things right, while the bad person gets things wrong, but especially in relation to pleasure. For pleasure is shared with the animals, and it is involved in all the objects of choice, since the *kalon* and the advantageous also appear pleasant. [*Nicomachean Ethics* II 3, 1104b30-1105a1] (Cooper, 1999, p.265)

Nobility was presented in Chapter 22/Part IV as a learning point along the path.

Peterson and Seligman (2004) set out to develop a list of strengths and virtues that might be valid across different cultures. Six broad virtues appeared consistently on their lists: wisdom, courage, humanity, justice, temperance and transcendence. While these are abstract, they serve as a way to organize specific strengths of character, defined as specific ways of displaying, practicing and cultivating the virtues.

Peterson and Seligman (2004) suggest 24 principle character strengths, each supporting one of the six higher-level virtues. These are: (1) Wisdom (curiosity, love of learning, judgment, ingenuity, emotional intelligence, perspective); (2) Courage (valor, perseverance, integrity); (3) Humanity (kindness, loving); (4) Justice (citizenship, fairness, leadership; (5) Temperance (self-control, prudence, humility); and (6) Transcendence (appreciation of beauty and excellence, gratitude, hope, spirituality, forgiveness, humor, zest). Haidt (2007, p. 168) says that the real power of this classification is that it points to "specific means of growth toward widely valued ends without insisting that any one way is mandatory for all people at all times." Thus, the classification schema can serve as a tool for diagnosing diverse strengths and helping people discover paths to excellence.

Good Character is Actionable

The quality of good character is actionable, that is, matching our actions with our thoughts and feelings such that they create good behaviors between ourselves and others. *Without action good character would not be discernible.* MacFlouer (2004-16) says that in our interactional world to identify someone with good character there must be a threat to goodness such that the one observed exhibits a strength in character through self-sacrifice. An individual with good character will respond with such; someone that lacks good character will show that lack by either taking no action or inhibiting positive response.

This idea of responsibility as a virtue and its relation to action is not a new one. Arthur Schnitzleer, starting his professional life first as a physician and morphing into a noted Austrian poet and dramatist, is credited with saying that there are only three virtues: objectivity, courage and a sense of responsibility. Objectivity is the ability to move beyond self and look at the larger picture, very much having to do with systems thinking. In Chapter 9/Part II we introduce courage as a cognitive conveyer intertwined throughout the modalities of change. Courage is about choices made and actions taken in an uncertain environment, a presence of mind. A sense of responsibility—for ourselves and others—puts us in a place of choice, choosing the way we respond to the perturbations and opportunities of life, and moving into our role as co-creators. Viktor Frankl (1948/1975) says that recognition of responsibleness as the essence of existence through existential analysis begins with inversion of the question: What is the meaning of life? He contends that,

> ... man is not he who poses the question, What is the meaning of life? But he who is asked this question: for it is life itself that poses it to him. And man has to answer to life by answering for life; he has to respond by being responsible; in other words, the response is necessarily a response-in-action. (p. 24)

While this responsibility in terms of action is very much in the NOW, it is both in terms of proactive and reactive. Frankl's (1969/1988) *Logotherapy* or existential analysis is intended to bring individuals to an awareness of responsibleness through becoming conscious of something spiritual. "For it is only from the viewpoint of man's spirituality, or existentiality, that being human can be described in terms of being responsible." (Frankl, 1948/1975, p. 24) This is the self becoming conscious of its self.

Taking a consilience approach, we share here, offered in the form of verse, key elements of the expansion of good character as we journey through life.

> Is it spirit? Is it form?
> Beauty, goodness and truth.
> We *seek* the cloak of virtue
> And journey through our youth.
>
> Are you listening? Can you hear it?
> Is it ringing in your ears?
> We *weave* the cloak of virtue
> From music of the spheres.
>
> I am aching. I am waking.
> I cannot hold it in my hands.
> We *wear* the cloak of virtue.
> My character expands.
>
> There is beauty. There is balance.
> Good character abounds.
> We *are* the cloak of virtue.
> Morality compounds.
>
> Life of service. Path of Oneness.
> We feel compassion grow.
> We *share* the cloak of virtue
> And consciousness bestow.

How do you create good character? What is the function of the action that shows caring to others? Since each individual is unique, the elements of good character are also going to be unique. We recognize that character is created and, referring back to Aristotle (1962/4th cent., 1103b), character is developed through practice.

> Men become builders by building houses, and harpists by playing the harp. Similarly, we grow just by the practice of just actions, self-controlled by exercising our self-control, and courageous by performing acts of courage.

Perhaps that is exactly the purpose of experiential learning (Bennet et al., 2015b; Kolb, 1984).

Buddha offered a set of activities called the "Eightfold Noble Path". With practice, these activities would create a person of good character (through right speech, action and livelihood) as well as a mentally disciplined person (through right effort, mindfulness and concentration). Clearly this early guidance, from both the East and West, demonstrates an understanding of the need for practice and repetition. This also demonstrates the need for both explicit and tacit knowledge sharing. As Haidt (2007, p. 160) explains:

> Moral education must also impart tacit knowledge—skills of social perception and social emotion so finely tuned that one automatically *feels* the right thing in each situation, *knows* the right thing to do, and then *wants* to do it. Morality, for the ancients, was a kind of practical wisdom.

With such an education, the concern of inclusivity voiced by Haidt becomes nil.

Certainly, empathy, *objectively* trying to experience the inner life of another, is a critical factor of good character. Note the relationship of empathy with the virtue of objectivity introduced above. Empathy was introduced in Chapter 22/Part IV as having three different types: (1) a cognitive-based form called *perspective-taking*, that is, seeing the world through someone else's eyes; (2) literally feeling another's emotions form called *personal distress,* caused by "emotional contagion"; and (3) recognition of another's emotional state and feeling in tune with it called *empathic concern*. While our responses to others are not always cognitive in nature, as suggested by type (2), clearly type (1) is a choice and type (3) is a skill set that can be developed. All three types require the element of compassion.

Underlying the concept of good character is the element of motive. Motive is not easily recognizable and often hidden, even from the individual who is taking action. However, as we define knowledge as the capacity (potential or actual) to take effective action, the result of the action itself in terms of effectiveness can be linked directly back to the choice to take action. Good motive is when you seek to improve a situation for the betterment of others, so you can measure the value of character of a person by the benefit to others. For example, if the result of action is to control or reduce the freedom of others or force others to act negatively, this is reflective of a negative motive and bad character.

Exploring Good Character through Core Values

Over the years, several of the authors had the opportunity to work with the Singapore Armed Forces as they focused on inculcating core values across the service. Since all of this material has now been published and presented at various conferences around the world, we will use this experience as a way to further explore the concept of good character.

The core values of an organization define their *unique character*, who they are and what they strive to become, serving as a common bond of identity. Because of their conceptual level of thought, they strengthen an organization's capacity to adapt to new challenges, and help determine how knowledge and skills will be used. As Commander of the Army Lt. General Desmond Kuek (2006) stated, "There are three things about a leader that don't and won't change: our sense of Mission which is our reason for being, our Values that define who we are and what we stand for, and our emphasis on our People which means developing them in mind, body and heart."

Potentially more prominent in a Defense organization, rationalizations, faulty beliefs and unclear thinking can erode core values and our sense of right and wrong, and even lead to compromised standards and unethical or despicable acts of cruelty in war. Connecting core values to patterns of past actions can serve as a guide for future actions. The individual soldier, sailor or airman who regularly reflects on his values is likely to channel behaviors in that direction. What we think about and reflect upon is what we become (Bennet et al., 2015b).

The core value set of Singapore Armed Forces (SAF) must be considered as a balanced set for guiding individual's decisions and right course of action. For example, the core value of Professionalism (being competent and knowing your job well so that you are not led down the wrong path) must be balanced with the core value of Ethics so that a job is not just done, but is the right thing to do.

The SAF core values begin with **Loyalty to Country**, **Leadership** and **Discipline**. While descriptions of each of the core values certainly include language specific to the mission of the SAF, the concepts underlying these values support the development of good character. We defer to the SAF *Core Values Handbook*, widely-available, for descriptions of the SAF core values. Note that descriptions of core values used in this text **emerged from the leaders**, at all levels of the organization, who were living these values. *Loyalty to Country* is concerned with protecting all that is cherished: our way of life, homeland, family and national interests. *Leadership* mandates the highest character, competency and authenticity from leaders at all levels. Leading by example and inspiring, motivating and developing people are foundational. Other phrases include: visioning, transforming and planning, teamwork and teambuilding, choices and good judgment, handling new paradigms, flexibility and adaptability. *Discipline* includes personal mastery, mental stamina, courage, inner strength and physical toughness. As can be seen, these aspects of the core values can easily be extrapolated over to any country or organization, and have very much to do with character and service to others.

The remaining core values provide specific examples related to good character. These are **Professionalism**, **Fighting Spirit**, **Ethics** and **Care for Soldiers**. Professionalism—knowing our roles and responsibilities and *giving the best in all that we do*—requires a systems perspective, creating new ideas and solving problems through innovation, the use of networking and the *sharing of ideas* [knowledge]. Other descriptive language includes: open communications, continuously striving for excellence, creativity, learning, and meeting challenges. *Fighting Spirit* involves courage, tenacity and resilience to do what is right. It engages the hearts, minds and bodies with conviction, whether facing fear and uncertainty or everyday mundane tasks, pressing on and never giving up.

Ethics represents the personal and professional integrity that promotes wholeness and soundness. In the context of the military, ethics is shown through exemplary conduct and willingness to take responsibility and be accountable for our actions. It concerns the *moral will* to do what is right even at personal costs, being honest and accurate, having integrity in dealings with others and not misusing position or power against others for selfish gains. It entails respect for all others regardless of their background and culture. Key words and phrases include: honesty, truth, integrity, selflessness, taking responsibility, accountability for actions, doing what is right, trustworthiness, moral will, and uprightness of character.

Care for Soldiers embodies genuine care and concern in the well-being of others, supporting physical, emotional and mental fitness and health. Key words and phrases include: respect, dignity, safety, welfare, moral responsibility, personal touch, morale, well-being, using heart, coaching, training, armed with knowledge, sharing knowledge, building confidence and cohesion, and showing and acting with empathy.

****

TOOL 34-1: DEVELOPING A GOOD CHARACTER ACTION SET

This tool is designed to raise awareness and aid in understanding our own character and the character of those around us. We will use the descriptive phrases and words included in the core value set referenced above.

STEP (1): Slowly reread the descriptions, including key words and phrases as provided, of the SAF Core Value set (as introduced in the paragraphs above this tool). Reflect on each descriptive phrase/word *asking the following question*: (a) Do I consider this an important aspect of good character? [If so, highlight that phrase/word.] *Then ask yourself these questions and listen to your answers*: (b) Is this an aspect that is a part of my thoughts, feelings, and actions? (c) Do I recognize and respect this aspect in the behavior of others? (d) What is an example of an action that conveys this concept?

STEP (2): Prepare a chart with the highlighted aspects in the left column (a), and a column for the responses to each of the three additional questions: (b), (c) and (d). Review the aspects listed in column (a) where "yes" appears in columns (b) and (c), *and* where you provided an example in column (d). These reflect aspects that through life you have developed as part of your good character. These aspects now comprise your current Good Character Action Set (GCAS).

STEP (3): Now go back and look at those aspects where (b) and (c) disagree and/or you were unable to come up with an example in column (d). These reflect aspects that you think/feel are important but are not yet embedded in your action set, or easily recognized in the actions of others. The good news is that now these have been brought into your awareness. Now let your unconscious go to work. In the morning as you start your day, review one aspect in this grouping and make a mental note to try and identify an example of that aspect in action in another person. This may take several days. If so, remind yourself of the aspect each morning, and keep looking. When you come up with an example, then reflect whether that is a behavior you would choose to add as part of your GCAS. Remember, you are individuated and have choice. The aspects you choose to embed as part of your GCAS will have their own personal flavor/approach in service to others consistent with the purpose and meaning you have identified as your direction in life.

STEP (4): In steps (1) through (3) above, we used an initial core value set to focus on good character and stimulate the bisociation of conceptual ideas and actions (examples). This is the way we search for truth (see Chapter 24/Part IV). Through experiencing and learning, open yourself to identifying behaviors that you think/feel reflect good character and then search for the underlying concepts that support your thought/feelings. In this way, continue to raise your awareness of your character and the character of others, and to expand your GCAS.

****

All People Are Not Created Equal

So far, we have looked at good character from a general viewpoint, noting the importance of individuation in terms of difference, but not addressing individuation in terms of capability. With apologies to historical documents (where the intent was focused on equal rights), *all people are not created equal*. Nor would we want them to be!

As defined by Merriam-Webster (2016), equal is, quite simply, the same in number, amount, degree, rank or quality; not changing, the same for each person. As we now know, people are verbs, not nouns, and, whether reflecting from the viewpoint of the physical, emotional or mental planes, changing every instant of our lives! In the context of this discussion, this might mean that it is quite easy for some people to achieve aspects of good character without thought or feeling or effort, sort of on automatic. From this viewpoint there is little, if any, growth and expansion. This "acting" may connect back to motive, with some underlying need to "appear" a person of good character but without the element of goodness, or the focus of giving others what they need. Or, this may have very much to do with capacity and capability. *Each individual carries the responsibility for acting with good character to the best of their ability*, coming up with the best ideas and solutions for the circumstances. And since good character is a choice and can be developed, this is a large responsibility. However, each individual has developed different levels of physical, mental and emotional sense that can be brought to bear in different situations. So, this development will be different for each individual. Doing the best you can *means just that*. With better developed senses comes greater responsibility; greater capability brings with it the opportunity for greater caring.

Reflecting on past actions can help you discover your level of capability. For example, *ask*: In a similar situation, what am I capable of doing? Could I have done more? Could I do more now? Reflecting on the past can help us project into the future.

<<<<<<<<>>>>>>>

INSIGHTS: **Creating good character is a process of changing ourselves into becoming more caring to others and understanding patterns of goodness**.

<<<<<<<<>>>>>>>

While the focus has been on developing good character in ourselves, by now we recognize that as social beings in continuous interaction with each other, our thoughts and actions are permeable, affecting others even as they affect us. As we attempt to discover the truth about our own capability and live that truth, this is a good reason to associate with people who have good character! While it is important not to compare ourselves to others—nor to judge others—observing, and reflecting on, other's actions can help us build an understanding of *who we choose to be* and, using D^2, who we choose not to be. Conversely, there is the recognition—and the responsibility that comes with that recognition—that *others may emulate our behaviors*. This offers the opportunity for greater service as a group, learning and growing through interacting with others who have different capabilities.

Final Thoughts

Creating good character is really a process of changing ourselves into becoming more and more capable of being caring to others, acting in ways that others need such that goodness is created between them and still others. This moves into the conceptual thought of the higher mental plane, laying the groundwork for understanding patterns of goodness and expanding our consciousness as we deepen our connections with others.

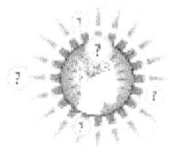

Questions for Reflection:

How might you use the classification developed by Peterson and Seligman in developing good character?

What character-building activities do you engage in?

Ask yourself: Are there any areas where my actions do not match my thoughts and feelings?

Chapter 35
Conscious Compassion

SUBPARTS: TOWARDS A GLOBAL ETHIC ... MOVING INTO COMPASSION ... JUDGING AND COMPASSION ... DEVELOPING CONSCIOUS COMPASSION ... COMPASSION AS A TOOL FOR CHANGE ... FINAL THOUGHTS

TABLE: 35-1. A CONCEPTUAL MERGING OF "CONSCIOUS" AND "COMPASSION".

FIGURES: 35-1. FROM SYMPATHY TO UNCONDITIONAL LOVE: A CONTINUUM WITH AN INCREASING DEPTH OF CONNECTION ... **35-2.** AS JUDGING GROWS TO AWARENESS WITH DISCERNMENT, COMPASSION GROWS.

TOOLS: 35-1. DISCERNING JUDGMENT ... **35-2.** ACHIEVING ZERO LIMITS THROUGH *HO'OPONOPONO*

Compassion leads to, and is a companion to, unconditional love as the highest virtue of the emotional plane. As we explore the virtue of compassion, we explore the depth of the social connection continuum, which moves through the Intelligent Social Change Journey from sympathy to empathy to compassion, and which will continue into a future phase of humanity as unconditional love. Compassion, focused on the emotional part of human nature and expanding from empathy, is a state of being connected through morality and good character, yet is also inclusive of *taking* action, *giving selfless service*.

We begin the exploration of conscious compassion by first looking closely at the Global Ethic emerging from a group of committed religious and spiritual leaders at the turn of the century and a closer look at the concept of compassion. We then explore the *depth of social connection continuum* before a brief discussion of judging, discernment and discretion. Several tools are included: Discerning Judging, an awareness-building tool, and Achieving Zero Limits through *Ho'oponopono*, based on the Hawaiian practice dealing with reconciliation and forgiveness. Finally, we take a deeper look at conscious compassion, and compassion as a tool for change.

Towards a Global Ethic

In 1999 the Assembly of Religious and Spiritual Leaders signed a declaration, "Towards a Global Ethic," which, for the first time, contained universally-accepted norms of behavior and responsibility, an ethics for humanity. The Global Ethic is *a call for humanity to live a more mature expression of moral life through the transformation of consciousness.*

This call, never more needed than in the changing, uncertain and complex environment of today, is not just to those who profess specific beliefs or practice specific religions. *It is a larger call to humanity*, and it is reverberating right above our upper threshold. With a soft push upward, and the slightest widening of the eyes and opening of the heart, we can embrace this expression.

Beversluis (2000, p. 241) describes this step upward as a Universal spirituality.

> What is needed is a universal spirituality that enables humankind to actualize its potential for the inner, transformative experience, to achieve the fruition of the human adventure in **contemplative consciousness** [emphasis added].

A Universal spirituality does not mean everyone believing the same or following the same expression of their beliefs. Nor does it mean recognizing a super-spirituality. Rather, as Beversluis (2000, p. 241) describes,

> The aim of describing a global spiritual life is not the reduction of the rich variety of humanity's inner life to one common form or generic type. That would be neither possible nor desirable … the goal … is to identify common standards of practice for the transformation of consciousness, so all authentic spirituality is in itself transformative. True spirituality, in its social dimension, is a deep and personal appropriation of the moral life, and makes each of us better than we were before.

Many of the luminaries emerging out of the last century would agree with the need for a Universal spirituality. This provides direction, moving ahead with an undergirding of moral fabric. For example, as Templeton (2002) says, "Universal principles are like compasses; they always point the way" (p. 257).

In the 1999 Assembly, eight elements were identified as essential to a Universal spirituality:

(1) An actualized moral capacity and commitment;

(2) Deep nonviolence and reverence for all life;

(3) A sense of interdependence and spiritual solidarity;

(4) Spiritual practice;

(5) Mature self-knowledge;

(6) Simplicity of life;

(7) Compassion and selfless service; and

(8) A witness to justice.

Spiritual energy weaves itself throughout the physical, mental and emotional planes. Recall in Chapter 3/Part I we described spiritual as standing in relationship with others pertaining to matters of the soul, with the soul representing the animating principle of human life in terms of **thought and action**, specifically focused on its **moral aspects**, the **emotional part of human nature**, and **higher development of the mental faculties.** Using this description to look at the eight elements of a Universal spirituality, we discover that (1) and (2) are primarily focused on moral aspects; (3) and (5) are primarily focused on higher development of the mental faculties; (1), (4), (6) and (8) are focused on actualized experiences, putting our spiritual nature into effective action; and (7) is focused on both the emotional part of human nature *and* putting our spiritual nature into effective action, both part of the same universal spiritual concept.

This represents an important characteristic of compassion. Yes, compassion is a state of being connected to morality and focused on the emotional part of human nature, yet it is also inclusive of a state of acting, *giving selfless service*.

Looking at the roots of the term "compassion" more closely, the prefix "com" denotes "with" or "jointly". Thus, when it is combined with "passion" the term clearly presents as "with passion". This begs an *object of that passion*, with passion considered an intense or overpowering emotion, a keen interest in a subject or activity. Similarly, the simple definition of compassion (*Encarta,* 1999)—sympathy for the trouble/suffering of others, *often including a desire to help*—insinuates activity. In this context, suffering is to feel pain or great discomfort in body or mind; to experience or undergo something unpleasant or undesirable; to be adversely affected by something. In the biblical context, the term "Passion" (capitalized) refers to the ultimate suffering of Jesus Christ on the cross.

According to Beversluis (2000), the transformation of an individual living an intense inner life leads to *spontaneous development of a sensitivity to other's needs*. This individual becomes capable of thinking and acting beyond self-interest, with the ability to *discern* what others require. As Beversluis (2000, p. 243) contends, "This pattern of behavior is found in every valid expression of the spiritual life and is one of the infallible signs of its genuineness."

Moving into Compassion

During the linear cause-and-effect phase of the Intelligent Social Change Journey (Phase 1), sympathy is required. Sympathy is (1) the feeling that you care about and are sorry about someone's else's trouble; (2) a feeling of support for something; and/or (3) a state in which different people share the same interests, opinions, goals, etc. (Merriam-Webster, 2016). When implementing Phase 1 change, supporting and caring for the people involved in the change helps to mitigate the force of resistance, improving the opportunity for successful outcomes.

Sustainability in the co-evolving state of Phase 2 requires empathy. Empathy, and the neuroscience findings connected with this concept, was introduced in Chapter 22/Part IV as a learning point along the Intelligent Social Change Journey. Empathy refers to the capacity to put oneself in the shoes of another, that is, to understand and even vicariously experience the emotions, ideas, beliefs and opinions of another. Recall that Riggio (2015) offered that there were three types of empathy: (1) a cognitive-based form called perspective-taking, that is, seeing the world through someone else's eyes; (2) literally feeling another's emotions, which is called *personal distress*; and (3) recognition of another's emotional state and feeling in tune with it, which is called *empathic concern*. All three of these types provide a direct understanding of another individual, a heightened awareness of the context of their lives and of their desires and needs in the moment at hand. Both sympathy and empathy have Greek roots in the term *pathos* which means feeling or suffering.

The creative leap of Phase 3 requires the ability to tap into the larger intuitional field that energetically connects all people. This can only be accomplished when energy is focused outward in service to the larger whole, requiring a deeper connection to others. **Compassion deepens our connection to others**. In the discussion of forces in Chapter 3/Part I we recognized that the fundamental cause of conflict is separation. Underlying this statement is the understanding that we are social creatures living in an entangled world. Recall that we are in continuous interaction with those around us, and the brain is continuously changing in response. Our brains are linked together, with interconnectedness and sociability existing at every level of brain function (Mahoney & Restak, 1998).

This movement from sympathy to empathy to compassion is part of a larger continuum based on an increasing depth of connection which is developing our sixth sense, an inner sense focused in the heart energy center. See Figure 35-1. As we move up the continuum toward unconditional love there is an increased balancing of senses across the physical, mental and emotional planes. As can be seen above, there is a correlation between this continuum and the phase changes of the Intelligent Social Change Journey. This means that as we move from linear cause and effect to co-evolving with our environment it is necessary to deepen our understanding of others, moving from sympathy to empathy. And as we move toward opening to the intuitional plane for the creative leap, it is necessary to develop a deeper connection with others; compassion helps us achieve this deeper connection.

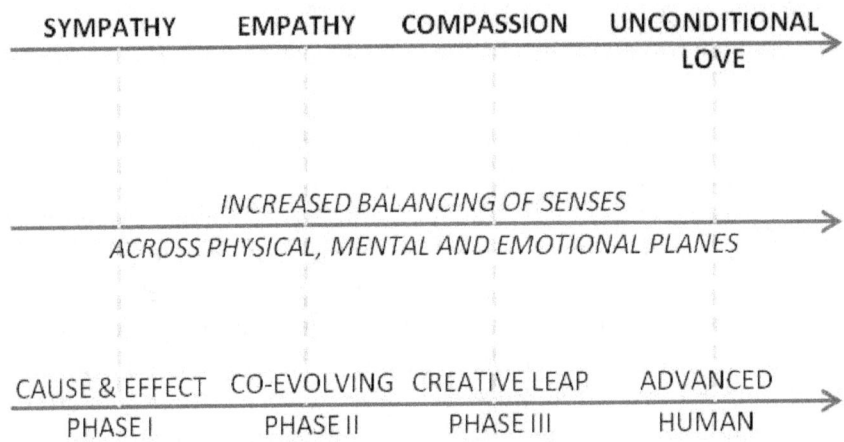

Figure 35-1. *From sympathy to unconditional love: a continuum with an increasing depth of connection.*

The movement from sympathy to empathy to compassion to unconditional love can be slowed or stopped through *compassion fatigue*, a loss or loosening of sympathy for the misfortune of others because too many demands have been made on the feelings of an individual (*Encarta*, 1999), that is, *overwhelment* can harden the heart. An example is the actions of some German military members during World War II, whose belief sets did not support their actions.

Judging and Compassion

The innate ability to evoke meaning through understanding and comprehension—to evaluate, judge and decide—distinguishes the human mind from most other life forms. To judge

is taken as the act of forming an opinion, interpretation or conclusion. The ability to judge enables us to discriminate and discern—to see similarities and differences, comprehend and form patterns from particulars, and purposefully create, store and apply knowledge.

There is an element of judging in every decision we make. For example, Klein says that building up expertise in a knowledge domain requires: (1) feedback on decisions and actions, (2) active engagement in getting and interpreting this feedback, that is, judging its value, not passively allowing someone else to do so, and (3) repetitions, which provide the opportunity to practice making decisions and getting feedback (Klein, 2003). While not necessarily widely recognized, judgments are used far more than logic or rational thinking in making decisions. This is because all but the simplest decisions occur in a context in which there is insufficient, noisy, or perhaps too much information to make rational conclusions. Further, judging is very much connected with emotional context related to preferences, that is, likes and dislikes.

Understanding that judging serves as a valuable human tool for operating in this world, in relation to compassion, we move the focus of this discussion to the judging of others. **Judging others is the opposite of compassion**.

The *act* of judging others and their actions requires something or someone to judge against. When one individual is judging another person, it is in the context of a scale, with the individual who is judging generally located somewhere in the middle of that scale. If the individual that is judging is egotistical, arrogant or insecure with himself, there may be a need to judge others as less in order to prove personal superiority or (artificially) feel better about himself. Alternately, if an individual's self-regard is low, an individual may judge others above herself, which will prove or justify her feelings and add to her insecurity. Thus, as Wayne Dyer so succinctly said, "When you judge others, you do not define them; you define yourself." (Templeton, 2002, p. 240)

Often, the people we are judging are showing us *a part of ourselves that we do not like*, or that they are comfortable with things we are unable to do or that *we dislike in ourselves.* As exampled by Wilrieke (2016),

> We may judge a busty lady for wearing a tight shirt that emphasizes her bosom for dressing cheap, when we are jealous of her physique or her courage to dress as she pleases. We may judge a working mom for not staying at home with her kids when we are a housewife who always dreamt of a career but gave it up when she became pregnant. We may judge a couple kissing openly in the streets because we dream of being in love, but are too afraid to open our heart for someone.

The act of gossip may accompany the act of judging. Gossip is the sharing of negative opinions in order to justify those negative opinions or justify self. Again, gossip is more about the individual who is gossiping than the subject of that gossip.

When we get into patterns of judging and gossiping it may be difficult to catch ourselves in the act, and when we are in the company of others who do so, it is easy for similar behaviors to creep into habit. The short tool "Discerning Judging" can help.

****

TOOL 35-1: Discerning Judging

Remember, change begins with awareness, and only you can change yourself (see Chapter 6/Part I). This exercise is focused on exploring negative thoughts and feelings that occurred in the past about an individual, and how those differ from the thoughts and feelings you have about that same individual today. This exercise will only work if you are forthright and honest.

STEP (1) Find a place where you can be comfortable and uninterrupted. Have a pad of paper and pen in front of you.

STEP (2): Write down the names of people with whom you have had conflict or about whom you have had negative feelings IN THE PAST. Indicate an approximate date of conflict or negative event. Leave a couple of spaces after each name.

STEP (3): Starting at the top of the list, one-by-one think about the event that triggered the conflict or negative feelings. **Imagine yourself back in that event**, and quickly jot down FROM THAT VIEWPOINT the thoughts and feelings *about that person* you were experiencing. Be honest. You can trigger your memory by thinking about the location, details leading up to that event, and your personal responses to that event.

STEP (4): When you are done, put that list aside and forget it for 15-20 minutes. Purposefully focus your attention on something positive and of interest IN THE NOW. Get up and have a drink of water and a snack.

STEP (5): Now, go back to your list, and from this new frame of reference review each name and what you have written, asking: Is this judging (criticizing) or is this discerning (perceiving)? Mark a "J" or a "P" beside each descriptive phrase.

STEP (6): For each place you have marked a "J", now describe this person from your current frame of reference.

Repeat this exercise as needed.

****

As can be seen by the short discussion and examples above, judging is a capacity that carries with it a large responsibility associated with how it is used. In Figure 35-2 below, judging is used in the context of judging others. As we mature and learn who we are, the judging of others gives way to awareness and discernment, that is, in our interactions it is no longer necessary to contrast others on our personal scale, while still important to have knowing of who they are (values, beliefs, etc.). The level of awareness and trust, of course, is dependent on the relationship in which you choose to engage with others. Discernment is to make out clearly, to perceive or recognize difference. As Templeton (2002, p. 240) says, "Discernment can help us comprehend where another person is on his or her path of growth and eliminate any need to be upset because he or she may come from a different place. Discernment perceives; judgment criticizes."

As judging turns to awareness, enabling discernment and discretion without judgment, compassion grows. See Figure 35-2. This is because we are developing an understanding of the other without constructing any forces with respect to our own inner feeling or shortcomings. We no longer are holding up the measurement scale with ourselves in the middle of that scale. Rather, we are learning to honor, and have compassion for, diversity and choice of both ourselves and others.

We cannot achieve compassion when we retain strong negative emotions. Sometimes when we are caught in the middle of a situation where strong emotions have been embedded, it is difficult to move beyond that place, and it may still be difficult years after the event is long gone. This is because emotional tags, regardless whether they are negative or positive, create strong connections among neurons. However, as introduced in Chapter 19/Part III, emotions are intended as a guidance system, and not meant to hijack an individual's judgment, decisions and actions.

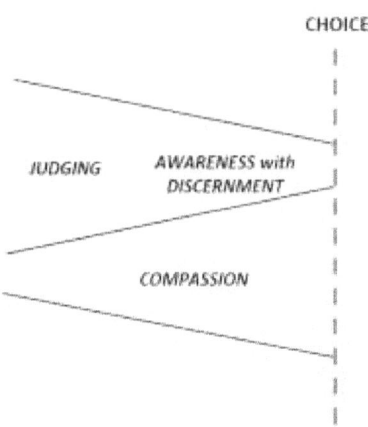

Figure 35-2. *As judging grows to awareness with discernment, compassion grows*

The Dalai Lama reminds us that we should act on the world with calm and clarity. This means getting rid of or controlling any destructive or disturbing emotions which will create more harm for the individual and others. Goleman provides the example of the use of anger.

If it mobilizes you and energizes you and focuses you to right social wrongs, then it's a useful motivation. However, if you let it take over and you become enraged and filled with hatred, those are destructive, and you'll end up causing a lot more damage than good. (Suttie, 2015)

Universal compassion holds out the possibility that people can change. While believing in universal compassion, the Dalai Lama emphasizes that there is a distinction between the act, which is unacceptable, and the actor, within whom is the potential for change. He also says that universal compassion is a hard goal to achieve.

It goes against natural mechanisms that make us favor our own group—our family, our company, our ethnic group, etc. So, the first step is to overcome that tendency and to become more accepting of and caring toward a wider circle of people. Caring for everyone is the final step ... (Suttie, 2015)

Again, we see this is a **call to action**. As the Dalai Lama calls out, *Don't just talk about it, do something*. (Goleman, 2015)

Ho'oponopono is an ancient Hawaiian practice dealing with reconciliation and forgiveness. Originally it required a mediator, and was a mental cleansing to address ills that had manifested in the physical, mental or emotional bodies. A more recent version of this is that introduced by Vitale and Len (2007) in their book *Zero Limits*. For situations where it is difficult to move beyond judging, you can use the zero limits version of *Ho'oponopono*, which helps bring the connections among people, and people and events, to a zero point, that is, where there are no memories. According to Vitale and Len (2007), this Self-I-Dentity state is based on taking responsibility for everyone's actions, not just your own. Any judging or negative feelings are resonant between the self and the other individual, or the self and the event.

****

TOOL 35-2: Achieving Zero Limits through *Ho'oponopono*

This is one version adapted from Vitale and Len's (2007) adaptation of *Ho'oponopono*.

STEP (1): Have a trusted friend (who will act as a coach) join you for this exercise in a quiet place where you will not be overheard or interrupted. On a piece of paper write the following mantra in four lines: *I'm sorry. Please forgive me. Thank you. I love you.*

STEP (2): Closing your eyes, imagine the other individual or event of concern on the other side of the room. Describe the connection between yourself and the individual or event. What kind of cord or structure is connecting you? What is the texture? What is the color? Is it heavy or light? Now open your eyes.

STEP (3): One-by-one, focusing on the CONNECTION BETWEEN you and the individual or event, complete the sentence for each part of the mantra, that is:

I'm sorry for/that … (one thing).
Please forgive me for … (one thing).
Thank you for … (one thing).
I love you because … (one thing).

REMEMBER … **Do not judge yourself!** The focus is on the *connection* to the person or event. For example, "I'm sorry that this happened/that you were in pain" or "Please forgive me for not knowing what was happening/having the skill set that might have helped". The "Thank you for …" may be general in nature and not necessarily related to the relationship or event. For example, "Thank you for being a good mother" or "Thank you for being responsible and paying your taxes." Similarly, "I love you …" can represent a simple concept such as "I love you because you always look clean/have pretty hair/are polite to strangers/work hard", or represent a higher-order concept such as "I love you because you are a child of God/Allah." As you repeat the cycle something closer to the person or event may come to mind.

STEP (4): Go through Step (3) a total of three times, each time providing a new ending for each part of the mantra. Your coach can remind you of the beginning of each part of the mantra. *Your* focus is on the *connection,* and coming up with the ending of each part of the mantra.

STEP (5): When you have completed three cycles, close your eyes, imagine the individual or event on the other side of the room, and describe the connection between yourself and the individual or event. It will have changed.

This sequence may be repeated periodically if judgment of an individual or negative feelings about an individual or event still remain.

****

Developing Conscious Compassion

Perhaps the best way to fully understanding the concept of conscious compassion is to conceptually merge the concepts of "conscious" and "compassion". In Table 35-1, columns 1 and 2, we have selected the various descriptors of these terms as referenced earlier in this book. In column 3 we have brought these concepts together as four descriptors of the intent of the term conscious compassion.

Conscious	Compassion	Conscious Compassion
* a state of awareness * a private, selective and continuous change process * a sequential set of ideas, thoughts, images, feelings and perceptions * an understanding of the connections and relationship among them and our self	* sympathy for the trouble/suffering of others, *often including a desire to help* * a state of being connected to morality and focused on the emotional part of human nature * inclusive of a state of acting, *giving selfless service* * includes sympathy: the feeling that you care about and are sorry about someone's else's trouble; a feeling of support for something or someone * includes empathy: the capacity to put oneself in the shoes of another, that is, to understand and even vicariously experience the emotions, ideas, beliefs and opinions of another	* active awareness and understanding of others thoughts and feelings as situations present themselves in the context of life * a moral responsibility and desire to intelligently and wisely care for and support others. * recognition and understanding of the connections and relationships among people and events, and the potential outcomes of actions taken * a conscious choice to give selfless service

Table 35-1. *A conceptual merging of "conscious" and "compassion".*

Exploring the multiple definitions provided in Table 35-1, we can now define conscious compassion as *an intelligent choice to give selfless service based on active awareness and understanding of others thoughts and feelings, the relationships among people and events, and wisdom.* This does not insinuate a separation from emotions, but rather the intelligence and wisdom of an individual that has embraced emotions and feelings as an integral part of life, using them as a guidance system and fuel to intelligently and wisely act.

<<<<<<<<>>>>>>>

INSIGHT: **Conscious compassion is an intelligent choice to give selfless service based on active awareness and understanding of others thoughts and feelings, the relationships among people and events, and wisdom.**

<<<<<<<<>>>>>>>

Since conscious compassion engages discernment and discretion in support of intelligent activity, *choosing not to act is a choice*, and, indeed on some occasions, this may be the intelligent and wise choice. When action is taken, recall the discussion of givingness in Chapter 22/Part IV. Giving is always of ourselves, and wise giving occurs when the recipient is participatory, either immediately (as an exchange or partnering) or in the future (pay-it-forward).

Compassion as a Tool for Change

In his book *Kindness, Clarity, and Insight*, His Holiness the Dalai Lama addresses compassion as a tool for change:

> Deep down we must have real affection for each other, a clear realization or recognition of our shared human status. At the same time, we must openly accept all ideologies and systems as a means of solving humanity's problems. One country, one nation, one ideology, one system, is not sufficient. It is helpful to have a variety of different approaches on the basis of deep feeling of the basic sameness of humanity. We can then make a joint effort to solve the problems of the whole of humankind. (Gyatso, 1997, p. 60)

The Dalai Lama and Daniel Goleman, a psychologist and best-selling author, collaborated on a book titled *A Force for Good: The Dalai Lama's Vision for Our World*, which is a call to action. In a conversation about this book, Goleman was asked why compassion was so important. Goleman referenced research at Stanford, Emory, and the University of Wisconsin as well as work at the Max Planck Institute which shows that *there is specific brain circuitry that controls compassion*. This research also showed that **when the circuitry of compassion becomes strengthened that "people become more altruistic and willing to help out other people."** Thus, the feeling (and act) of compassion becomes a tool for change. As Goleman exclaims, "This is so encouraging, because it's a fundamental imperative that we need compassion as our moral rudder" (Suttie, 2015).

Goleman (2015) uses the term *muscular compassion* to denote that compassion is action oriented, for example, for attacking social issues like corruption and collusion in government, issues that require compassion. This is consistent with the distinction made earlier in this chapter that while compassion is a state of being connected to morality and focused on the emotional part of human nature, it is also inclusive of a state of acting, *giving selfless service*. Thus, the term muscular compassion is considered a close synonym for conscious compassion.

Final Thoughts

Conscious compassion is an intelligent choice to give selfless service based on active awareness and understanding of others thoughts and feelings, the relationships among people and events, and wisdom. As we move through the Intelligent Social Change Journey, we move from sympathy to empathy to compassion, *consciously and purposefully choosing* to engage compassion, developing a deeper connection to others and fully embracing our collective creativity to move into the future together.

Questions for Reflection:

How do you personally develop conscious compassion through connections to morality and the emotional parts of human nature?

How might you use compassion as a tool for change?

Chapter 36
The Changing Nature of Knowledge

SUBPARTS: KNOWLEDGE AS A MEASURE OF SELF GROWTH ... SPREADING THE KNOWLEDGE MOVEMENT ... IT'S GLOBAL ... THE SPIRITUAL NATURE OF KNOWLEDGE ... KNOWING ... ONENESS

FIGURES: 36-1. THE SHIFTING PERCEPTION OF KNOWLEDGE AS WE MOVE THROUGH THE ISCJ ... **36-2.** THOUGHT BITE: "KM IS SIGNIFICANT BECAUSE IT FITS RIGHT UPON THIS HISTORICAL OPPORTUNITY" ... **36-3.** GROWING THROUGH CHANGE.

By way of a quick review, in the Preface of this book we introduced knowledge as the capacity (potential or actual) to take effective action, by definition irrevocably connecting knowledge and action. Further, we have forwarded that knowledge is context sensitive and situation dependent. Since we live in a world of change, knowledge is not static but emergent. Our minds—as associative patterners and co-evolving with a dynamic environment—are continuously creating and recreating knowledge for the moment at hand. Further, we also now understand that knowledge is a force, and that forces can both push us backwards and propel us forward. Such is knowledge, which can be limiting or expanding, depending on how we choose to create and direct it.

Our perception of knowledge changes as we expand through the Intelligent Social Change Journey. When we start the journey in Phase 1, the connections among information are clear and linear, and as we develop our logic we effectively build, block after block, our knowledge. Everything is connected to what we previously had learned, and it feels like we can just keep on expanding and get larger and larger amounts of information to effectively apply in our personal and professional experiences. We discover along the way that cooperation and collaboration enable us to build larger structures, and so that expansion continues.

<<<<<<<<>>>>>>>>

INSIGHT: **Our perception of knowledge changes as we expand through the Intelligent Social Change Journey**.

<<<<<<<>>>>>>>

When we enter Phase 2, we're caught up in the flow of co-evolving. In an increasingly changing, uncertain and complex environment we learn to rapidly adapt our knowledge to fit the current situation. Our perception of knowledge shifts as we recognize that knowledge is also incomplete, and by sharing knowledge with others, we have much more knowledge available for our use, more options and choices. Our creativity begins to blossom as we bisociate ideas. Recognition of the patterns among events and underlying behaviors improves our decisions and actions. Information can no longer be explored in simple cause-and-effect relationships; it is necessary to develop larger and larger concepts as we search for a higher level of truth. This requires deeper connections to others, and an empathy emerges through our continuous interactions with others. While Figure 36-1 captures the idea of a calm flow, we know that this is only a (small) part of the co-evolving journey!

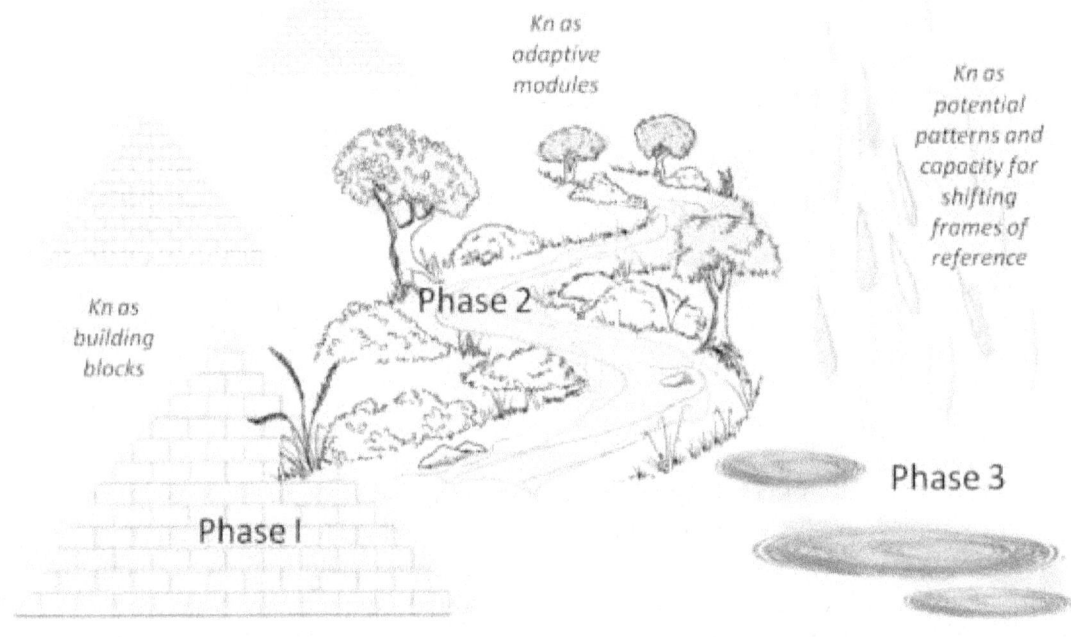

Figure 36-1. *The shifting perception of knowledge as we move through the ISCJ.*

As we prepare to expand into Phase 3, there is a huge perception shift in relation to knowledge. We now are guided by higher conceptual thinking in concert with an ability to tap into the intuitional plane. Knowledge, the capacity (potential or actual) to take effective action, is no longer based on how much we learned in school or even what we have experienced, for as we leap from puddle to puddle, from pond to pond, shifting our frames of reference to accommodate our learning, the direction of events change and the context of life *may or may not* represent a continuum.

The flexibility we learned while operating in the NOW of Phase 2 serves us well as we shift from one frame of reference to another, fully engaging our creative imagination and the excitement of discovery as we co-create our reality. We understand the connections among all people, and that we are part of a larger ecosystem for which we have responsibility. Through conscious expanding and planning, we have the ability to join together knowledge and apply it in ways that are unique and bring about inclusiveness. We move through the experiences of the world with compassion and love, honoring diversity and respecting individuation while simultaneously sharing what we are learning with the collective. It's not necessary to store that knowledge as information, block after block, in our heads or in our systems. It IS necessary to explore the connections among things and, as information changes second-by-second, sustain relationships with others and have access to ever-expanding resources through engaging in conversations that matter. As we co-create together, we move closer and closer to intelligent activity, and as a humanity consciousness expands.

As can be seen, knowledge is no longer a building block based on what was known, but rather a tool in support of conceptual thinking and intelligent activity. There is an expanding beyond patterns, a growing knowing and understanding of underlying rules of the Universe, what perhaps we could describe as heuristics, and the ability to tap at will into the flow of known and new thought when it is needed. This is the ultimate "potential" part of knowledge, all starting with development of the mental, fired by the passions of the emotional, and counterbalanced by the compassion and love of the spiritual. And then, we choose to act.

<<<<<<<>>>>>>>

INSIGHT: **The ultimate "potential" part of knowledge starts with development of the mental, is fired by the passions of the emotional, and counterbalanced by the compassion and love of the spiritual.**

<<<<<<<>>>>>>>

Thus, should we choose, knowledge is in service to intelligent activity, and that intelligent activity supports freedom of thought, and more learning and knowledge that, when creatively engaged, leads to innovation. This flow connects people and connects thoughts, and has the potential to expand the consciousness of all those joining together.

Knowledge as a Measure of Self Growth

Through every phase of the Intelligent Social Change Journey the value of personal and/or organizational knowledge resources can be measured in terms of the effectiveness of actions. Recall from Chapter 2/Part I, that knowledge itself is neither true nor false, and its value in terms of good or poor is difficult to measure other than by the outcome of its actions. Knowledge includes a special form of information and all information is energy; how it is used determines its value. Hence, good knowledge would have a high probability of producing the desired and anticipated outcome, and poor knowledge would have a low probability of producing the expected result. Note that the concept of "good" or "bad" is not connected to morality but to anticipated outcome of the user. (See the discussion of the growth path of knowledge sharing in Chapter 12/Part II.) After an outcome has occurred, the quality of knowledge can be assessed by comparing the actual outcome to the anticipated outcome, with the probability in terms of effectiveness ranging from zero to one.

From an individual viewpoint, this measure provides a way of assessing the level of comprehension an individual has relative to a particular domain of reality or situation of interest. As we move through Phase 2 and into Phase 3 of the ISCJ, knowledge can be selectively used as a measure of effectiveness in terms of (1) our ability to tap into the intuitional field and access what is needed; (2) our ability to cognitively translate what we learn in terms of identified needs and opportunities; and (3) our ability to act on it.

While (1) and (2) work together, they are quite different things, with (2) providing a measure of the effectiveness of (1), and (3) providing a measure of the effectiveness of both (1) and (2). Let's explore that relationship a bit more. Recall from Chapter 28/Part IV, that intuition is the ability, without any time delay, to determine the causes of effects regardless of the complexity of those effects. This is a higher awareness, a deeper understanding, very much supported by our five senses of form and our two inner senses focused from the heart and crown energy centers. The intuitional plane, which is informed by spiritual energy, is a higher vibrational field beyond the physical, emotional and mental planes that are a part of our everyday lives (see Figure 28-2 in Part IV). How to tap into this field is the focus of Part IV.

Whether earned or revealed, connections with this field in terms of intuition can present themselves in many ways. For example, when you have a desire or need, a book may "fall" into your awareness. This idea of "falling" was shared by one of the authors who had a serendipitous experience (see the discussion on serendipity in Chapter 22/Part IV). When hunting for the answer to a specific issue, the author walked into a bookstore and was standing in front of a rather large selection of books in the area of focus when, quite literally, a book *fell* off the bookshelf. Looking around, there was no one in proximity who might have facilitated the event. Picking the book up off the ground, the open pages just "happened" to be exactly what was needed, that is, the information provided in the open pages of the book could be understood in the context of the issue at hand, and could be translated by the author into specific actions to take. Thus, the effectiveness of (1) was validated by the ability to achieve (2).

Then, when these actions were taken, the effectiveness of both (1) and (2) was determined by the outcome of those actions. Did what was intended happen? If not, did this action move a situation toward (the direction of) the outcome that was intended? On a probability scale of 0-1 (or 0-100% if you prefer), what was the level of effectiveness? Thus, knowledge (the capacity to take effective action) can be measured in terms of movement toward the expected outcome.

If you are an individual committed to the expansion of consciousness and you are seeking to achieve controlled intuition, there are, of course, other measures which knowledge supports. These would include systems measures related to time and effort, as well as relative outcome measures. Again, effectiveness can be explored and values assigned by considering your intent, your consequent actions, and the outcome of those actions.

Note that tapping into the intuitional field as described in Chapter 28/Part IV and expanded in Chapters 29 and 30/Part IV is highly contingent on an individual's current physical, mental and emotional state, counterbalanced with the spiritual, and the ability to sustain a high level of consciousness. Remember, we are holistic beings. The entangled physical, mental, emotional and spiritual systems cannot be separated from each other. "The human reality is a dynamic holistic system subject to the continuous ebb and flow of intellectual, emotional and spiritual influences." (Stebbins, 2010, p. 2) (See Table 6-1 in Chapter 6/Part I.)

Spreading the Knowledge Movement

The focus on the importance of knowledge moved solidly into our organizations at the turn of the century with the *Organizational Learning (OL)* and *Knowledge Management (KM)* movements, both centered around creating a knowledge-centric organization, that is, building the capacity of an organization to acquire (learn) the knowledge necessary to survive and thrive in its environment. This is much the same role the personality has in the early life of an individual (see Chapter 4/Part I). Recognizing knowledge as a basic resource, and the value of learning and knowledge to the organization, KM and OL brought knowledge into the heart of the organization, and with it came a re-focusing on *the importance and value of people and diversity*. In particular, the early connections of KM to information technology proved a catalyst for gaining management attention, thus the name "Knowledge Management", although it was clear that knowledge could not be managed. With the continued advancement of technology and the reality of global connectivity came increased collaborative entanglement and growing recognition of the importance of social knowledge (Bennet & Bennet, 2007b). In short, no matter what it is called or how it is defined, this focus on knowledge has and is serving as a catalyst to change the world.

For example, the increase of knowledge sharing across organizations and around the world is notably the greatest contribution to expanding the potential for innovation. A critical tenet of KM and OL, knowledge sharing was accelerated with the advent of communities of practice and interest that emerged out of social learning theory (Wenger, 2000; Wenger et al., 2002). Moving into the new century, humanity entered a new era of social connectivity and interaction, with knowledge—at the very core of our existence—playing a large role.

Many communities are global in nature, encompassing the diversity of culture, education, religion, age, sex and experiences. Addressing these changing times and the remarkable opportunities they bring with them, Houston (2016, p. 1) expresses the importance of knowledge sharing,

> To succeed we can no longer go it alone, but must partner with one another to share innovative and creative ways in which to rethink and restructure our individual existence within the context of our expanding global communities. To do this requires a heightened awareness, an awakened sense of purpose, and a **dedicated commitment to actively seek out the possible** [and the impossible].

She goes even further in suggesting that we embrace the *wisdom circle movement* to help spread communities "devoted to developing human potential able to address the enormity of the Earth's problems" (Houston, 2000, p. 96). As has been proven by literally hundreds of organizational studies beginning with the emergence of total quality leadership, working in groups such as teams and communities creates a synergy, what Houston calls transformational synergy, that enables the group to move faster and go farther.

> Through the evocation of one another, we expand our base of concern, developing an enhanced relationship to our planet and intensifying our recognition of its needs as well as our willingness to respond creatively to those needs. Working in community, each person holds the dreams and excellence of everyone else in the group .... (Houston, 2000, p. 97)

The Knowledge movement may be serving as a key to do just that ...

In 2005 the Mountain Quest Institute sponsored a research study that involved in-depth interviews with 34 Knowledge Management Thought Leaders, the KMTL study referenced several times in this book. These Thought Leaders (TLs) worked in and with industry, academia and government across four continents. The term *thought leader* was used by Booz, Allen & Hamilton to describe top executives, authors and academicians interviewed between 1995 and 1997 to address big concerns such as defining values and vision, managing people and risk, adapting to changing markets and new technology, and assessing performance and portfolio mixes (Kurtzman, 1998). By 2003, Dearlove (2003) forwarded that thought leadership is an idea that has delivered, or has the potential of delivering, significant and lasting benefits. Our understanding of the role of a thought leader was expanded when Durham (2004) noted that thought leader inferred as much a *social role* as the command of knowledge, going beyond subject matter expertise to imply leadership and a willingness to assert direction. As she noted,

> Thought leaders can articulate vision ... and hone in on the core issues. They possess social capital ... influence ... actively mentor others ... generate novel ideas and connections. Further, they have earned the respect of their colleagues, and their leadership is not only asserted but acknowledged. (Durham, 2004, p. 306)

The thought leaders that were part of the original KMTL study and a more recent follow-on study, who are called out by name in the Acknowledgements section of this book, understand the importance of connection and contribution. As one TL describes:

> If you think of knowledge broadly as all of the understanding that we as human beings have gained through experience, observation or study, thinking of that broad, broad definition, then what we are doing either in the production of individual knowledge or in the development of this discipline that helps us to find and apply knowledge, are little drops of rain that start to flow down the hill, then come together in little streams that eventually become big rivers flowing into the ocean. From that point of view, I think that we, whether as thought leaders or participants, are making a contribution. In some cases, it is as little drops of rain, and in other cases it may be monsoons.

These thought leaders also recognize that the KM field is providing a path forward, serving as ***a platform for energizing other people apart from ourselves***, and that **the more energy you create in others, the more it brings back to you.** One TL describes, "KM is making us more like nodes in multiple networks where we're much more in control of our own destiny." While this social dimension is critical to the journey toward intelligent activity, it is also having a strong impact on those who participate. As one TL describes, "It has profoundly changed me ... it enriches my *awareness of what livingness is* by bringing in this whole social dimension."

Whether we draw on science fiction or an inner belief set, we know we are part of a larger network. One TL exclaims: *And that just constantly amazes me. I have collaborations with people I don't know.* When engaged intelligently, this amazing networking multiplies brain power and creates new opportunities. *So much innovation comes from intersections, taking disparate people and bringing them together. People across different cultures, across different languages, are participating . . . Different outlooks, different philosophies, different experiences, all these differences that bring about creative abrasion* (Leonard-Barton, 1995).

One thought leader noted that social media is still in its infancy, or perhaps the reference is to something larger. "We are in our infancy. It is what Peter Russell was talking about, the global mind, where he compared the evolution of the telephone system and the Internet system, increasing the connectedness of people and, consequently, **thought patterns**. But it looks like connectivity is only one dimension. We have to expand that to *contactivity*, where we include some of the other senses." Nowhere was this clearer than in the experience shared in Chapter 14/Part III, where seven people considered "influencers"—followed by millions of people via various social media—were unplugged for 48 hours. As one participant realized following this experience, "There's no 'social' in social media."

It's Global

This focus on knowledge is not confined to superpowers. Countries around the world are leveraging their mental abilities and knowledge. Spain has been doing this for decades, a country with relatively few natural resources that's been an economic powerhouse. In Asia, Singapore, also a country of few natural resources, became the first "Most Admired Knowledge City" in the world! South Korea has literally burst out onto the world scene, with an incredible percentage of people now connected to the Internet. Part of what we are seeing is countries from an economically poor area sharing and using knowledge, and embracing innovation. As one TL noted, *It's made the world so small, just incredibly small, because now we connect with people . . . we've had conversations we couldn't have had before . . . this is a KM movement ... and it is changing the world.* At no time in history have people ever had so much potential knowledge immediately available regardless of their level of learning and experience.

<<<<<<<◇>>>>>>>

INSIGHT: **At no time in history have people ever had so much potential knowledge immediately available regardless of their level of learning and experience.**

<<<<<<<◇>>>>>>>

Just how the focus on knowledge is changing the world is directly addressed by a number of thought leaders. For example, one said, "I think that as people have more experiences where their humanity is honored, and where, let's call it, the larger intelligence that infuses all of life can be accessed in our human exchanges and made available, that's a good thing in terms of our capacity for sustaining life on this planet." Another said that this focus on knowledge is bringing questions onto the planet that we need to ask. *Just the simple acknowledgement that another human being has a different thought world than we do—and maybe there's something we need to understand about each other's thought world in order to work together better—that's pretty powerful.* **Maybe there's something we need to understand about each other's thought world?** This is a powerful thought, and questions do bring with them enlightenment.

Agreeing that this movement is still in its infancy, one TL noted, *This focus on knowledge is only at the very, very beginning of what it can actually accomplish in terms of this wider systems perspective of **providing a level of consciousness for mankind**.* It feels "almost as if I'm being pulled forward. I'm not pushing myself anymore. I feel as if I've come into a space which has a life of its own. And it just feels right down to my core. I'm on the right track." And that track is ***taking humanity to the next phase*** *of whatever humanity is becoming.* Knowledge, then, is seen as a *vehicle for co-evolution as a species.*

If we think about it at its largest level, and look at what's happening with the Internet as synapses of the collective mind, and you think of whatever that largest consciousness is within which even the planet sits, and you think of field theory in terms of the implicate order or even as the different lenses on this type of larger intelligence, whether we want to call it God or Source or super field or generative intelligence or implicative order or whatever, that's the ***life affirming urge***. *We're accessing **that** when we're seeking these ways of knowing together.*

From this brief sharing of their thoughts, it's not surprising that **all** of these thought leaders talk about *making a difference in the world through sharing their knowledge with others so those others can share their knowledge with others* and their organizations. For example, Leif Edvinsson describes this as *nourishment and cultivation of the future.* In this same vein, Debra Amidon offered, "Now with the focus on knowledge, innovation and collaboration, I think we have the potential to **create the platform for world peace**, and I think that's what many along this journey are trying to do. They are really looking to make a difference." While Debra transitioned in 2016, her words ring true in our ears today. And the others with whom we seek to share are also sharing. One thought leader believes that "everybody has something to contribute very worthwhile in our quest to have more wisdom about the world … I find something worthwhile in everybody that I meet."

<<<<<<<>>>>>>>

INSIGHT: **As we value knowledge, we value people; as we value creativity, we value cooperation and collaboration; and as we value innovation, we value our future.**

<<<<<<<>>>>>>>

Figure 36-2 is a "thought bite" which provides a synopsis of thought leader responses from the KMTL study that refer to *the potential for world change brought about by this focus on knowledge*. From these thought bites, it is clear that OL and KM emerged during this momentous time in the history as preparation for entering what can be called the Golden Age of Humanity (Bennet, 2004). The acceptance and growth of what OL and KM represent is indicative of the changing nature of the global environment and humanity at large.

The Spiritual Nature of Knowledge

At several points in this text we have bought up the need for balance, and, in particular, now that we as a humanity have so rapidly and successfully forged ahead in development of our mental faculties, the need to ensure a spiritual counterbalance to avoid the pitfalls of arrogance, prevent the cessation of learning, and continue our expansion of consciousness. (See Chapter 4/Part I, and also Chapter 32.)

As introduced briefly above, and from the extensive data collected during the KMTL study, the focus on knowledge occurring in the KM field, is supporting a higher calling. For example, the specific terms "spirit," "spirituality," and "religion" appear 84 times, many as part of a larger related conversation. Spiritual concepts were also referred to in terms of "light" or "living in the light." Perhaps the most obvious connections, however, are the spiritual aspects that emerge throughout the conversations, presentations and writings of these thought leaders. For example, one thought leader shared, "I do believe that the human being is of full dimensionality." He told a story about his mentor, who spoke a lot about spirituality and the need for the human being to be *fully recognized in all of those dimensions*. Another TL explains,

> From the spiritual point of view, I think there's a strong drive to grow, to expand. I forget who said it, but to *release the imprisoned splendor* as it's called, not only from within each person as an individual—which I think is something we individually work at—but also collectively in terms of the human race. And one might say *knowledge is the life blood of doing that*.

<<<<<<<>>>>>>>

INSIGHT: **Now that humanity has so rapidly and successfully forged ahead in development of our mental faculties, there is the need to ensure a spiritual counterbalance to avoid the pitfalls of arrogance, prevent the cessation of learning, and continue our expansion of consciousness.**

<<<<<<<>>>>>>>

"KM is Significant Because It Fits Right Upon This Historical Opportunity."

THE WORLD IS CHANGING ...
- Collective world change
- World as living network
- Moving into new global governance ... dynamic relationship between civil societies, nation states and businesses
- Knowledge will be global discriminator

Be the change you want to be ...
-Mahatma Ghandi

- Paradoxical moment ... Power darkening planet ... forces at war around us ... Moment in evolution of potential extreme importance.
- Most dangerous times in our history ... The best of times and worst of times at the same time
- We as a human species are reinventing ourselves

Knowledge and Knowledge Management are "predecessors to higher-level understanding and meaning" ... They offer:
- The promise of a difference in human experience
- An opportunity for evolution into a qualitatively different reality.
- Nourishment and cultivation of the future.
- The potential to create a platform for world peace.

Characteristics of KM from a world view: Honors humanity; Has a human and humane agenda; Reaffirms faith in people; Enriches awareness of livingness; Honors value of human judgment.; Uses tools of meaning from belonging to human society; Multiplies brain power; Is reducing ignorance; Helps us recognize we are a part of the world in a very deep way.

To help transform the world we need to: Honor the world; Generate a further level of consciousness; Get across this idea of understanding other people's perspectives; Find better ways of embracing the Knowledge movement and beyond.

Knowledge management is ... Bringing questions onto the planet. Certain questions have the power to change the world ... Providing a systems perspective for *raising the level of consciousness* for man. Part of the new consciousness. A new way of looking at the world ... Ushering in *advances for humanity*. Helping us move as a world towards responsibility and peace ... A quest to have more wisdom about the world ... *A vehicle for co-evolution as a species*. Providing the possibility to overcome the fundamental contradiction between biological constitution and civilization.

Embedded in KM is some kind of spiritual wonder of what this world is about.

Figure 36-2. *Thought bite: "KM is significant because it fits right upon this historical opportunity."*

This is consistent with the understanding we have gained through this book. And, if while acting in the physical knowledge is the life *blood,* and by definition interwoven with the *life force* introduced in Chapter 18/Part III, from where does knowledge come? Pondering this question, one thought leader asked, "What is this knowledge that comes to us from seemingly nowhere? The nowhere is, of course, somewhere. Then, it becomes a matter of how we define the borders of our knowledge. I believe we should search outside the traditional lines, the traditional tangible realm, to get closer to the *real* source of knowledge."

So where does spirituality intersect Knowledge Management? Madanmohan Rao sees this relationship as one reason why many people are attracted to the KM field. "One of the few things that outlasts us human beings after our deaths is the knowledge that we leave behind. Some people think KM is about converting knowledge into action, and then using this to define products and patents and copyrights. [And it certainly is.] Other people think knowledge networking is great because you can share this knowledge with other people and make the world a better place—you accept people and get them to share their knowledge, just as you share your knowledge with them. [And this *does* happen.] But, **embedded in the knowledge movement is some kind of a spiritual wonder of what this world is about**."

There is a lengthy discussion in the KMTL research findings about discovering *hidden knowledge*, "knowledge that seems to have a significant impact on the way we live and act, regardless of which religious sect you are speaking of." This hidden knowledge is passed on from master to student with a set of techniques, and is often codified. For example, Zen is codified in terms of koans; the Confucian approach is parables; and in the Judeo-Christian context it is in the stories in the Torah, the Old Testament and the Bible. Even the Alchemical concept of turning lead to gold is symbolic, and has nothing to do with lead *or* gold (see Chapter 31). Lead and gold were symbols of a transformative process within the individual to bring certain qualities of the mind and heart under control to enable that individual to grow spiritually and develop. These symbol systems are knowledge systems. As one TL explains,

> Within this hidden knowledge is an incredible capability to convey very abstract feelings, concepts, ideas, affection through a reasonably rigorous set of exercises. This is fourth world knowledge, what Jung would call the supraconsciousness, which is a world of spiritual entities and spiritual abstractions that are available to people if they can **exercise their mind appropriately** and **keep their physical form in a certain level of balance**. KM, then, at the level of changing the core of individuals who have decided to develop more, [offers] a lot to study and research in the more esoteric realms as well.

As we know, symbols and metaphors contain a huge amount of meaning for those that are in the know, and they are incredibly powerful for those who are initiated in their meaning and use. (See the discussion of Symbolic Representation in Chapter 21/Part III.) For example, Reiki symbols used for spiritual and energy healing are amazingly powerful if you are attuned to their energies. This is part of the hidden knowledge referenced in the quote above. As another example, *the Internet is the outward, somewhat material, manifestation of what is happening worldwide in a non-material, inner way.*

Knowing

The word and concept of *knowing* is used in so many ways in our language. Indeed, even within the pages of this book you will find a variety of meanings in its usage. The concept we focus on in these few paragraphs is that presented in the treatment that is Appendix E. This is a knowing beyond self, yet connected at the core of self and informing self. In this context, knowing is considered a *sense* that is supported by our tacit knowledge and development of our higher mental faculties. It can poetically be best described as: ***seeing beyond images, hearing beyond words, sensing beyond appearances, and feeling beyond emotions***.

Figure E-1, a nominal graphic showing the continuous feedback loops between knowledge and knowing, was introduced in Chapter 5/Part I and is in Appendix E. Thinking about (potential) and experiencing (actual) effective action (knowledge) supports development of embodied, intuitive and affective tacit knowledge. Knowing begins with expanding our seven senses and increasing our ability to consciously integrate these sensory inputs with our tacit knowledge. That tacit knowledge is the result of past learning experiences residing in the unconscious, *entangled with* the flow of spiritual tacit knowledge, representing development of our higher mental faculties and continuously available to each of us. In other words, knowing is the *sense* gained from experience that resides in the *unconscious*, **including the energetic connection our mind enjoys with the *superconscious*.**

While this term "superconscious" has been used by others, the authors struggled a number of years ago with whether to use the term "superconscious" or "supraconscious", as several other notable researchers propose. The prefix *super* conveys the idea of exceptionally powerful, with outstanding and excellent qualities; the prefix *supra* conveys the idea of being above. Since we recognize the connectedness and Oneness of humanity, and that through experience, consciousness—whether at the level of the individual or humanity—has the potential for continuous expansion, we chose to use the term *superconscious*.

Recall that we have two inner senses, both of which potentially connect to the superconscious and support knowing. They deserve a reiteration in this discussion. The sixth sense of the human is connected to the heart energy center and is a very real sense of Oneness, recognizing an energetic connection to all living things and a higher order of existence. For example, within a specific religious context, this would include the recognition—and some level of belief or understanding—of God or Allah. However, it is not necessary to believe in this context to understand Oneness and connection, which is a part of our everyday lives. For example, we recognize that the human is part of the larger ecosystem of Earth; we now operate in a global business environment; and we are increasingly open to our responsibilities to each other as a larger humanity, all of which convey the recognition of being a part of something larger, and a sense of Oneness.

The seventh sense of the human, which is focused from the energy center residing above the head—often referred to as the crown energy center—serves as a direct link to the larger Universal mind. As an analogy, consider the role of one neuronal firing in the mind of the human; then extrapolate that across to consider the human mind as one firing in a larger Universal mind. As small as a single firing is in terms of the Universe, it is just as important as it is small, for at this "point of action" that single neuron, individuated and one of a kind, is co-creating the reality in which it interacts.

<<<<<<<◇>>>>>>>

INSIGHT: **Considering the human mind as one neuronal firing, as small as a single neuronal firing is in terms of the Universe, it is just as important as it is small, for at this *point of action* that single neuron, individuated and one of a kind, is co-creating the reality in which it interacts.**

<<<<<<<◇>>>>>>>

The subconscious and superconscious are both part of our unconscious resources, with the subconscious directly supporting the embodied mind/brain and the superconscious, through the two inner senses, focused on tacit resources involving larger moral aspects, the emotional part of human nature and the higher development of our mental faculties. (See Chapter 3/Part I.) When engaged by an intelligent mind, which has moved beyond logic through conceptual thinking into conscious and unconscious processing based on trust and recognition of the connectedness and interdependence of humanity, these resources are immeasurable

In Figure E-1 (Appendix E), the superconscious is described with the terms: spiritual learning, higher guidance, values and morality, and love. An aspect of considering the larger perspective is the expanding idea that there is something else in existence that is powerful and pervasive. In a number of world religions, attention is given to external communications "inspiring" the human mind. For example, in Christianity some adhere to the idea of the *Light of Christ* or the *Spirit of Truth* as a Universal influence available to all. Additionally, the role of the *Holy Ghost* for individual guidance is so fundamental that this is a communication resource attributed directly to deity.

Oneness

With the advent of Quantum physics in the early twentieth century, scientists discovered that subatomic particles held no meaning when in isolation, rather only in relationship with everything else. You could not take a reductionist approach to matter; it was indivisible. *So much for the Newtonian worldview of separateness.*

People were already beginning to think globally. For example, the idea of six degrees of separation has intrigued people since 1929 when Frigyes Karinthy wrote a short story called "Change" that challenged anyone to discover within five steps a single person to whom he was not connected.[36-1] Researchers have taken on the challenge, only more focused on proving that Karinthy was right, that there *are* only six degrees of separation among any two people in the world

As we slid through the end of the last century toward new beginnings, aided by the extensive contribution of sites such as Ancestry.com, FamilyTree.com and MyHeritage.com, the ubiquitousness and invisibility of the Internet has accelerated our remembrance of connectedness. As introduced above, the Internet is an example of an outward or somewhat material manifestation of what is happening worldwide in more of a non-material, inner way. Indeed, perhaps information *is* that key which flows and connects it all, with knowledge implying the effective application of that information as we deepen our connections with each other and move toward intelligent activity.

Because of the accelerated development of the mental when people had greater access to other people and their knowledge, it only makes sense that at the same time the Internet was flaring into existence, our understanding of the mind/brain and our consciousness was on the rise. We were beginning to discover the tremendous power and untapped potential of ourselves, what Laszlo (2009, p. 99) describes as,

> … a consciousness that recognizes our connections to each other and to the cosmos … a consciousness of connectedness and memory … [that] **conveys a sense of belonging, ultimately, of Oneness** … a wellspring of empathy with nature and solidarity among people.

This is the height of individuation, which we had largely achieved as we moved into the 21st century, coupled with a growing sense of Oneness as social media capabilities expanded, a path which is laid out before us but, because of our arrogance, is difficult to fully embrace. Life and learning are dependent on interaction, whether forceful or expanding. The good news is that the recognition of Oneness brings us into a non-dual space, with fewer forces responding to cooperative and collaborative co-creation. (Duality is addressed in Chapter 38, the final chapter of this book.)

The highest level of creativity occurs when there is a free flow of ideas. *The diversity of ideas comes from individuation; the creative bisociation of ideas, and the resulting innovation, comes from cooperation and collaboration.* The goal, then, is to reach Oneness in understanding and compassion, while simultaneously individuating and collaboratively co-creating.

<<<<<<<>>>>>>>

INSIGHT: **The diversity of ideas comes from individuation; the creative bisociation of ides, and the resulting innovation, comes from cooperation and collaboration.**

<<<<<<<>>>>>>>

Verna Allee conjures up a powerful image of Oneness as she speaks about the urgency for the planet. She forwards that one of the most symbolic and powerful images to come forward in the last century was the image of the Earth from space. While young people of today have grown up with that image, she says to those of us who are older, "You and I can remember when it was new. You and I can remember when we stood there with our mouths standing open looking at this incredible blue jewel floating in a vast darkness. As a human society, as a species, that image evoked a shift of consciousness on this planet. It's not something that's *going* to happen. It's something that really *already has happened* in a very fundamental way. We got it down to the toes of our interdependency, we got the fragility of that beautiful blue planet and the connectedness . . . it truly is *one living planet* and we're all part of it, and we're all dependent on each other, and what I do right here *does* affect the other parts of the world. **What we have not been able to do is reconcile our business and economic models with that understanding**,

What we see occurring today in spiritual discussions and supporting literature, which was in the past relegated to structured religions or structured groups, is the more pervasive use of the term "Oneness". This Oneness is not perceived as a subject-object mechanistic connection. Rather, it is closer to being immersed in an energy field (for example, a light or heat field) where everyone is giving off and receiving energy; where sinks, sources, resonances and interdependencies may occur between, among and throughout the entire space.

This concept of connectedness is so prevalent in spirituality that English and Gillen (2000, p. 1) define spirituality itself as awareness of connectedness, an "awareness of something greater than ourselves, a sense that we are connected to all human beings and to all of creation." His usage of the word "sense" is very relevant, for the sixth sense, that inner sense discussed above focused in the heart energy center long associated with love, is all about connectedness. You will recall that this sixth sense is developed as we expand from sympathy to empathy to compassion—the deepening of connections that is foundational to the Intelligent Social Change Journey.

Oneness is also being realized through our growing ecological understanding of the Earth, and in business through the growth of a global economy. Similarly, in a learning group, connectedness is perceived as "a sense of belonging for each individual and an awareness that each one cares for the others and is cared for ... a shared understanding" (Wlodkowski, 1998, p. 70). (See the discussion of care for others as a value in Chapter 32.) Thus, this connectedness or Oneness as a state-of-being would *manifest itself in a life of service*. In its highest order, connectedness would include an understanding and appreciation for the autopoietic aspects of an individual's framework of reality as well as expanded states of consciousness. Autopoiesis is the property of complex living systems that structurally adapt and co-evolve with their external environment while maintaining their organization.

Looking at Oneness through the framework of the Intelligent Social Change Journey (ISCJ), we first focus on the cause-and-effect relationship, which is based on separateness. In the second phase we focus on co-evolving relationships, which are based on the understanding that we are all connected and part of a larger system. In the third phase we move to a co-creating model, which is based on Oneness. See Figure 36-3. As we look at this model of growth and expansion, we recognize that it is built on understanding gleaned from a number of different fields of thought. For example, from systems thinking we now know that a system (Life) cannot sustain itself without growth. From symbiotic thinking we recognize that a system can only be recognized by identification of what is and what it is not. An object is defined by the space around it, and the space around it is space because of the object within it. We also recognize that learning and growth bring change, and at an energy level we are changing every instant of our lives. Figure 36-3 suggests the expansion occurring in the ISCJ as we open to new frames of reference. This graphic will be expanded upon in the following chapter from the viewpoint of consciousness.

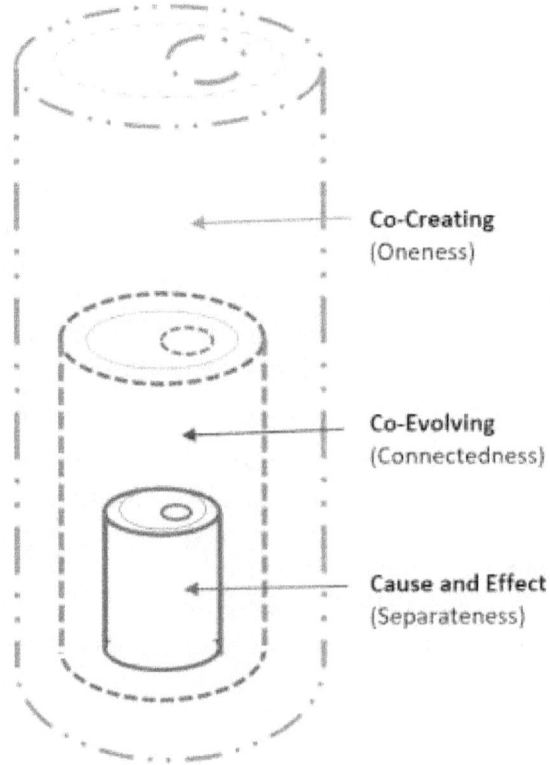

*A system (Life) cannot sustain itself without growth.

Figure 36-3. *Growing through change.*

Taking the consilience approach embraced throughout this book, we can look at knowledge sharing as the connective tissue supporting Oneness. While we have learned how this occurs through cooperation and collaboration at the physical level, through deepening connections with others at the emotional level, and through the search for higher truth at the mental level—all virtues—this knowledge sharing is also occurring at the intuitional level. For example, knowledge itself can be instantly shared among the senses. We are all part of one Quantum field, each emitting weak radiation that carries with it information regarding all aspects of life. As forwarded in Chapter 18/Part II on flow and as McTaggart (2002, p. xvii) describes, "On our most fundamental level, living beings, including human beings, [are] pockets of Quantum energy constantly exchanging information with this inexhaustible energy sea." When operating from the viewpoint of an individuated consciousness, and depending on the level of empathy and compassion developed, there is the ability to sense what others think and feel (and have learned) through *their* individuation. This open sharing through all the senses produces a continuous flow of new thoughts, which in turn is bisociated with individuated thoughts, *spurring on the process of co-creation*. And, as we know, when acted upon offers the potential for invention and innovation.

Final Thoughts

We as a human species are reinventing ourselves, and it is clear that this focus on knowledge is ushering in advances for humanity. This experience is transcendent. As Verna Allee reflects,

> We have this new world view that's coming forward, but we're very much stuck in a building where there's another kind of world view operating, so how do we reconstruct, how can we take the elements of that old structure and system and re-harness them into this new understanding?

This is, of course, what is happening in our world today. We indeed live in a paradoxical moment. While the challenge is large, the payoff could be a new, different and magical future, a new world for all of life.

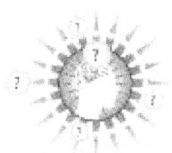

Questions for Reflection:

How can you tap into your inner knowing?

Are you able to sense beyond appearances?

How well do you leverage the diversity of ideas through collaborative co-creation to generate innovation?

Chapter 37
Consciousness Rising

Without creation life goes backwards. Without consciousness life doesn't grow.
"Learning is creation, growth is creation ..."
Consciousness allows us to connect ourselves with others.
-Niles MacFlouer (2004-16)

SUBPARTS: INFORMATION FIELDS AS CONSCIOUSNESS FIELDS ... EXTRAORDINARY CONSCIOUSNESS ... NEW ROLE FOR PERSONALITY ... BEYOND ASSOCIATIVE PATTERNING ... ASSOCIATIVE ATTRACTING ... THE HOLOGRAPHIC UNIVERSE ... FINAL THOUGHTS

TABLE: 37-1. RELATIONSHIP OF PHASES OF THE INTELLIGENT SOCIAL CHANGE JOURNEY WITH LEVELS OF CONSCIOUSNESS

FIGURE: 37-1. CONCEPTUAL MODEL RELATING KNOWLEDGE AND CONSCIOUSNESS ... **37-2.** CONSCIOUS RISING ... **37-3.** RESONANCE IS A QUALITY OF THE FIELD

From the characteristics of consciousness introduced in Chapter 4 and Chapter 5/Part I, and as punctuated throughout this book, it is clear that consciousness is emergent. While certainly born with personality traits, to the best of our knowledge, an infant does not have awareness of self. As the self grows and makes good choices, developing virtues and cooperating and collaborating with others through knowledge sharing, so, too, does consciousness expand.

What does it mean to expand in consciousness? In the context of our evolving and expanding Intelligent Social Change Journey, we build on the lessons we learn as we engage forces at the physical, emotional and mental levels. Learning to co-evolve with the challenges and opportunities of an increasingly complex, uncertain and changing environment, we finally recognize that all of our experiences and learning has prepared us for a new way of being, emergence of an inner power, an intuitiveness and connectedness that opens us to a larger role as co-creators. This is reflective of the ultimate vision of Lao Tzu, who believed that "if each and every one of us could realize and gain control of our evolutionary power, it would **invisibly unite us and allow us to become a collective, compassionate, and fully aware social and universal organism** [emphasis added]" (Wing, 1986, p. 13).

As we expand through the Intelligent Social Change Journey, coming full circle in our physical, emotional, mental and spiritual development and moving closer to our moment of choice as a humanity, we pause briefly to consider the concepts of consciousness that have been presented over the course of these books. This chapter will focus on five areas. First, we explore the connections between information fields and consciousness fields, revisiting the concept of the emergence of consciousness to see what can be learned from the human experience that might provide clues to higher consciousness fields. Second, we introduce the term extraordinary consciousness, and how that applies to people in terms of expanding consciousness. Third, we readdress the concept of *personality*, exploring the potential of a new role for this old friend of the individuated human. Fourth, looking from the viewpoint of expanded consciousness, we revisit the idea that the mind/brain is an associative patterner and introduce the concept of associative attracting. Finally, we look at the exciting discoveries from cell biology that encourage us to more fully consider the idea of a holographic Universe.

Information Fields as Consciousness Fields

In Chapter 5/Part I we describe consciousness as a process inclusive of who we are, what we believe, what we say, how we act and the things we do, and forwarded a working definition as a state of awareness and an understanding of the connections and relationships among that of which we are aware and our self. In Chapter 23/Part IV we acknowledge consciousness as the field in which everything—including material reality—exists. Then, in Chapter 28/Part IV, we introduce the idea of controlled intuition, the ability to tap at will into the intuitional plane, and talk specifically about the Field of Ideas, relating that field to the Noosphere, the Zero Point Field, the Quantum Field, or the God Field. In Chapter 36 we introduce Knowing and explore connections to the larger Field from the perspective of the unconscious. That which is "unconscious" includes the subconscious (referring to embodied, affective and intuitive tacit knowledge, which are primarily earned knowledges supporting earned intuition) and the superconscious (referring to spiritual tacit knowledge, and alluding to something else in existence that is powerful and pervasive). As we think about these ideas, the question is begged: Is "tapping" into the intuitional plane, the Field of Ideas (with all of its various names), and the superconscious the same concept looked at through different frames of reference? And, specifically, trying to develop a level of discernment, are these information fields or indeed consciousness fields?

The incompleteness of our knowledge, limits of our understanding and the difficulty of imagining multi-dimensional issues from our conscious stream of thought, as well as the difficulty of describing what might be emerging with a limited vocabulary, makes exploring these questions quite challenging. Yet, since defining concepts and describing ideas is what brings them into reality for further exploration, let's pursue a few possibilities.

<<<<<<<>>>>>>>

INSIGHT: **The incompleteness of our knowledge, limits of our understanding and the difficulty of imagining multi-dimensional issues from our conscious stream of thought makes exploring questions related to consciousness quite challenging.**

<<<<<<<>>>>>>>

Laying the groundwork for this journey in Chapter 2/Part I, we introduced information—viewed as any non-random pattern or set of patterns—as the connective tissue of the Universe. The "Field of Ideas" specifically insinuates an information field, albeit an "interconnecting, information-conserving and information-conveying cosmic field" (Laszlo, 2004, p. 3). Similarly, Zero Point, as perceived by the authors of *Zero Limits*, refers to a *state wherein memory or inspiration occurs* (Vitale & Ihaleakala, 2007). At least one aspect of these fields, then, is that they can be considered information fields. The *Akashic Field* is recognized as a field that somehow records every aspect of life, a field of organized memories (patterns), and a cosmic information field that *informs*. Laszlo (2004, p. 3) says the A-Field (as he refers to it) is not limited to just the physical world, but "informs all living things—the entire web of life. It also *informs our consciousness* [emphasis added]"

Other "fields" are specifically described as consciousness fields. For example, Jean Gebser (1985), a Swiss philosopher, describes the larger consciousness field (beyond human) as four-dimensional integral consciousness. Integral consciousness is a core concept of the integral worldview, which shows the influences of evolution on the development of consciousness and culture. Integral philosophy emerges from the work of Ken Wilbur (2000) with the important contribution of spiral dynamics from Don Beck (2002). Integral consciousness liberates the internal domain of consciousness from external biological constraints wherein the human is "able to embark on the path of a whole new type of mental, emotional and spiritual evolution." This development is occurring within consciousness and culture, "in a domain that is best described as the *internal universe*" (McIntosh, 2013). American mystic Richard Bucke (2010) describes the Field as cosmic consciousness and, as an essential part of the Universe, Eckhart Tolle (2004) describes this as the intelligence and organizing principle for the emergence of form through evolution, *with consciousness expressing through form*. Thus, the consciousness of the human expressing through form can be considered part of the larger consciousness of the Field.

<<<<<<<<>>>>>>>>

INSIGHT: **Consciousness expresses through form.**

<<<<<<<<>>>>>>>>

As introduced in Chapter 4/Part I, **consciousness is a process, and not a state**. From the individual perspective, it is private, continuous, always-changing and felt to be a sequential set of ideas, thoughts, beliefs, images, feelings and perceptions (Bennet, 2001) with an understanding of the relationships among these and the self. Recognizing that we are a verb, it is at any instant the sum total of who we are, what we believe, how we act and the things we do (Dunning, 2014). Because we live in a world we perceive as solid, it is hard for us to get our hands around the idea that consciousness is a process representing our actions, beliefs, thoughts and words. Even the concept "get our hands around" represents the idea that it is something tangible, which is not the case. This idea of solidity is, of course, an illusion. Thus, consciousness is intangible, yet through self-reflection and observation can be measured in a specific context in the instant at hand.

The levels of consciousness developed by Hawkins (2002) provide a "measuring" approach. Recall that the levels of consciousness (Hawkins, 2002) represent calibrated levels correlated with a specific process of consciousness—emotions, perceptions, attitudes, worldviews and spiritual beliefs. These levels, ranging from 0 to 1,000, are a mapping of the energy field of consciousness. The 200 level, which is associated with integrity and courage, is the balance point between weak attractors with negative influence and strong attractors with positive influence. Examples of weak attractors (starting at the lowest level) are shame, guilt, apathy, grief, fear, desire, anger and pride. Examples of strong attractors (starting at the lowest level) are willingness, acceptance, reason, love, joy, peace and enlightenment. For purposes of this discussion, we repeat the table introduced in Chapter 5/Part I below as Table 37-1.

These levels are not intended to be criteria for judging others; they are indicators of our progression toward expanded consciousness as we move through the Intelligent Social Change Journey. Looking at consciousness as a set of ideas, thoughts, beliefs, images, feelings and perceptions and an understanding of the relationships among these and self, as we deepen our relationships with others (moving from sympathy to empathy to compassion and unconditional love), these relationships become more complex and entangled, bringing us closer to perceiving Oneness. Along this journey, how you perceive the world and your ideas, thoughts, beliefs, images, and feelings simultaneously affect your perception of self and how you interact with the world, AND are affected *by* your perception of self and interactions, providing both input and the effect of output.

Phase of the Intelligent Social Change Journey	Levels of Consciousness (Hawkins, 2002)
PHASE 1: Cause and Effect (Requires Sympathy) • Linear, and Sequential • Repeatable • Engaging past learning • Starting from current state • Cause and effect relationships	20-150: Moves through Shame, Guilt, Apathy, Grief, Fear, Desire and Anger 175: Pride 200: Courage
PHASE 2: Co-Evolving (Requires Empathy) • Recognition of patterns • Social interaction • Co-evolving with environment through continuous learning, quick response, robustness, flexibility, adaptability, alignment.	[*Moving out of negativity*] 250: Neutrality 310: Willingness 350: Acceptance 400: Reason 500: Love [*Interest in spiritual awareness*]
PHASE 3: Creative Leap (Requires Compassion) • Creative imagination • Recognition of global Oneness • Mental in service to the intuitive • Balancing senses • Bringing together past, present and future • Knowing Beauty; Wisdom	540: Joy 600: Peace [*Good of mankind becomes primary goal*] 700-1,000: Enlightenment

Table 37-1. *Relationship of Phases of the Intelligent Social Change Journey with Levels of Consciousness (repeat of Table 5-1).*

In Chapter 5/Part I we introduced the threshold of consciousness with the levels of consciousness. The threshold of consciousness refers to a definable attention space within which each individual thinks, talks and acts that has upper and lower thresholds. Recall that if a proposed new idea or strategy is above the upper threshold, it cannot be comprehended and, even if it comes into awareness, has no perceived value. If a proposed new idea or strategy is below the lower threshold, it is so well-understood, so common, that it may be dismissed as unimportant; it does not command your attention. At any given moment, this threshold adjusts to accommodate new learning and focus. What we are focusing on, and the related thoughts and feelings all connected to our beliefs and perception of self, are what determine our level of consciousness at any given moment in time.

<<<<<<<<>>>>>>>

INSIGHT: **What we are focusing on—and the related thoughts and feelings connected to our beliefs and perception of self—are what determine our level of consciousness at any given moment in time.**

<<<<<<<<>>>>>>>

Let's consider the consciousness of a two-year old child, who has not yet had the opportunity to develop mental faculties nor learn to navigate the intricacies of our emotional guidance system. Something that is wanted is not forthcoming, so the child throws a temper tantrum. "I want it, and I want it now!" In our scenario, let's say the wanted item is a piece of candy to which the child is allergic. Even if provided a logical reason, the two-year old cannot fathom the meaning, cannot understand the relationship between what is being said and its self, but is operating at a level of desire (125) and anger (150). Actually, that scenario is all too familiar in the instant economy of today for people of all ages! Back to our scenario, an experienced adult will try to refocus the child's attention, which can rapidly jump, for at least a short while, to joy (540) when a favorite toy is introduced. As can be seen, there is a correlation of the level of consciousness and the context of the situation at hand, and a fluctuation as attention is shifted. While these fluctuations also occur in adults, it is the focus over time as we make conscious choices that supports (or deters) our journey of conscious expansion.

Pushing this understanding a bit farther, and recognizing that we simultaneously operate from the physical, emotional and mental planes, let's see what happens in terms of focused attention and levels of consciousness when we are out of balance, and then with the *rise of consciousness*. Consider (A), (B) and (C) below. Levels of consciousness (Hawkins, 2000) are indicated in parentheses.

(A) In this scenario as a child we are spoiled such that our emotional development is stymied. Our emotions are out of control, and we are not required to develop the potential of our mind. Cause and effect are still a part of our learning, although, similar to the two-year-old, it is more about making sure we get whatever we want. In this particular situation, the individual is focused on ownership of material goods, and has developed an overwhelming pride (175) in this regard, a self-centeredness and selfishness which has moved beyond egotism to arrogance. Thus, **the focus of attention is on the physical**, which is what is valued by the self

AND *how the self is valued*. Then, as with life, the unexpected occurs. There is a car accident, and though you survive, you are now a cripple for life. Since your value of self was based on the physical, this event is devastating. Your bounty of "friends" who have partied with you regularly continue their preferred behaviors with others; and your anger (150) plummets into fear (100) and grief (75) and then into apathy (50). As you begin to move through the pain, there is someone there who supports you, previously ignored or tossed aside, but who is there in your time of need. Working through the various emotional responses, you pull a spark of courage from within (200) and, still carrying an abundance of emotions, a part of you reaches for a place of new beginnings, a neutral place (level 250) that ever so slowly, with the continuous support and love of those you now recognize as family and friends, morphs into a willingness (350) to try new things.

(B) Much like a rebirth, although it is still you in terms of personality and self, you engage your creative imagination, a new frame of reference which is **focused from the emotional plane** and not dependent on the limits of the physical body. Your emotions are still virile, but now you learn to harness them and, even, appreciate them as the pendulum swings from negative to positive and back, and they help you discover what you like and don't like about life, about others, and about yourself. As you explore and expand the limits of your imagination, you begin to see connections among things, even a reason, a purpose (400), for the events of your life. Art becomes very important to you. There is such beauty of form captured in this Carlotti,[37-1] in that Rembrandt. Then you see exquisite beauty in a Van Gogh; and while at first there is a related material aspect of possession, or the desire to possess, you quickly move beyond that, captured by the intrigue of the artist's intent and feelings. You are deepening your connections with people and now enjoying extensive conversations with others. As you move into greater understanding of the fullness of what it is to be human, you discover love (500). At first, it's romantic in nature—the individual who has helped you expand, who is always there for you. Then, deep feeling and respect emerges for the amazing artists you are conversing with, and you begin to develop caring and deeper friendships.

(C) In the midst of these new emotions, the *ideas* of others capture your attention, and through bisociation of these ideas with your inner thoughts you begin to create larger concepts and discover higher truths. **Focusing from the mental plane**, but bringing along the lessons of the physical and emotional planes, you are excited with a continuous flow of ideas and are filled with joy (540) as you brainstorm with others, opening the door to a diversity of thoughts. While honoring your passion for art, which moves you into a state of peace (600), you simultaneously reach for larger ideas, eager to learn from others and share with others. There are no limits to this growth and expansion other than the choices of your focus and attention. Along the way, you consciously embrace wise giving and begin to reflect on your learning and growth, and *how you can make the world a better place for others*. As you are blessed with the continuing journey of life and the entanglement of friends and loved ones, you begin to see your connection to something larger (700).

In the above scenarios, we can see the emergent quality of consciousness from the perspective of an individual. In (A) consciousness is at a very low level, and as we progress through (B) and (C) there is continuous expansion. There is also no question that (A), (B), and (C) all take place in an information field, although what is brought into awareness, and what is focused on, shifts and changes. What we can also see in these scenarios are links between the physical plane, the emotional plane, the mental plane and the spiritual.

Emotions *do* serve as a guidance system, helping us to understand and develop preferences (likes and dislikes), as developed and explored in Chapter 19/Part III. However, they are also serving a critical function in awakening/expanding consciousness in terms of self and *the relationship of self* to external and internal situations and circumstances. Thus, the "I want" of the two-year-old is the beginning of awareness of self. However, emotions do not work alone in this regard, but are connected to, at first, cause-and-effect reactions, and then to larger conceptual thought.

Thus, a second insight from these scenarios is that development of the mental is critical to emergence and expansion of consciousness. While the two-year-old did not have the mental capability to perceive self beyond the level of "I want", the adult in scenario (B) was able to harness the emotions and, through beauty and development of the mental faculties (C), begin to perceive a larger purpose and potential of self.

A third insight is that through deepening relationships with others coupled with a diversity of thought and higher conceptual thinking, our consciousness expands such that we have the ability to perceive ourselves as part of a larger consciousness field. Thus, the Intelligent Social Change Journey is critical to the expansion of consciousness, both in terms of mental development (expanding from cause-and-effect through co-evolving to the creative leap) and in terms of deepening relationships to others (moving from sympathy to empathy to compassion).

Can we make the leap to say that the larger fields we have identified as information fields are also consciousness fields? Referring to consciousness in human form, Laszlo forwards,

> Today consciousness is ready to create form without losing itself in it—it can remain aware of itself, even while creating and experiencing form. Thus, the next stage in the evolution of human consciousness is the state of awakening—the consciousness of mastering the art of 'awakened doing.' (Laszlo, 2009, p. 56)

This refers to the advancement of human consciousness to take on qualities of the larger field of consciousness, playing an expanded role in co-creation. Laszlo's wording infers that in the past humans have lost themselves in consciousness, unable to stay aware of themselves while experiencing form at the physical level. No doubt many of us have had these moments. The idea of "lost" also insinuates that *before* coming into form consciousness was "found," implying that the larger field to which we are returning is a consciousness field. Thus, clearly, Lazlo considers this larger field a consciousness field. Mastering the art of "awakened doing" means a higher awareness of our role in co-creating, an expanded level of consciousness. In the human state of consciousness of the past, we were asleep; but "today" we're ready to see the larger picture in an awakened mode.

Pierre Teilhard de Chardin was quite clear in defining the Noosphere as "a human sphere, a sphere of reflection, of conscious invention, of conscious souls" (de Chardin, 1966, p. 63). By definition, then, the presence of consciousness at the individual or soul level is attributed to the Noosphere. Similarly, while acknowledging it as containing a shared accumulation of information, McTaggart (2002) attaches qualities of consciousness to "The Field" in terms of it carrying on incessant dialogue and intelligent, creative and imaginative interactions with people. She goes so far as to suggest this may be the point of consciousness of the human. This is consistent with findings from cell biology that a cell has no behavior if disconnected from the environment, describing a simulation information field. These concepts are expanded below in our discussion of the Holographic Universe.

Reflecting on these scenarios, as well as the thought of the authors cited above and others called out earlier in this text, we are in a position to speculate on the answer to our question. As forwarded, consciousness is emergent—*an emergent quality of an information field*. Thus, **the potential of consciousness exists in the larger field, no matter what we call that field**. We could say that consciousness is a quality of the Field. Since consciousness fluctuates, this would mean that the level of consciousness may depend from which level of the *in-formation* field you focus. We wrote "in-formation" in deference to David Bohm, the "great maverick physicist" as Laszlo calls him. Bohm refers to the information field as in-formation, meaning a message that forms the recipient. As Laszlo (2004, p. 3) describes,

> In-formation is not a human artifact, not something that we produce by writing, calculating, speaking, and messaging. As ancient sages knew, and as scientists are now rediscovering, in-formation is produced by the real world and is conveyed by a fundamental field that is present throughout nature.

Laszlo (2004, p. 3) goes on to describe a Universe that is not of just vibrating strings and particles and atoms, "but is instead constituted in the embrace of continuous fields and forces that carry information as well as energy."

Seife (2006) points out in *Decoding the Universe* that the study of information theory is gaining more attention because it is information that is at the heart of existence, not the material things which merely carry it. For example, after extensive investigation of the very small, we finally find the structure of DNA and realize that the inherent design of the double helix serves to help with the reliable storage and copying of information from one generation to the next (Lewis, 2012). Our existence is more closely tied to information than to our historic study of Newtonian physics. However, this appears consistent with our emerging understanding of Quantum, where individual consciousness is considered a subfield of the larger Quantum field, an unlimited field of possibilities. All Quantum fields are controlled by thought (MacFlouer, 2004-16). When thoughts within this larger field are heading in the same direction, they group together and create a subfield; uniquely different from the infinite field, pursuing a probability, yet pulling along related elements outside that probability. Consciousness is such a subfield, and is self-defining, self-creating, self-conscious, self-controlled, self-sustaining—and also self-limiting.

Extraordinary Consciousness

The concept of "extraordinary" is a very human term. From the viewpoint of people, "ordinary" consciousness represents the customary or typical state of consciousness, that which is common to everyday usage, if consciousness could possibly be considered common! Polanyi sees tacit knowledge as *not* part of one's ordinary consciousness (Polanyi, 1958). Recall that the term "tacit" is a descriptive term for those connections among thoughts that cannot be pulled up in words, a knowing of *what* decision to make or *how* to do something that cannot be clearly voiced in a manner such that another person could extract and re-create that knowledge (understanding, meaning, etc.) An individual *may or may not* know they have tacit knowledge in relationship to something or someone. But even when it *is known*, the individual is unable to put it into words or visuals that can convey that knowledge. Thus, as we know, tacit knowledge resides in the unconscious.

It is the ability to tap into unconscious resources, described in terms of the subconscious and the superconscious, that moves us beyond ordinary consciousness to what we call *extraordinary consciousness*, specifically, (1) acquiring greater sensitivity of and access to information stored in the unconscious in order to facilitate the awareness and application of that information and knowledge; (2) developing the ability to access and translate information available in the larger Field, AND (3) achieving controlled intuition, the ability to tap at will into the *flow of information* relative to the NOW, whether past, present or future (see the discussion of controlled intuition in Chapter 28/Part IV).

Extraordinary consciousness may be created through such techniques as meditation, lucid dreaming, guided visualization, hemispheric synchronization (see Appendix D, Accessing Tacit Knowledge), and other ways of quieting the conscious mind, and by doing so allowing and encouraging *accessibility* to information in the unconscious. Such techniques create a heightened sensitivity to, awareness of, and connection with our unconscious mind with its memory and thought processes.

Thinking about consciousness as a flow, extraordinary consciousness represents increased sensitivity to and awareness of tacit knowledge, that which is not accessible to ordinary consciousness as currently defined. A characteristic of consciousness is to be *aware* of the nature and structure of information and understand that information in relationship to self. Time plays an important role in this understanding. From the physical plane perspective, the focus is on the past, the memory of what has occurred as it happened. From the emotional plane perspective, the focus is on the present and the past, how we feel then and now about what happened, and the creative ideas in the NOW linked to and sparked by the past and present. While remembered from the past, emotions and feelings can only be experienced in the NOW. Even if we perceive a future situation that has emotional links, the feelings connected to that imagining are occurring in the present. From the mental plane perspective, we are looking at the why, remembering the past, perceiving the present and exploring the future. Expanding beyond ordinary consciousness to extraordinary consciousness gives us the opportunity to perceive from all three planes and from the past, present and future simultaneously, bringing our thoughts into balance.

Extraordinary consciousness delimits ordinary consciousness, increasing sensitivity to, and awareness of, that which is tacit—that which is in the unconscious—whether embodied, affective, intuitive or spiritual (see Appendix B). It is important to recall that these tacit knowledges are inter-linked; humans are holistic decision-makers. With this larger sensitivity and awareness of that which is tacit comes increased understanding of the interdependence associated with patterns of information, some of which would be patterns of patterns, possibly hierarchical in nature, although they might be represented by any three-dimensional patterns in space.

Figure 37-1 provides a visual representation of the relationships among knowledge, consciousness and extraordinary consciousness. The dotted lines represent a movement from ordinary consciousness into extraordinary consciousness, at whatever level that may occur. The wavy lines represent the fluctuating boundary between explicit and tacit knowledge, with implicit knowledge describing that which was thought tacit but triggered into consciousness by external events (incoming information). A fascinating aspect of this model is that what we called extraordinary consciousness when we first developed this model is quite ordinary today, with new, extraordinary possibilities emerging every day.

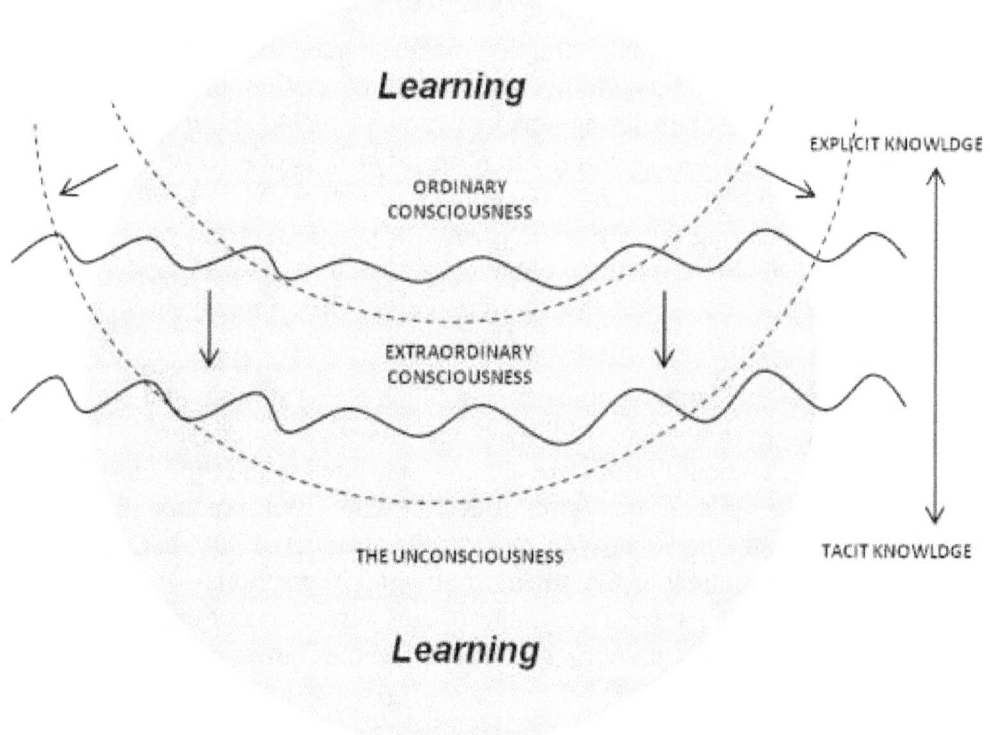

Figure 37-1. *Conceptual model relating knowledge and consciousness.*

While there is much thinking and experimentation needed to truly understand wisdom, it is increasingly clear that extraordinary consciousness—expanding our sensitivity and awareness of that which is tacit—appears to open the door to expanded wisdom. (See the discussion of wisdom in Chapter 27/Part IV.) Ultimately, consciousness relates to our connectedness and relatedness to each other, to the world we perceive within us and around us, and to the larger Universe. This state of connected consciousness is described by physicist-philosopher Peter Russell (2009) as *recognition of the self as the light of consciousness*—the same light that shines within each individual. When the mind sinks into the silence of pure consciousness, the state of Samadhi or "still mind", the markers of individuality that separate us are no longer present, and we become One with all beings.

New Role for the Personality

As a working definition introduced in Chapter 4/Part I, personality is a set of emotional qualities and/or ways of behaving that make a person different from other people. In search of a clearer understanding, we build on the definition forwarded by Caprara and Cervone (2000), considering personality as *a psychological complex system which displays a unity and continuity in terms of past, present and future both as perceived by the individual and as the individual is perceived by others*. This definition enables viewing the personality from the perspective of the individual (a collection of attributes and inclinations) as well as the perspective of the observer (a social construct based on a set of perceived differing psychological characteristics).

Further, we agreed that "human beings are not blank slates at birth, and our slates become increasingly rich and multidimensional as we grow and learn" (Carroll, 2016, p. 393). Personality traits are already imprinted at the time of birth and then, of course, these traits are thereafter affected by the environment and experiences of life. Thus, the personality is very much a product of both nature and nurture. As time passes—and responsive to environmental interactions—personality becomes ever more complex, a system of structures and processes that emerges from multiple subsystems, specifically involving interdependencies between the person and the environment.

<<<<<<<◇>>>>>>>

INSIGHT: **As time passes, and still in the survival, pleasure and avoidance of pain role, the personality becomes ever more complex, a system of structures and processes that emerges from multiple subsystems, specifically involving interdependencies between the person and the environment.**

<<<<<<<◇>>>>>>>

As situations occur and actions are taken, groups of thoughts (knowledge) are "chunked", that is, patterns are created in the unconscious as to how to respond to these situations. As similar situations emerge, based on feedback and response, more and more neuronal connections are created related to how to effectively handle these situations. Embedded in the unconscious—waiting to be triggered—these chunked groups of thought come to the fore when they are needed. The more an individual experiences similar situations, the stronger these patterns become, eventually quite capable of driving actions which are not recognized until they occur (and often not then), and can become more and more difficult to change by a conscious decision or an act of will (Bennet et al., 2015a). As Rowan describes, this experience of being "taken over" by a part of ourselves "lasts as long as the situation lasts—perhaps a few minutes, perhaps an hour, perhaps a few hours—and then changes by itself when we leave this situation and go into a different one." (Rowan, 1990, p. 7)

While this concept is not new to the *field of psychology*, it has been called by many names including, for example, Freud's (1938) ego, id and superego; Jung's (1990) archetypes; Lewin's (1936) subregions of the personality; Tart's (1975) identity states; Goffman's (1959) multiple selfing; and Kihlstrom and Cantor's (1984) self-schemas. Similarly, other authors make reference to ego states, retroflection, internal objects, imaginal objects, the hidden observer, the emotionally divided self, the false or unreal self, energy patterns, deeper potential coming to the surface, subidentities, small minds, little I's, agencies within the mind, possible selves, prototypes, alter-personalities, and a community of self (Rowan, 2000). Building on the work of Assagioli (1975), Brown (1979), Redfearn (1985), Rowan (2000) and Wilber (2000), we use the term sub-personalities to represent this concept. These sub-personalities exist as what Wilber (2000) refers to as an *unconscious "I"*.

It is important to recognize that these become automated responses to life situations coming from the unconscious, which responses may or may not be appropriate for the situation at hand at the current time. While undoubtedly these responses served at some level of effectiveness in the past—and with conscious awareness can serve as knowledge tools (Bennet et al., 2015a)—remember, we are verbs, not nouns, always changing; AND the environment and situations within which we interact are always changing. You may recall experiencing these types of responses. For example, they can present emotionally/mentally where you pretend to be someone you are not or say something you don't really mean, or even physically where you react in similar situations with a response before any conscious thought is given to the response!

Remember that as the self emerges, evolving in concert with interactions with the environment, the personality is kept quite busy integrating incoming information from the 21 senses operating on the physical, emotional and mental planes. Working through the self, learning through lived experience and developing the lower mental faculties, somewhere in the mid 20's learned and earned wisdom begins to emerge. During this growth, the personality is working through the self as it is expanding. As consciousness expands, the sub-personalities—unconscious responses focused on navigating similar repeating situations—are no longer necessary, and can limit the growth inherent from learning.

<<<<<<<<>>>>>>>

INSIGHT: **As consciousness expands, the sub-personalities—unconscious responses focused on navigating similar repeating situations—are no longer necessary, and can limit the growth inherent from learning.**

<<<<<<<<>>>>>>>

Hopefully—but not always since each human has choice—the personality has now served its primary purpose during the early part of life, that is, survival (self-perpetuation), pleasure (self-gratification) and the avoidance of pain (self-maintenance). Given this point of growth is reached, while the processing of incoming information through the senses continues in the subconscious, the personality now has the opportunity to take on a new role. This, of course, assumes a balancing of the senses has occurred (see Chapter 32), and raising the consciousness of self is in concert with this expansion.

From the Viewpoint of Alchemy. Let's explore the personality in terms of the Alchemical cycle. While the terminology and descriptive terms used in our earlier discussion of personality are somewhat different, there is also a consistency in the primary points. For example, in the language of Alchemy (and the Kabbalah), the personality is described as composed of learned behaviors and beliefs from this life. Recall from the short review above, that we differentiated the personality and the self, noting that the personality—charged with self-maintenance, self-perpetuation and self-gratification—was preprogrammed with pre-existing properties, with these traits thereafter affected by the environment and experiences of life. While the personality grows ever more complex, much of this complexity is in the unconscious (in terms of sub-personalities) and development ceases altogether as the self, destined to become a co-creator through conscious choice and change, emerges and expands. This is where we discover a strong consistency in these frames of reference, which also demonstrates the power of taking a consilience approach!

In Alchemy, the ego is considered the part of us that we are born with that has wants and desires for survival, pleasure and avoidance of pain, which is how we define the "personality" in our earlier discussion. In the Alchemical cycle, the personality becomes an impediment, and thus it has to go through a kind of "death", "sacrifice" or "surrender" to the *true self* in order for us to evolve. The Alchemical Fermentation stage is referred to as the "Death of the Personality." For this death to occur, it is necessary to clean up and get mastery over the negative ego, *which is influenced by the subconscious*. The "personality" in the language of Alchemy is thus considered masks, false identities, learned or patterned behaviors, coping strategies that form through life (sub-personalities), cementing in AFTER the age of reasoning (sometime between 6-10 years old). These false identities are due to the influence of the negative ego on the self, which creates splotches and warps/distortions on the lens of personality through which our true self is filtered.

Recall the analogy of the caterpillar, which must "die" or be obliterated and start from the beginning again in a new form, building a new identity, asking: *Who Am I? What Am I? What is my purpose?* In Alchemy, this "true self" is called *individuality* to distinguish it from personality, with the realization that this individuality is one node on a greater web of connectivity and Oneness. This is the *identity* of the butterfly instead of the *personality* of the caterpillar. Note that this does not refer to just a fusing, merging or expansion, but rather is a *complete breakdown or annihilation of the old personality that was built of false or limiting beliefs and assumptions*, and that this process is in service to *discovery of the greater truth of self*.

<<<<<<<◇>>>>>>>

INSIGHT: **This process is a *complete breakdown or annihilation of the old personality that was built of false or limiting beliefs and assumptions*, and is *in service to discovery of the greater truth of self*.**

<<<<<<<◇>>>>>>>

This is very much related to the expanding levels of consciousness (Hawkins, 2002), with each level an exponential function of the previous level, moving through a kind of death, a neutrality, before emerging on the other side into ever-expanding higher levels of consciousness (see Chapter 5/Part I).

From a more pragmatic viewpoint, this "death" is the elimination of negative ego traits and the backlog of unprocessed stuff buried in the subconscious as we heal from old traumas. Recall that the higher the development of our conceptual mind, the further back we can go and the more patterns we can recognize from the past and project into the future. In this state we are able to release the tethers of the NOW and leap into new patterns of reality. The personality becomes transparent (rather than filtering or masking) such that the true self can shine through, unimpeded, and be expressed into the world through positive ego. Positive ego, influenced by energies of the spiritual plane, is the part of us that has a desire to express our uniqueness, positive self-image, and drives us to become better and achieve more of our potential and purpose in the physical. Positive ego is the more conscious self.

Using the language introduced in this book while continuing our consilience approach, the personality that we have known, which ceased to develop around age 10, can indeed be an impediment to the emerging self. Imagine the limitations of choice when viewing life through the narrow lens of survival, pleasure and the avoidance of pain! This personality and its pre-programming must be "surrendered" if the self is to move into a position of choice. However, as an impediment, **the personality also serves as a force** to propel development of self as preferences are discovered, choices are made and individuation occurs. We liken this to the emergence of the butterfly. One author recalls a PowerPoint presentation that has circulated for years relating a story to this process.

The presentation goes something like this. When the time is ripe for the butterfly to emerge, a small hole appears in the shiny chrysalis, through which the butterfly struggles to force its body. A man is watching this struggle, and when it appears the butterfly is unable to make progress, he takes a pair of scissors and cuts a slit for the butterfly to easily emerge, which it does. Only, the butterfly is tiny, with a withered body and shriveled wings. The man continues watching, waiting for and expecting the transformation into a firm body and strong wings. However, this does not occur, and the "almost" butterfly spends the rest of its life crawling around in that withered body. When we look at the biological factors involved, we realize it is the *struggle getting through that tiny hole* that forces fluid from the butterfly's body into the wings in preparation for flight. When this struggle does not occur, the fluid never passes, the wings never develop, and the butterfly is unable to fulfill its potential.

When we as humans *are* finally able to move beyond and surrender the personality (unconscious traits and sub-personalities), many of the traits of our everyday lives may appear to be the same as earlier traits attributed to the personality—and no doubt in our normal vernacular the term "personality" would still be used to describe these traits. However, once the personality is surrendered, *who we are is a product of choice with simultaneously individuated preferences and deepening connections.* (See the discussion of Oneness in Chapter 36.)

<<<<<<<◇>>>>>>>

INSIGHT: **When the initial role of the personality is surrendered, who we are is a *product of choice* with simultaneously *individuated preferences and deepening connections.***

<<<<<<<◇>>>>>>>

The personality, born anew and reflecting the choices of self (the Alchemical *individuality*), now fuses directly with the higher mental body *and* is directly connected to the spiritual plane. In this new role, the personality is open to the higher consciousness field described previously as the Noosphere, Quantum Field or God Field, but which has been labeled many different ways (see Chapter 16/Part III). This is the Universal field of Oneness to which the self—still focusing from and operating on the physical, emotional and mental planes—now has greater access through its own personality (the Alchemical *true self*). There is the recognition of Oneness, that is, that we are all part of a larger Universal ecosystem in terms of not only the physical, emotional and mental planes but inclusive of the spiritual counterbalances, *and there is an expansion of love and wisdom.*

In a final expression, the lower self fuses with the higher Self, and having fully developed mental faculties, reaches into the intuitional plane (MacFlouer, 2004-16). With the lower and higher mental planes, the reborn energy of personality and individuality now playing a *connecting role* rather than a subconscious supporting role, and the lower self and higher Self all working together in a *continuity of consciousness*, the individual has the ability to achieve controlled intuition, that is, to tap into the intuitional plane at will, taking what is learned and effectively acting on it (see Chapter 28/Part IV).

The usage of a capital "S" of Self in the previous paragraph begs exploration. In experience, in life, there is always the concept of *more,* a precept of growth. For example, consider your wants and desires. As you achieve or acquire one thing, there is always another desire emerging in your stream of thought, another want engaging your feelings. This same expansive pattern has appeared throughout the conversation of this book. Remember, we are verbs, ever learning and changing. For example, from the viewpoint of the mental plane, we begin with development of the lower mental thought of logic and cause and effect, and move into higher mental thought with recognition of patterns and development of concepts, and then explore the concept of Universal rules represented by heuristics. From the viewpoint of the emotional plane, in exploring our deepening connections with others we move from sympathy to empathy to compassion towards unconditional love.

<<<<<<>>>>>>

INSIGHT: **In experience, in life, there is always the concept of *more*, a precept of growth.**

<<<<<<>>>>>>

This same pattern appears in the expansion of consciousness as we begin with the personality, grow with the emergence of self, and expand into a higher Self, moving towards rejoining our soul. Recall in Chapter 4/Part I the definition of spiritual was described as pertaining to the Soul, or "standing in relationship to another based on matters of the soul" (Oxford, 2002, p. 2963). Soul was forwarded as representing the *animating principle of human life in terms of thought and action*, specifically focused on its moral aspects, the emotional part of human nature, and higher development of the mental faculties. From the philosophical aspect, it is the vital, sensitive or rational principle in human beings (Oxford, 2002, p., 2928). Thus, this concept of a higher "Self" alludes to the *more* that moves us closer to the core of what it is to be human and what it is to be alive. Figure 37-2 builds on Figure 36-3, suggesting the ever-expanding "more" in terms of mental development (expanding through logic, concepts and heuristics towards Universals), deepening connections (expanding through sympathy, empathy and compassion towards unconditional love) and individuation (expanding through personality, self, Self and towards the Soul). We have now added an important piece to the expansion of consciousness as we move through the Intelligent Social Change Journey.

This is the concept of *consciousness rising*. Historically as humans we have used three to five percent of our brain during normal functioning, with the rest of our mental faculties operating in subtle ways. Yet, while it is difficult to imagine from our frame of reference, there is a continuous "more" available on this journey of growth. **There is no limit to the expansion of consciousness!** As information is passed through the balanced senses, communication channels are used and strengthened. The sources available to the individual expand, as does their consciousness. And the only limits as we continue to focus from the physical, emotional and mental planes, and even as we tap into the intuitional plane and fully co-create our reality, are those we place upon ourselves.

<<<<<<<>>>>>>>

INSIGHT: **The only limits to expansion of consciousness are those we place upon ourselves.**

<<<<<<<>>>>>>>

Beyond Associative Patterning

From the viewpoint of the physical, mental and emotional planes, what is different? The subconscious continues to process incoming information through the seven senses. However, while the associative patterning process continues, the personality plays an expanded role. Recall that the unconscious (the personality) is working 24/7 for the self. Because the personality is no longer tethered by a focus on the physical, mental and emotional planes, it now has greater access to the higher field of thought—whether the conscious mind is actively participating or not—and can proactively and aggressively access thoughts in the Field that resonate with the focused thought of self. Through vibration there is an attraction of thought to thought, a resonance, much like the bisociation of ideas in dialogue and conversations with others.

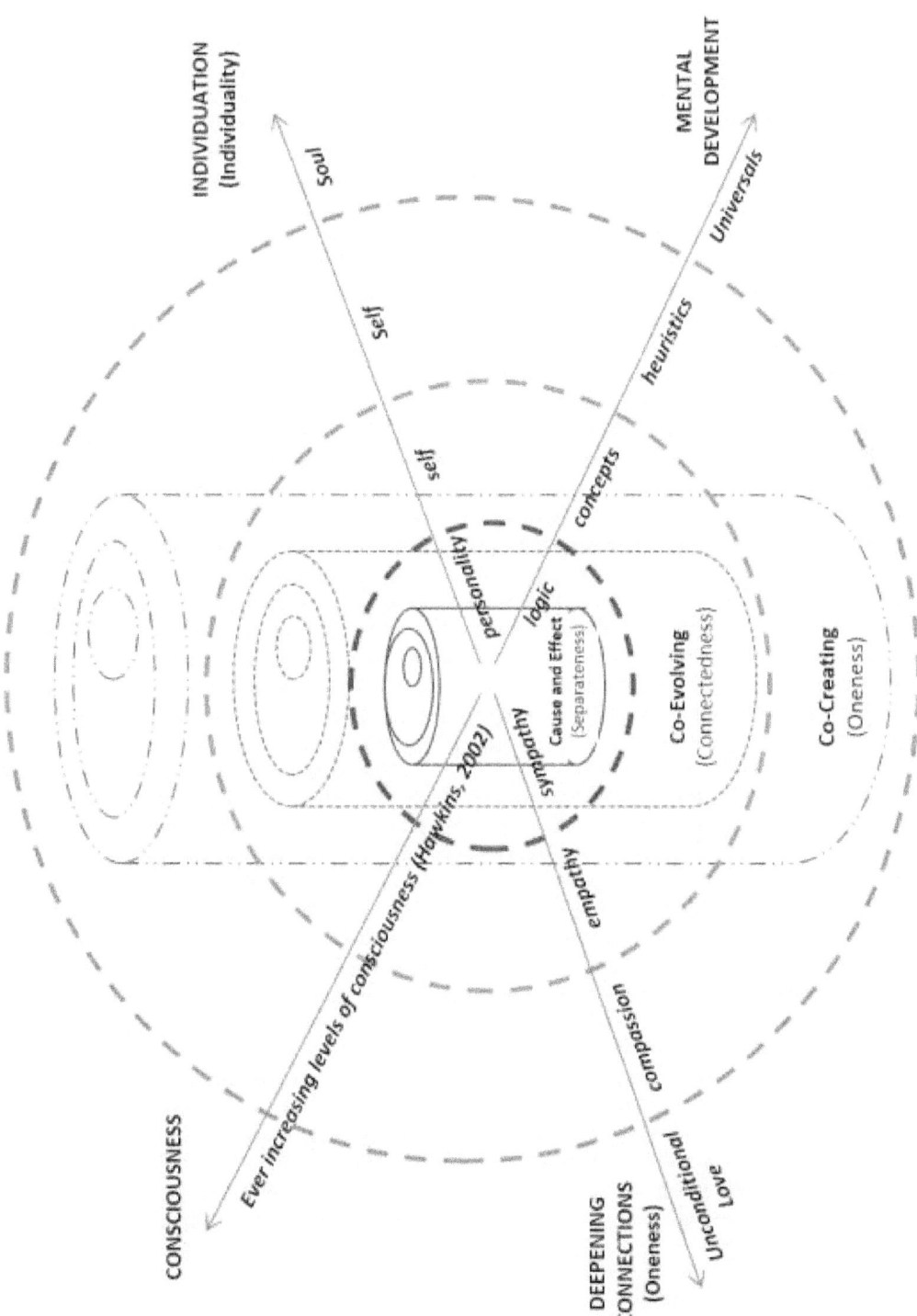

Figure 37-2. *Consciousness Rising.*

Let's briefly review some of the learning about resonance in the earlier Parts of this book.

In Chapter 3/Part I we acknowledged the human urge to seek close relationships built on personal resonance, an event moving far beyond surface meaning to connecting values, beliefs and dreams. A mechanism that aids in the synchronism of two individuals is the adaptive oscillators that are part of our physiology. These oscillators are created by stable feedback loops of neurons. There is a state of mutual entrainment that occurs, which is a measure of stability that oscillators have when they lock in with each other (Buzaki, 2006). *This is the resonance of connection that can lead to empathy, compassion, and love.*

<<<<<<<◇>>>>>>>

INSIGHT: **The resonance of connection can take the form of empathy, compassion and love.**

<<<<<<<◇>>>>>>>

In our discussion of tacit knowledges in Chapter 5/Part I, we referred to the need to deepen areas of resonance between the self and the unconscious, which refers to the self moving into the lead in terms of focus and choice and, through expanded consciousness, deepening the connection with tacit knowledges. *This is a resonance between the conscious choices of self and the processing preferences of the personality.* Inducing resonance is introduced as one of the four ways to engage tacit knowledge in Tool 5-1 (see also Appendix D). *This is a resonance between an incoming idea and the beliefs, values, etc. within the individual.*

In Chapter 10/Part II we talked extensively about the resonance of ideas, which plays a large role in today's global world in developing and sustaining trust. Idea resonance, an emergent quality of our new paradigm, refers to value built on relationship of, respect for and resonance with ideas. Ideas with which we resonate are generating energy as well as expending energy (Chapter 21/Part III). *This is a resonance among people based on similar or complementary ideas that excite the mental and/or emotional planes.*

In Chapter 14/Part III we introduced collaborative entanglement as a social phenomenon analogous to the natural activities of the brain. In the associative patterning process information coming into the individual through the senses resonates with internal patterns that have strong synaptic connections. When resonance occurs, the incoming information is consistent with the individual's frame of reference and belief systems. Collaborative entanglement describes this same process from the point of view of a community. *This is a resonance among people in a lived relationship based on possibilities consistent with mutual frames of reference and belief systems.*

Building on the idea of resonance, in Chapter 17/Part II we considered reverberation as a repeating echo that may have far-reaching or lasting impact. Harmonic reverberation occurs when two or more individuals or groups between or among whom no forces exist reflect and consider the thoughts and feelings of the other, with an emergent quality representing the best of multiple streams of thought and feelings. *This is a resonance among people based on the comingling of ideas resulting in the emergence of something more.*

In the learning points along the way of Chapter 22/Part IV, Cozolino (2006, p. 203) notes that empathy is a "muddle of resonance, attunement, and sympathy." *This resonance, then, is with the relationship of circumstances and another individual in terms of feelings and understanding.*

In Chapter 26/Part IV from a neuroscience perspective we forwarded that significant social relationships stimulate learning and knowledge creation and shape the brain (Bennet et al., 2015b). For learning, the brain actually seeks out an affectively attuned "other", someone with whom we resonate. *This is a deep resonance among individuals based on trust and respect.* We go on to say that continuous creativity thrives on exposure to a broad range of knowledge and experiences—places and people and thoughts in resonance with *who we choose to be. This is a resonance based on possibilities.* Also from a neuroscience perspective, we noted in Chapter 28/Part IV that mirror neurons facilitate *neural resonance between observed actions and executing actions* (Bennet et al., 2015b).

In Chapter 17/Part II we introduce Sheldrake's (1989) hypothesis of formative creation proposing that memory is inherent in nature, with a collective memory inherited from previous generations. This process of the past becoming the present—involving formative causal influences transmitted through both space and time—is called morphic resonance. *This is a resonance among ideas from the past and focused thought in the present.* Through morphic resonance, our thoughts have the capacity to influence other people, making it more likely for others to think in the same way we are thinking (Sheldrake, 1995). *This represents a resonance among thoughts and people occurring in the NOW.*

Thus, regardless of the lens through which we look, resonance is a quality of the Field within which we live. See Figure 37-3.

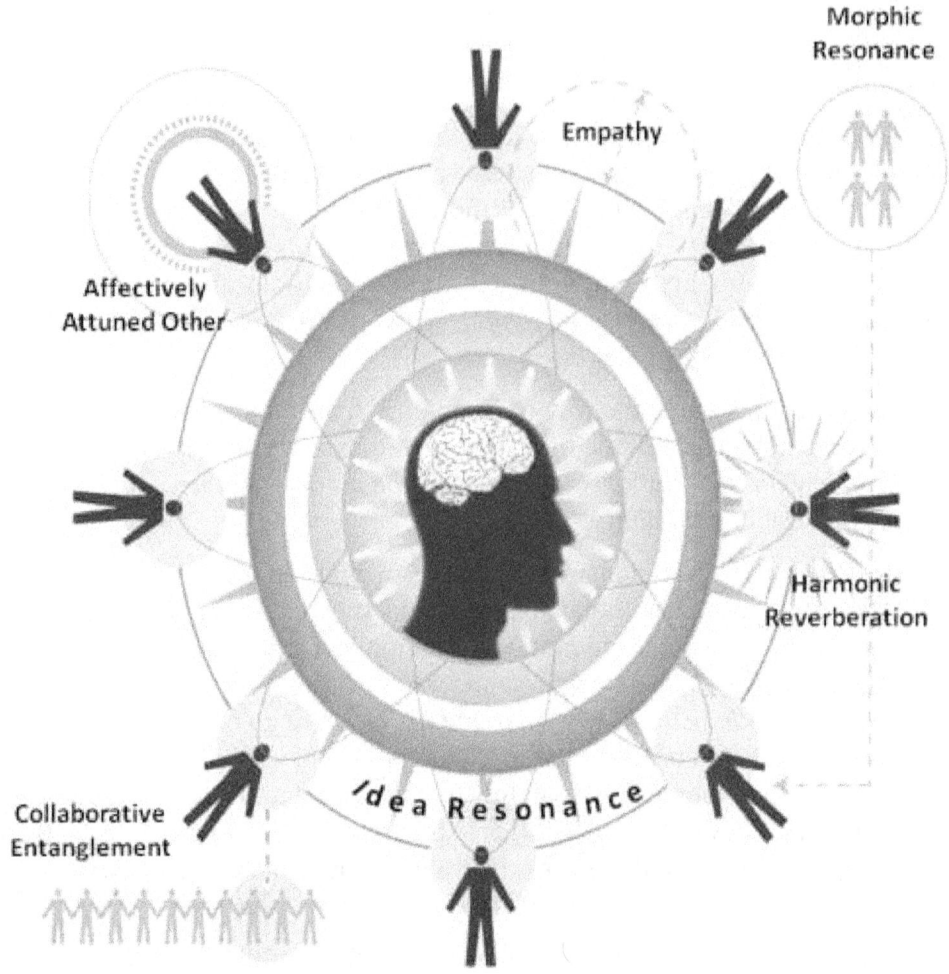

Figure 37-3. *Resonance is a quality of the Field.*

When discussing the field of ideas in Chapter 28/Part IV, we recognize that thoughts as thought forms with specific characteristics are already there in the field, waiting to be discovered, and note that when there is a resonance between the thought and the thinker, a connection occurs. We reference McTaggart (2000), who refers to an incessant dialogue that we carry on with the Field, in which we can gain access to a *shared accumulation of information.* "In that sense, our intelligence, creativity and imagination are not locked in our brains but exist as an interaction with The Field" (McTaggart, 2002, p. 139). In Chapter 36, we talk about this field as the connectedness of all things, a Oneness.

This field is also "within." Recall in the discussion of Time and Space in Chapter 16/Part III, a difficulty in understanding space in the physical plane is the fact that while our material bodies exist in space, space also exists in these same bodies; space is a property of all material bodies. Thus, as a body moves through space, it takes with it all of its properties, even the space which is within it. If you will, imagine the Field as space. Of course, it is much more than the concept we currently have of space, but for the sake of this analogy let's imagine it as space. The Field, then, exists both outside of us and inside of us, and as we move around, we carry it with us. Thus, we are always connected to the Field. Similarly, bringing in the idea of morphic resonance, we are always connected to the past as well as the ever unfolding present.

Now, imagine ideas (thoughts) as lightening bugs. This is an interesting analogy since we often picture ideas as light bulbs. Even more appropriate, when we watch lightening bugs the light flashes on and off in a continuous flow of punctuated movement. Such are ideas, where there is a flash that seems to quickly go away, then, as we keep watching (focusing) perhaps another in the general area. Even when we are not focusing, when we close ourselves off in our houses for the night, the lightning bugs are still moving and still flashing their lights. So it is with ideas.

Associative Attracting

Recall our conversation of thought forms in Learning Points Along the Way (Chapter 22/Part IV). Change begins with thought, then **energy follows thought** and becomes thought forms. Thus, the material world is an effect, not a cause. These thought forms are sent out into the environment where they attract sympathetic vibrations, that is, those who resonate with the thought being produced. Each thought that is a definite thought produces both a floating thought form and a radiating vibration. Thought forms differ in both density and quality, with *color* having to do with the emotional quality of the thought; *form* having to do with the intent of the thought; and *distinctness of outline* having to do with the degree of concentration of the thought (Besant and Leadbeater, 1999).

<<<<<<<<>>>>>>>

AN INSIGHT REMINDER: **Energy follows thought**.

<<<<<<<<>>>>>>>

Thus, we as energy beings (Chapter 18/Part III) are continuously creating thought forms and a radiating vibration connected to those thought forms. We literally live in a sea of thought forms! This is somewhat analogous to the sea of information bombarding us continuously in our interconnected world. The good news is that only those thought forms that resonate are attracted to each other, and that point of attraction has very much to do with the threshold of consciousness within which we operate (Chapter 5/Part I).

Recall the discussion of levels of consciousness developed by Hawkins (2002) (Chapter 5/Part I). Serving as a map of the energy field of consciousness, these are calibrated levels correlated with a specific process of consciousness—emotions, perceptions, attitudes, worldviews and spiritual beliefs. The progression is as follows: 20 (Shame); 30 (Guilt); 50 (Apathy); 75 (Grief); 100 (Fear); 125 (Desire); 150 (Anger); 175 (Pride); 200 (Courage); 250 (Neutrality); 310 (Willingness); 350 (Acceptance); 400 (Reason); 500 (Love); 540 (Joy); 600 (Peace); 700-1,000 (Enlightenment). It is the 200 level associated with courage and integrity that serves as a balance point between weak and strong attractors and negative and positive influence (Hawkins, 2002), and it is at the 500 level that the happiness of others becomes an essential motivating force.

The level at which we vibrate has an upper and lower threshold, dependent on the specific focus of the NOW, which is reflective of emotions, perceptions, attitudes, worldviews and spiritual beliefs interacting with the world. Thus, consistent with the highs and lows that move in and out of the experience of living, the thought which we send out and that which we attract can vary from instant to instant.

Engage your creative imagination to picture a field full of poignant, tiny flashes of light. As a thinking energy being, you, too, are producing these tiny flashes of light that have the ability to join with other flashes resonating at the same level of consciousness. Energy follows thought, with thought forms weaving reality and energizing action. This is the process of **associative attracting**. In the language of information technology, we have a personal crawler that is out there attracting and attracted to thought forms in resonance with our personal vibration. Through conscious choices, the unconscious is directly tapping the field and connecting to partial thought that resonates with the direction of those choices. This personal crawler carries vibrational attraction, both reaching out and pulling in. Thus, associative patterning continues as information comes in through the senses in the course of living and experiencing, while simultaneously associative attracting is occurring through a radiating vibration.

When we have achieved the point of fusion where our self has expanded sufficiently in consciousness to tap into the intuitional plane at will, and our personality has taken on its new role, we now have access to higher vibrating thought forms. The higher the level of our thought, the higher the level of thought forms conveyed to others and brought in through our senses. As we recognize higher order patterns, we discover higher truths.

While all this sounds very grand, the development of the mental faculties underway as we have moved through the Intelligent Social Change Journey *does* come into play! We are here to live and experience. We have this amazing physical body, a powerful and sometimes surprising set of emotions, and a miraculous mind/brain that at this point in our development is just beginning to discover itself!

<<<<<<<>>>>>>>

INSIGHT: **We have a miraculous mind/brain that at this point in our development is just beginning to discover itself!**

<<<<<<<>>>>>>>

We ask again and again in conversations with ourselves, our families, our friends, our colleagues, and with the world in general: *How can we make a positive impact on the world? How can we move through the challenges that face humanity?* "I'm just one person", we say. Of course, if we were, in fact, alone and separate, this would be absolutely true. However, this is not the case. As we now understand, we are part of a larger Field, with our own personal attractor so that we can discover others of like mind and heart, and cooperate and collaborate together to ensure we head toward intelligent activity.

Indeed, there is a great deal of responsibility that comes with all the learning occurring throughout the ISCJ. With consciousness, comes responsibility. The higher level of ideas that we now, at will, have access to are meant to be used, to be acted upon. For example, one of the gifts of this physical world is innovation. We take information, the basic building block of the Universe, connect that information to a need or opportunity, engage our creativity as we bisociate two separate conceptual patterns and connect an emerging idea to that identified need or opportunity, and develop that idea into an effective product or process. Such is innovation, which represents the creation of new ideas and the transformation of those ideas into useful applications for others.

Recalling the conversation in Chapter 20/Part III, while innovation can certainly equate to "success", however that may be defined by the innovator, it *always* equates to service. Innovation is in service to others. Innovation produces processes and products that others will use to make or do something better, generally to make their lives better in some way, and perhaps providing the opportunity for *them* to improve other's lives in some way. Thus, innovation requires letting go of our ideas, sharing them, applying them, passing on the form in which they are applied, taking responsibility for them, and, as appropriate, expanding on them through iterative feedback loops. To accomplish all of this within the world in which we live requires development of the mental faculties counterbalanced with the spiritual. As we move through the Intelligent Social Change Journey, this is what is occurring.

The Holographic Universe

Just as humans are a verb, creating knowledge for the instant at hand, our Earth and our Universe is continuously creating in each instant. As Duane Elgin, a futurist and social scientist, describes:

> Our vast cosmos is a unified organism that—in its totality of matter-energy, space-time, and consciousness—is being recreated anew at each moment. We cannot take our existence for granted. Our cosmos is a dynamically maintained system of matter and consciousness that lives within and is sustained by an unbounded field of Life-energy—an infinitely deep ecology that I have called the Meta-Universe or the generative ground. (Elgin, 1993, p. 274)

The Universe is, then, an organism unified in all its parts. Physicist David Bohm takes this the next step. He views the Universe as a dynamic hologram. A hologram is formed when a single beam of coherent light is split into two parts, with one beam bounced off an object and the second beam aligned to interfere with the first beam's reflected light. The result is a wave pattern that can be recorded on file. When light is shown through this two-dimensional file an image that is three-dimensional is projected. For example, this is the phenomenon that occurs on credit cards etched on two-dimensional plastic films that recreate a 3D image when light bounces off of them.

Bohm (1980) says that everything, every experience emerges from the *implicate order*, an energy field that contains all possibilities, with each part of this hologram contained in each other part. This means even the smallest stream of light would contain the pattern of the whole. As physicist Erwin Schrödinger (1983, p. 21) describes, "Inconceivable as it seems to ordinary reason, you ... are all in all. Hence this life of yours which you are living is not merely a piece of the entire existence but is in a certain sense the whole."

More recently and building on Bohm's ideas, the work of Hal Puthoff, Fritz-Albert Popp, Jacques Benveniste and Karl Pribram show that the Universe is a **cobweb of dynamic energy exchange, with a substructure that holds all possibilities**, showing biology as a Quantum process. As McTaggart (2002, p. 95) describes:

> Nature was not blind and mechanistic, but open-ended, intelligent and purposeful, making use of a cohesive learning feedback process of information being fed back and forth between organisms and their environment. Its unifying mechanism was not a fortunate mistake but information which had been encoded and transmitted everywhere at once ... All the processes in the body, including cell communication, were triggered by Quantum fluctuations, and all higher brain functions and consciousness also appeared to function at the Quantum level.

Schempp's discovery that short- and long-term memory is not located inside the brain, but stored externally in the Zero Point Field (similar to the concept of the Noosphere, Holofield or Akashic Field) (Schempp, 1993) is consistent with these earlier findings. This would make the human brain a receiving mechanism, with the brain receiving and processing information through holographic transformation of wave interference patterns (Lazlo, 1995). It would appear that this confirms what was forwarded in Chapter 5/Part I. Recall that Lipton (2005) says that, similar to a computer, a cell has no behavior if it is disconnected from the environment. In his research, Lipton discovered that cells are not controlled by the nucleus as previously thought, but rather through receptor and effector proteins, a set of antennas, that appear on the outer membrane of the cell. Thus, Lipton sees consciousness as a simulation information field, still evolving, with identity, and ownership, being picked up in the environment. This begs the question: Are we part of a larger virtual reality?

Adopting the humility approach introduced in Chapter 4/Part I, what would it mean to us to be part of a virtual reality? First, it would mean that there are higher energetic beings of some nature (the true "I", if there is one) participating in this virtual reality. Could this in some way be related to the soul? Second, virtual realities are created within specific rule sets. What are these rule sets? Might our rule sets have a relationship to what we call science? Third, the virtual reality games that we create have a purpose, an end point to the game far beyond the life of a single game piece. What is the purpose of human life? As can be seen, trying to comprehend the meaning of this new understanding from cell biology is quite difficult. We are operating in new waters that require a shift in our consciousness in order to understand consciousness. There is still much to learn.

<<<<<<<>>>>>>>

INSIGHT: **We are operating in new waters that require a shift in our consciousness in order to understand consciousness.**

<<<<<<<>>>>>>>

The concept of the human cell exchanging information with a field of Quantum fluctuation suggests "something profound about the world". McTaggart (2002, p. 96) says it hints at

> Human capabilities for knowledge and communication far deeper and more extended than we presently understand. It also [blurs] the boundary lines of our individuality—our very sense of separateness. If living things boil down to charged particles interacting with a field and sending out and receiving Quantum information, where [do] we end and the rest of the world begin?

The implications of this are staggering, requiring a shift in every aspect of our thought and perhaps a coalescing of our spiritual beliefs and scientific understanding.

Final Thoughts

For humans operating in form, there has been an absolute level of consciousness, while consciousness itself has no limits. What might this shift underway mean in terms of consciousness expansion? Glancing back over the chapters that have unfolded in this book, we can perhaps get an idea. Here's what it might look like: Our consciousness is tremendously elevated. We are free to become more. Life moves into an ease and flow, with *time* a way of navigating that ease and flow at will. We have the ability to use knowledge in new ways in wider and wider circumstances. There is a power of mind, with the ability to change energy back and forth at will, from thought, to thought form, to thought, allowing enormous creativity and new found ways of activity that are perfectly balanced (MacFlouer, 1999). And as we move toward a new age, **we are co-creators of our reality becoming engaged in intelligent activity**, that is, *a state of interaction where intent, purpose, direction, values and expected outcomes are clearly understood and communicated among all parties, reflecting wisdom and achieving a higher truth.*

Questions for Reflection:

Are you able to engage fully in learning experiences without being pushed by need or negative events?

How can you pull more of your deep tacit learning into conscious decision-making processes?

If consciousness is a quality of the Field, and resonance is a quality of the Field, what is the relationship between consciousness and resonance? Are there any experiences in your life where you have experienced that relationship?

How do you think love affects harmonic resonance and your connections to the Field?

Chapter 38
The Bifurcation

We are faced with the fact ... that tomorrow is today. We are confronted with the fierce urgency of now .... Over the bleached bones and jumbled residues of numerous civilizations are written the pathetic words—"Too late." (Martin Luther King, Speech at Riverside Church, New York City, April 4, 1967)

SUBPARTS: FREEDOM AND CHOICE ... CHOOSING BEYOND DUALITY ... THE SPLIT IN THE ROAD ... IS HUMANITY READY FOR THE CREATIVE LEAP? ... CLOSING THOUGHTS

FIGURES: 38-1. THE HUMAN JOURNEY OF CHOICE ... **38-2.** CAN HUMANITY ADVANCE AT THE SAME PACE WITHOUT THE PUSH OF NEED, FEAR AND SURVIVAL? ... **38-3.** COMPLEXITY BEGETS COMPLEXITY, FROM WHICH EMERGES SIMPLICITY.

THE BIFURCATION BY ARTIST CINDY TAYLOR (2017)

At no time in history have Martin Luther King's inspirational words been more needed to ring out around the world. Lipton and Bhaerman (2009) demonstrate the lifespan of a civilization with a very simple graphic showing the rise of development, a leveling out as the civilization moves into rigidity, the insertion of challenges as the environment shifts and the rigidity (active resistance to change) continues, and the inevitable decline that follows inflexibility and the cessation of learning. Today, humanity is in the throes of global challenges and at a decision point regarding survival of our planet and our race. As Lipton and Bhaerman (2009) describe:

> Today's world situation reveals that we are deep in the throes of global life-threatening challenges that are directly linked to civilization's misperceived societal truths. We are entering a transition period between a civilization that is dying and one that is struggling to be born. From the ashes of the old civilization arises a new one—we are living the story of the Phoenix. (Lipton & Bhaerman, 2009, p. 206)

Indeed, a great upheaval is underway, ushering in a new era for humanity. As nuclear physicist Robert Oppenheimer wrote, "The world alters as we walk in it so that the years of man's life measure not some small growth or rearrangement or moderation of what he learned to childhood, but a great upheaval." (Copeland et al., 1999, p. 644) This time has been referred to by mystics as a Quickening, a Great Shift, a transformation, a time of transition, or the end of the world we once knew and the birthing of a new world. Humanity is in labor. And as with any birthing process, there are pains that come with it.

<<<<<<<<>>>>>>>

INSIGHT: **A great upheaval is underway, ushering in a new era for humanity.**

<<<<<<<<>>>>>>>

The expansion of human consciousness underway today was eagerly called forth as we neared the end of the last century, whether couched in cognitive or cultural terms. Recognizing that humans create reality, as early as 1977 industrialist Aurelio Peccei, founder of the Club of Rome, prophesized:

> There cannot be any salvation, unless people themselves change their values, mores, and behavior for the better. The real problem of the human species ... is that it has not been able culturally to keep pace with, and thus fully adjust to, the changed realities which it itself has brought about ... It is only by developing adequately human quality and capacities all over the world that our material civilization can be transformed ... This is the human revolution, which is more urgent than anything else if we are to control the other revolutions of our time ... (Peccei, 1977, p. xi)

This concept of conscious evolution is an important theme of our times. Evolution often comes in the face of crisis, where there is a huge pressure that puts us at risk of extinction unless we get really innovative and evolve; and there have been a lot of crises happening in the world since the turn of the new millennium. We see some people reacting with survival-based instincts and trying to cling to control, while others are doing away with old methods and responding with great innovations. These are truly unprecedented times.

At a 2011 university graduation lecture given by Barbara Marx Hubbard, she forwarded the idea that each successful evolutionary shift could be identified as a *consciousness raising experience*, the view that evolution results in a gradual (or sometimes rapid) rising of consciousness. Certainly, we can look back on the various evolutionary stages and see that, indeed, evolution has led to ever more complex and self-aware beings. Our consciousness, self-awareness, complexity and multi-dimensionality of thought have continued to increase over time as we and our technologies evolve.

Hubbard (2015) recognizes that humanity is poised to make a leap that is "as great as that made from the Neanderthal to the Self-aware human." Not only are we about to make another big leap, we are also now *aware* that we are evolving AND that we have the power to *co-create our own future*. This awareness and the ability to collaborate with our own process as co-creators presents us with an amazing opportunity: the chance to launch into a new age of conscious evolution, the *Golden Age of Humanity*.

The push now is towards a new level of harmony, a balancing of our senses that can lead to beauty. We are entering an era that seeks connection and integration rather than separation, that embraces synergy rather than conflict. With all our marvelous individuation and diversity, it is time to bring the pieces together into a greater whole rather than continuing to break things into separate parts.

<<<<<<<<>>>>>>>

INSIGHT: **We are entering an era that seeks connection and integration rather than separation, that embraces synergy rather than conflict**.

<<<<<<<<>>>>>>>

McWhinney (1997) recognized our realities as a product of second-order change, and that symbols, mental images, sensory impressions, events and naming give reality to our perceptions. He says this reality can move in two different directions: *conventionalizing* or *differentiating*. Conventionalizing moves toward a monistic position, bestowing order and rational integration, forming generalities and models, and "systematically organizing empirical knowledge to gain power over ideas as well as resources" (McWhinney, p. 64).

Differentiating is the opposite, leading to the creation of new symbols, concepts, relations and metaphors. This differentiation can emerge from recognition of patterns of behavior, or the bisociation of ideas (creativity). For example, Ben Franklin, Thomas Edison or Edwin Land of Polaroid had whole catalogs of differential ideas. As Wagner (1975, p. 44) says, "A differentiating symbolization specifies and concretizes the conventional world by drawing radical distinctions and delineating its individualities." Through deep differentiation, new wholes are generatively created, transcending the separation of subject-object and making the change distinct. This is a form of *reframing* (Watzlawick, 1974), similar to developing a new market for a product, only at this level developing the new human.

In *The Global Brain*, similar to Hubbard's conviction, Peter Russell (1982) said that we as a humanity had advanced in our evolutionary journey to where we were poised to make a leap to a global consciousness. He sees the Earth as a self-regulating living organism. As such, this leap is just as significant as the emergence of life itself. The Global Brain refers to the interlinking of billions of minds together as one system, although when this book was published this was still a dream. To leap, of course, involves inner spiritual development and transformation of the individual human consciousness.

José Argüelles (2009) says the future is already beginning. We would go further. The future is already here. Thinking in terms of the Earth as an ecosystem and the interconnectivity of humanity, we exist in a new stage of consciousness as *part of the Noosphere*, the energy field described by the French geologist/paleontologist, Pierre Teilhard de Chardin, as "a human sphere, a sphere of reflection, of conscious invention, of conscious souls" (de Chardin, 1966, p. 63).

As Russell (1982) predicted, this new phase of humanity is **dominated by consciousness**, and we are in the midst of the "sundry effects of the *biosphere-noosphere transition*, the chaotic and dissipative shift into the new order of planetary reality" (Laszlo, 2009, p. 98). Collectively, as a planetary organism, there is a new planetary consciousness emerging, a Oneness, which we individually as an evolving human spirit and collectively as an evolving humanity have the opportunity to embrace. This is our choice, what we describe as the Bifurcation, holding onto the past *or* flowing into the future.

Mulhall offers a vision of the future based on transhumanism, that is, **moving beyond human** into the realm of superintelligence and superhealth, which includes increased emotional and social well-being. The World Transhumanist Association (2001) describes transhumanism as a radical new approach to future-oriented thinking based on the premise that the human species does not represent the end of our evolution but, rather, its beginning. They go on to formally define it as follows:

> (1) The study of the ramifications, promises and potential dangers of the use of science, technology, creativity, and other means to overcome fundamental human limitations.

> (2) The intellectual and cultural movement that affirms the possibility and desirability of fundamentally altering the human condition through applied reason, especially by using technology to eliminate aging and greatly enhance human intellectual, physical, and psychological capacities … (World Transhumanist Association, 2001)

Many other changes come along with this transformation. Mulhall (2002, p. 107) says that transhumanists agree on one concept, that the

> … era of Homo sapiens as the only self-aware, technological lifeforms on earth may be about to end. We may be at the same relative stage as when Neanderthals met the first Homo sapiens, except this time the transition may be decades or centuries, not thousands of years. It may involve not just one

subspecies of posthuman, but many, each emerging in a time span that seems like spontaneous combustion compared to the rest of history until now.

The focus is not on what it is to be human *now*, but *on what we can rapidly become*, what may be a new species of human: posthumans or transhumans in an era of transhumanism.

Freedom and Choice

Sameness gives comfort; yet it is this same sameness that bores us and holds us back from being the verbs, the continuous learners, that we are or can be. Noting that nearly all change produces some level of fear, we agree with Walsch (2009, p. 44) when he says that "Life begins at the end of your Comfort Zone." When we feel uncomfortable with life, we know that change is beginning. Walsch's words reiterate the thought that began this book: "Life *is* change, and when there is nothing that is changing, there is nothing that is living" (Walsch, 2009 p. 47). The aspiration is to purposefully co-create the change you want to happen.

Humans are designed to question and doubt, with freedom of motives and choice (MacFlouer, 2004-16). In the cascade of choices available at every level of change, there are three direct factors—aspirations, insight, and incentives—that influence every choice that is made (Martin, 2000, p. 463). Individuals in any social situation are influenced, in conjunction with other factors, by their individual aspirations, all underpinned by a complex set of values, emotions and expectations. In a complex world where individuals do not know what they know (or don't know), we are influenced more and more by intuition and insights, thus aspirations often go hand-in-hand with insights. As Martin (2000) says, "Aspirations help define what insights are valuable, and such insights are pursued to the exclusion of other insights" (p. 461). Incentives provide the impetus to move forward in accordance with aspirations and insights, or disincentives may discourage such a choice. Thus, these three factors are mutually reinforcing in a cascade of choices, with each and all highly dependent on the situation and context at hand.

As introduced in the modalities of change in Chapter 8/Part II, a fourth factor influencing each of these three is learning capacity. Sustainability in a changing environment requires learning. When learning capacity is high, there are more choices, and a better chance of adjusting and responding to the needs and opportunities at hand, enabling choices that match aspirations, insights and incentives. A low learning capacity insinuates an inability or difficulty in adjusting and responding to changes that present themselves.

Agreeing that aspirations, insight, incentives and learning all directly impact choice, building upon beliefs, values and mental models experientially developed, there is still the freedom to choose. Nowhere was this more obvious than in the United States 2016 Presidential election. However, choice does not end with the results of an election. People are responsible for the governments under which they live. See the discussion of forces in Chapter 3/Part I, and, specifically, the example of the use of spiritual force. Informed by the physical, mental, emotional and intuitional planes, the balance between freedom and imposed and supported societal or governmental limits is an intelligent choice that drives actions.

This brings us to the CHOICE facing humanity today. See Figure 38-1. At the beginning of each of the five Parts of *The Profundity and Bifurcation of Change*, the Intelligent Social Change Journey was introduced as a developmental journey of the body, mind and heart, moving from the heaviness of cause-and-effect linear extrapolations, to the fluidity of co-evolving with our environment, to the lightness of breathing our thoughts and feelings into reality. We acknowledged that these phase changes might feel familiar to the journeyer. As babies, we were born connected to our mothers and families and to the larger energies surrounding us. This is a place we began breathing our thoughts and feelings into reality (Phase 3). Then in 4th grade, beginning the process of individuation, we looked to those around us as models, living in the NOW and very much co-evolving with, flowing with, our environment (Phase 2). By the mid-teens we were immersed in the learning of cause and effect, whether imposed by parents, schools, religion or society. There is a heaviness here; with rules to be learned, and consequences to actions taken outside those rule sets. As we move into adulthood, this is the starting point of the Intelligent Social Change Journey.

In Phase 1, within the framework of our local environment and with a focus on the geosphere (the physical), diversity thrives on freedom as we follow our passions and individuate as we are able, deciding what we do like and what we don't like. While there is much to learn in this phase, today, as a global world, the large majority of our youth move rapidly into the NOW and co-evolving of Phase 2. With a focus on the biosphere (living organisms), these young minds are not tethered by action and reaction; they understand concepts, the way things are connected and the relationship of those connections. Through their interactions with others around the world, they honor diversity and have developed an empathetic understanding of other cultures. People are people, each unique and creative, each with likes and dislikes, each with passions, and each choosing where to focus their energy and their creative juices.

Virtue grows from this Journey-nurtured diversity as we recognize the interconnectivity and interdependence of humanity, and as we strengthen our connections to the Noosphere (human thought and consciousness), we move toward an understanding of Oneness and the thoughts and actions that Oneness advances. For example, balance and beauty are choices that expand humanity beyond the limits of virtue to a larger frame of reference, helping us move fully into co-creating our collective reality. All along this journey is choice.

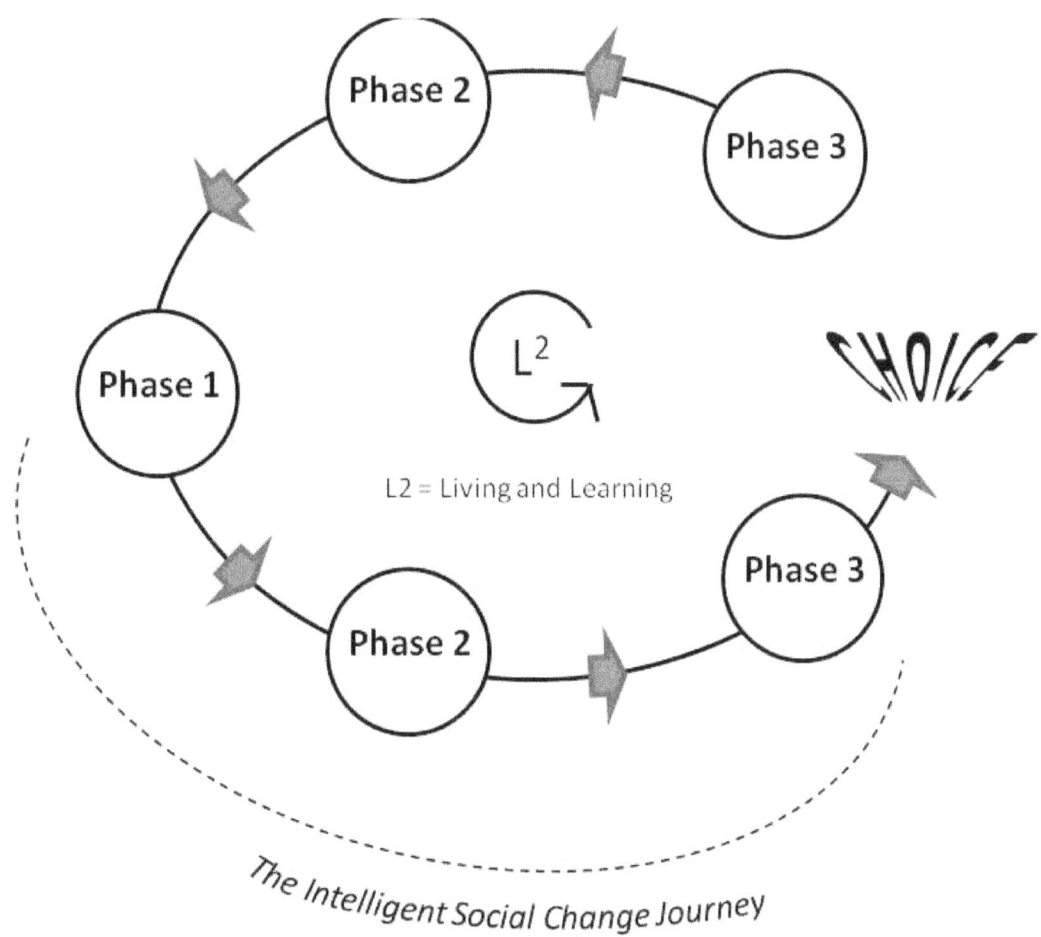

Figure 38-1. *The human journey of choice.*

<<<<<<<<>>>>>>>

INSIGHT: **Virtue grows from diversity as we recognize the interconnectivity and interdependence of humanity, and move toward an understanding of Oneness and the thoughts and actions that Oneness advances.**

<<<<<<<<>>>>>>>

Choosing Beyond Duality

In Chapter 12/Part II we quoted McWhinney (1997, p. 21) as saying "Conflict is intimately related to change, and change engenders conflict." They have a symbiotic relationship. Conflict is a condition of duality, which has both dampened our hearts and spurred us onward, placing us in competitive win/lose situations.

The concept of duality is the concept of opposites and contrast. Simple examples are black/white, good/bad, win/lose, and male/female. From a symbiotic viewpoint, the two opposites are part of a larger whole: one concept exists because the other exists. (See the discussion of symbiotic thinking in Chapter 22/Part IV.) Historically, we have often been driven to change, to create and innovate, by occasions (events and perceptions) related to need, fear and survival. Thus, our experiential learning journey is heavily based on the "push" factor of negative events and perceptions. And learn we have! Take a moment and reflect on what you would define as the greatest learning experiences of your life, times when you pushed through difficulties, perhaps significantly changing the course of your life.

However, if we have really learned these lessons, we question the continuing necessity of this, and reflect: *Have we experientially learned enough to make wise choices in a world not grounded by duality?* The authors have struggled for several years reflecting on this and related questions. Is duality necessary for effective choices? What would be the driving forces for growth and expansion in a life without duality? Note that our responses to these questions assume the *experience* of duality in the past, that is, the experiential learning associated with a full life of ups and downs, trials and tribulations, losses and successes, all of which have been used to propel us forward into expanded consciousness. Per symbiotic thinking, the concept and potential of non-duality exists *because the duality we have experienced exists*. Thus, we acknowledge the significance of these experiences, which have anchored in and then honed our beliefs and values, have opened us to new ways of thinking and being, and have helped us to individuate and understand and appreciate our choices. And we ask this question from a state of experiential learning and expanded consciousness.

Let's briefly view the experience of duality from the viewpoint of neuroscience. Generic experiences, those that are repeated day after day, are low-intensity, faint experiences, with the objects of those experiences quickly fading from memory. These are experiences with low-contrast stimuli. The intensity of neural responses in the mind/brain, that is, the rapidity of spikes produced by neuronal firings, is proportional to the level of contrast of the stimulus. Low intensity neural responses are evoked by low-contrast stimuli, and high intensity neural responses are evoked by high-contrast stimuli (Reynolds and Chelazzi, 2004). A higher level of activity means the formation of a more robust neuronal code (Fazekas and Overgaard, 2016a). Thus, higher contrast events have a higher level of neuronal activity resulting in a more concrete conscious experience. Of course, there is a threshold to be crossed. As Fazekas and Overgaard (2016b, p 8) explain:

> Neurons respond with an increased firing rate only to oriented edges with a contrast level that is above a threshold value. Above this threshold as the stimulus contrast increases, the neuron produces increasingly stronger responses (following roughly a flat S-curve).

There is, however, also a saturation point, where an increase in stimulus contrast ceases to increase the firing rate (Schlar and Freeman, 1982; Reynolds and Chelazzi, 2004). This is consistent with the focus and learning threshold of consciousness introduced in Chapter 5/Part I; where something (an idea, strategy, event, etc.) above the upper threshold is either not recognized or does not make sense.

Of course, intensity of contrast is only one factor determining the level of consciousness. Fazekas and Overgaard (2016, p. 7) say that "the quality of representations is determined by the robustness, the distinctness, and the stability of the neural code", with robustness related to *intensity* or amplitude, distinctness related to *precision* or variance and stability related to *temporal stability* or maintenance of the codes. Another example of intensity is attention. As introduced in Chapter 23/Part IV, we know that attention to various features also increases the concrete conscious experience (Asplund et al., 2014). Precision is focused on the unique quality of representations, what is being seen, heard, felt, tasted, smelled. Temporal stability is the length of time percepts are held; with unconscious representations decaying quickly and conscious representations being maintained for a period of time (Greenwald et al., 1996; Dehaene et al., 2006; Kiefer et al., 2011).

From this short discussion, it is clear that the level of contrast, the uniqueness of specific incoming information, and whether we are conscious of an event, all have a direct impact on the neuronal activity of the brain, and therefore warrant reflection when exploring the significance of duality in the experiential learning cycle. This very discussion of whether duality is necessary is paradoxical, that is, with non-duality defined by our understanding of duality. Recognizing the significance of contrast and the power of attention, the question becomes: *Are there attractors outside the context of conflict (duality) that can provide that contrast and keep our attention?*

Looking at the current world situation, we see the push of need, fear and survival woven throughout our systems. This is evident in the daily headlines, whether dealing with politics or economics, the ecosystem or in the experience of erratic and severe weather shifts. Looking through the lens of the Alchemical cycle introduced in Chapter 31, humanity is indeed primed for a push into a new way of being!

Conversely, looking toward a brighter future, we ask again: *Are these negative experiences necessary to sustain the depth of experiential learning happening today?* From a positive perspective, what is it that can capture our attention or provide the needed contrast to cause spikes in our neural activity? We suggest that for those who choose to no longer live in a reaction mode responding to need, survival and fear, who no longer require conflict in order to choose change, there is the *excitement of exploring the unknown*.

<<<<<<<>>>>>>>

INSIGHT: **The excitement of exploring the unknown has the ability to capture our attention and provide the needed contrast to cause growth and expansion.**

<<<<<<<>>>>>>>

Humans have an innate curiosity to discover new things, and an intense desire to explore the unknown. And there are other attractors as well. There are inner urgings to challenge and test ourselves, and, fulfilling the role of the co-creators we are, to create and innovate. And anticipation rivals boredom! In Figure 38-2 we introduce a number of attractors that can provide the *pull* to create and participate in extraordinary learning experiences.

Whether responding to the push or embracing the excitement of the pull, there is a choice to be made. This brings us to the moment at hand.

The Split in the Road

We are at the point of choice, and this choice is about who we are becoming, not who we are. For several generations, whether from an individual, organizational or global frame of reference, we've known the split in the road was ahead of us. In 1996, James wrote in her forward-thinking book, much of which is now taken for granted:

> Understanding the nature of change is harder now because we cannot see the signs and signals that were once so obvious. Getting off a horse to step into a car was a pretty clear indicator that the age of mechanized transportation had arrived. Now change seems invisible, hidden in transparent pulses in the air. The appeal of a retreat to the past is not surprising. But it's too late to go back. We know too much. The new road will stretch out ahead of us regardless of our ambivalence. (James, 1996, p. 15)

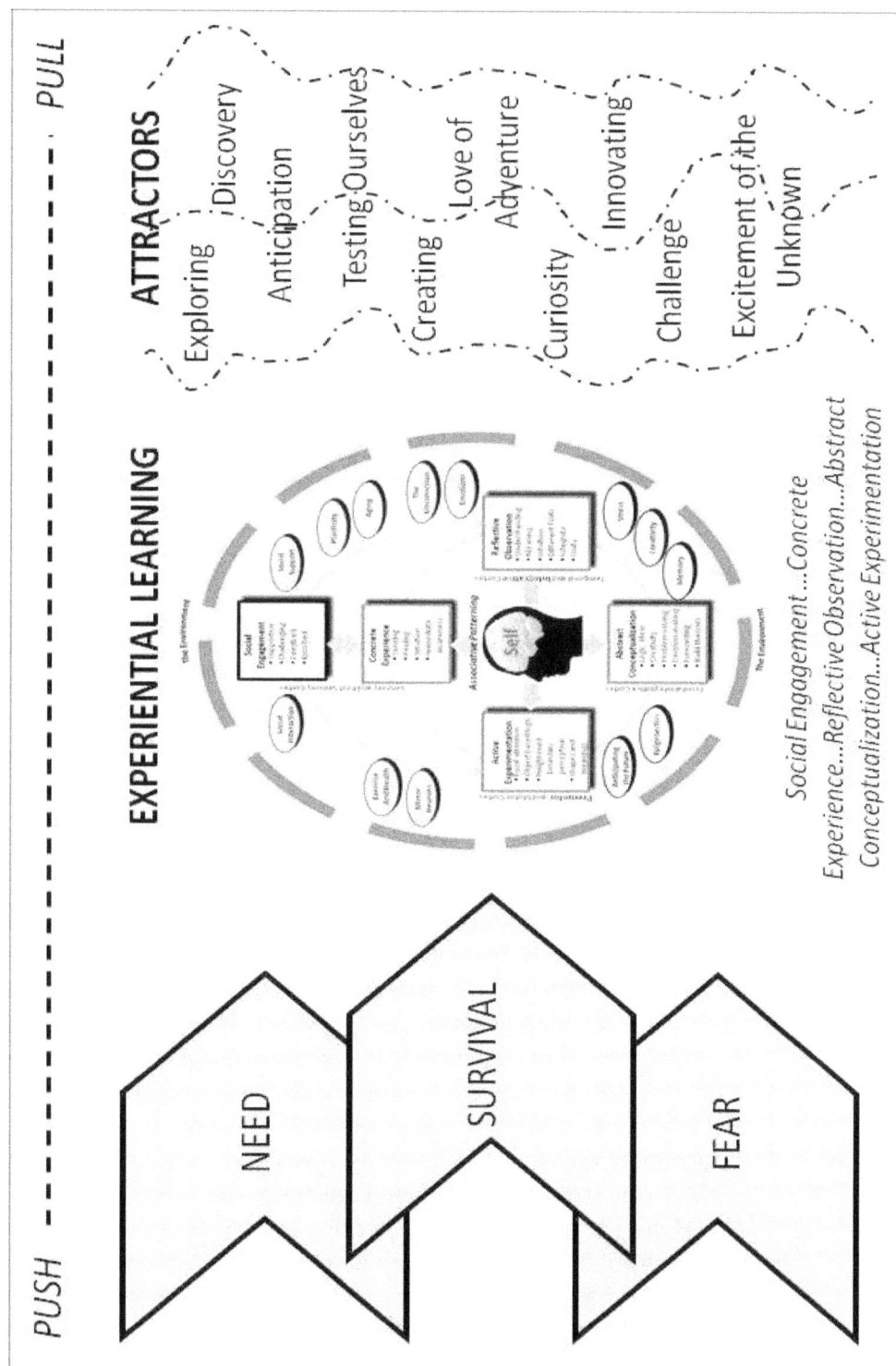

Figure 38-2. *Can humanity advance without the push of need, fear and survival?*

Many of us know this in our hearts, and many of us have noticed it in the shifting focus of the workplace. In 2005 a participant in the KTML study (Bennet, 2005) noted that Knowledge Management hit a moment in human evolution of potential extreme importance. In his words,

> We as humans are confronting in our history the possibility to overcome a fundamental contradiction between our biological constitution and our social vocation, between our animal constitution and our aim to build civilization, and this is a contradiction that has been pointed out frequently by scientists and thinkers and historians and social biologists. . . . KM brings the opportunity to look above why humans are reacting the way we do, **to generate a further level of consciousness** that will help us rethink the social systems that we created before in the more mechanical way we inherited from the past ... from the mental reflection on knowledge systems as the core upon which social human life, human societies are constructed, that we are now facing this opportunity.

Lipton and Bhaerman (2009) speak of the Bifurcation as a fork in the road, that is, **a balance point between the spiritual and material realms**. This is the balancing of the physical, mental and emotional, all interlaced with the spiritual beings that we are. This is the balancing of our five senses of form and two inner senses that connect us to the larger whole. In a poetic sense, this is the balancing of our minds and hearts. Thus, we explore the sense-making of poet Cindy Scott (2016a) in her poem "Balancing the Heart and Mind":

> How does one balance the emotional heart
> With the logical intellect of mind?
> Harmony between passion and the mental
> Is sometimes not easy to find.
>
> I physically live in a body
> Of temporal carnality,
> While peering into the peculiar realm
> Of my Spiritual reality.
>
> Armed with life's many learned lessons,
> With an awareness of where I am from,
> Helps me discern the trails of this life
> And those that are yet to come,
> 'Til I finally gain understanding
> Of the elegant path I am sowing,
> Expanding my focus to expedite
> My needed Spiritual growing.

The future is dependent on the choice that is made between two alternative paths. On the one hand, we can keep doing things the way we've done them in the past, certainly making some headway in terms of technology, only living by the law of the jungle in a pit of duality. As Lipton and Bhaerman (2009, p. 207) suggest:

> We may choose to stay in the same familiar world of dueling dualities, wherein religious fundamentalists and reductionistic scientists continue to polarize the public. This path will obviously continue to take us toward the same destination we are heading to now—imminent extinction.

OR *we can choose to think and act together*. This is returning to a point of balance.

> … as we return again to the balance point, we may choose to resolve our differences by seeking harmony over polarity. By combining formerly factious elements into a unified functional whole, we can open the door, transcend historic dualities, and experience an evolution that will provide for a higher-functioning, more-sustainable version of humanity. (Lipton and Bhaerman, 2009, p. 207)

These authors call for adoption of a new basal paradigm they calls holism, that is, a paradigm based on the integration of a new science and ancient spiritual wisdom (Lipton & Bhaerman, 2009). There are three primary questions (p. 211) holism addresses:

(1) *How did we get here?* (Holism answer: a combination of evolution and creation);

(2) *Why are we here?* (Holism answer: Experience and learning for humanity's continued evolution);

(3) *Now that we're here, how do we make the best of it?* (Holism answer: Balance based on the recognition of Oneness, all things are connected).

We encourage each of you to ask these same questions of your self: *How did we get here? Why are we here? Now that we're here, how do we make the best of it?* And perhaps one more question: *Where do we choose to go next?*

Is Humanity Ready for the Creative Leap?

Historically, we as humans work and strive to create change with only slightly visible results, then some event occurs which connects all this prior activity, and the understanding of value pushes everyone to a new strata of recognition, with the entire plane of behavior shifting upward to a new starting point. A good analogy is the growth of bamboo. For the first four years the young bamboo plant is watered with relatively little visible evidence of growth. But during this time, out of sight the roots are spreading, interconnecting and growing in strength. Then, during the fifth year, the bamboo plant streaks upward some 20 or more feet.

Humanity is at the sprouting point in terms of our expanding consciousness. We've done a great deal of work growing our mental faculties, and learning through our connections to others. We look through the lens of Ken Wilber to further explore this transition. Wilber (1999) says that humanity—both as individuals and as members of a historically located culture—is undergoing a process of psychospiritual development. This transition is not much different than the shifting developmental stages each of us experiences in life, that is, moving from a symbiotic state with our mother (Phase 3) to separation; from focus on an individual body to membership in a group (Phase 2); and then into development of the mental ego (Phase 1), from where we start the Intelligent Social Change Journey, moving from the logic of lower mental thinking (Phase 1) to the concepts of higher mental thinking (Phase 2). As we expand through these stages or phases, our idea of "self" shifts and changes. We have a higher awareness of being aware, and with consciousness comes responsibility. We move into a state of self-governance, anchoring and putting into action every level of our multidimensional self in our continuous search for higher truth. We move beyond the mental ego into the heart (Phase 3), embracing diversity and expanding our individuation, while simultaneously connecting more deeply with others through conscious compassion. And, as those connections deepen, we move ever closer to that unconditional love that once appeared illusive and, even, unobtainable for humanity.

<<<<<<<>>>>>>>

INSIGHT: **As our connections deepen, we move ever closer to that unconditional love that once appeared illusive.**

<<<<<<<>>>>>>>

There are two dimensions that Wilber says are necessary to transition from one stage to another: *the creative urge* and *the willingness to let go*, that is, be open to new thought and experiences (Wilber, 2000). Note the similarity of these dimensions to those required for innovation! This is not surprising. Certainly, the beginning of this transition is the global network of technology facilitating the movement of information around the world, and enriching the creative field from which innovation emerges. Coupled to this capacity are the attitudes of a new generation of decision-makers who are growing up green and growing up connected, and who are not satisfied with the world as it is (Tapscott, 2009).

Wilber (2000) identifies four factors that are particularly important to facilitate personal transformation. These are: fulfillment, dissonance, insight and opening. *Fulfillment* is the completion of basic tasks at the current stage, having the knowledge, a basic competency, to function adequately and be ready to move on. *Dissonance* is between the old (holding on) and the new (setting in), which could be emotionally charged through affective tacit knowledge. We now recognize that through choice, the excitement of the unknown can create this dissonance. *Insight* into the situation and what is actually wanted provides the direction to move forward and most likely draws on intuitive and spiritual tacit knowledge, and may involve consciously tapping into the intuitional plane. *Opening* refers to the quality of openness needed to move forward into a new awareness, learning and an expansion of consciousness.

Jean Houston (2000), scholar, philosopher and teacher, is more dramatic in her description of the choice upon us. She says that this time in Earth's history addresses the imperative "grow or die". As she quite eloquently describes:

> We are guests at a wake for a way of being that has been ours for hundreds, even thousands of years .... Our challenge is to cultivate the vision and lay out the practical steps necessary to move through the opening times that follow upon closing times .... the new millennium we have entered is the intersection between worlds, between species, between ourselves and forever .... we as a species stand at a crossroads faced with radical choices, any of which promise to make tomorrow look nothing like yesterday. (Houston, 2000, p. 2)

That wake is turbulent, an ending—breaking apart and crumbling—of all that we have known, the future that we expected. We are beyond our comfort level moving toward the unknown. Yet from this very place, when we look inside, we can perceive great potential, unlimited possibilities.

<<<<<<<>>>>>>>

INSIGHT: **We are at an ending, a breaking apart and crumbling of all that we have known, the future that we expected, and are moving toward the unknown.**

<<<<<<<>>>>>>>

We've entered the *Jump Time* that Houston (2000) describes, "a whole system transition, a condition of interactive change that affects every aspect of life as we know it" (p. 11). Recognizing that virtually every human system—organizational, economic, environmental, political, etc.—is undergoing a state of deconstruction and breakdown, the Jump Time phenomenon is focused on possibilities. Five forces are driving this jump into the future:

(1) The Evolutionary Pulse from Earth and Universe (realization that we are co-creators);

(2) The Re-patterning of Human Nature (tapping into the creative mind and engaging the full human capacity);

(3) The Re-genesis of Society (becoming and thinking global);

(4) The Breakdown of the Membrane (dissolving of old barriers); and

(5) The Breakthrough of the Depths (a spiritual yearning; balancing inner growth with outer accomplishments) (Houston, 2000, pp. 12-15).

In this journey, *the choices of each individual make a profound difference.* "Our individual life is part of the unfinished symphony of the cosmos" (Houston, 2000, p. 18).

This is the creative leap ahead for humanity. There is an influx of energy, an increase in forces, and the expansion of consciousness. Only, unlike the transition into puberty, we have a choice whether to hold onto the survival mode of our childhood personality focused on seeking pleasure and avoidance of pain, or to let our emergent self grab the reins and embrace a new way of being. Or do we? We know that a living system cannot stay in stasis; that we require growth to survive.

The possibility of a creative leap at the level of humanity is not a new idea, although it does take on new meaning as we begin to explore the ideas of Quantum theory. In 1972 Stephen Jay Gould of Harvard University and Niles Eldredge of the American Museum of Natural History challenged Darwin's concept of phyletic gradualism, which is the theory that changes within species evolve over long periods of time. Gould and Eldredge discovered through new evidence from fossils that new evolutionary forms had emerged over a few generations rather than through a long, slow process. This is *punctuated equilibrium*, accepted today as one kind of evolutionary change.

Or, in the language of complexity theory, we might describe this time in history as reaching a *tipping point*, when a complex adaptive system changes slowly until all of a sudden it unpredictably hits a threshold which creates a large-scale change throughout the system. Braden (2014) and others use the term *turning point* to remind us of the words attributed to Lao-Tzu (6th Century B.C.E. Chinese philosopher), "If you do not change direction, you may end up where you are heading." The *100th monkey effect* refers to a hypothetical phenomenon where a new idea or behavior spreads instantaneously across a group or among groups when a critical number of members in one group adopt that idea or behavior. This infers tapping into the Noosphere. In Quantum field language, we would talk about enough energies heading the same direction in a probability field such that a *Quantum leap* occurs. What is clear is that from whatever frame of reference we choose to look, we are poised for a creative leap at the level of humanity!

<<<<<<<>>>>>>>

INSIGHT: **From whatever frame of reference we choose to look, we are poised for a creative leap at the level of humanity.**

<<<<<<<>>>>>>>

Let's see what this might look like as a graphic. In Figure 38-3 we show the relationship of the expanding CUCA environment (increasing change, uncertainty, complexity and anxiety) and the creative leap that represents an *expanded state or level of consciousness*. In the current environment (lower left of figure), we are embedded in ever-increasing complexity, opining about how much simpler things were in the past. We all can identify with that thought. Note the familiar topics in the text box in the center of the graphic. The content of this book has been an attempt to surface and connect the amazing developmental journey underway in which we all play a leading role—whether as a participant, resister or observer—in preparing for this consciousness shift.

An insight is that the world-view at this expanded level of consciousness, represented by the upper pair of glasses, is quite different, such that the current condition of the world—the way things are—is simpler, providing a new "norm" and a new starting point for learning and increasing complexity. From that viewpoint, we experience the total complexity of today as chaste simplicity. *And we begin our journey of expansion anew.*

<<<<<<<>>>>>>>

INSIGHT: **From an expanded level of consciousness, the current condition of the world—the way things are—is simpler, providing a new starting point for learning and growth.**

<<<<<<<>>>>>>>

What is also insinuated in this graphic is that *this shift is coincidental with the point of singularity*, a time when humans have advanced technology so far and fast that it enables humans to transcend their biological limits (Kurzweil, 2005). Recognizing the current human limits to fully understanding the capabilities and possibilities of the human mind/brain, we contend that the Singularity, which we agree will happen soon, *is thought of and defined by our* **current** *limitations*. Recall the discussion in Chapter 22/Part IV focused on the Quantum concept with the example that behind a closed door "all that is possible exists", and that prior to

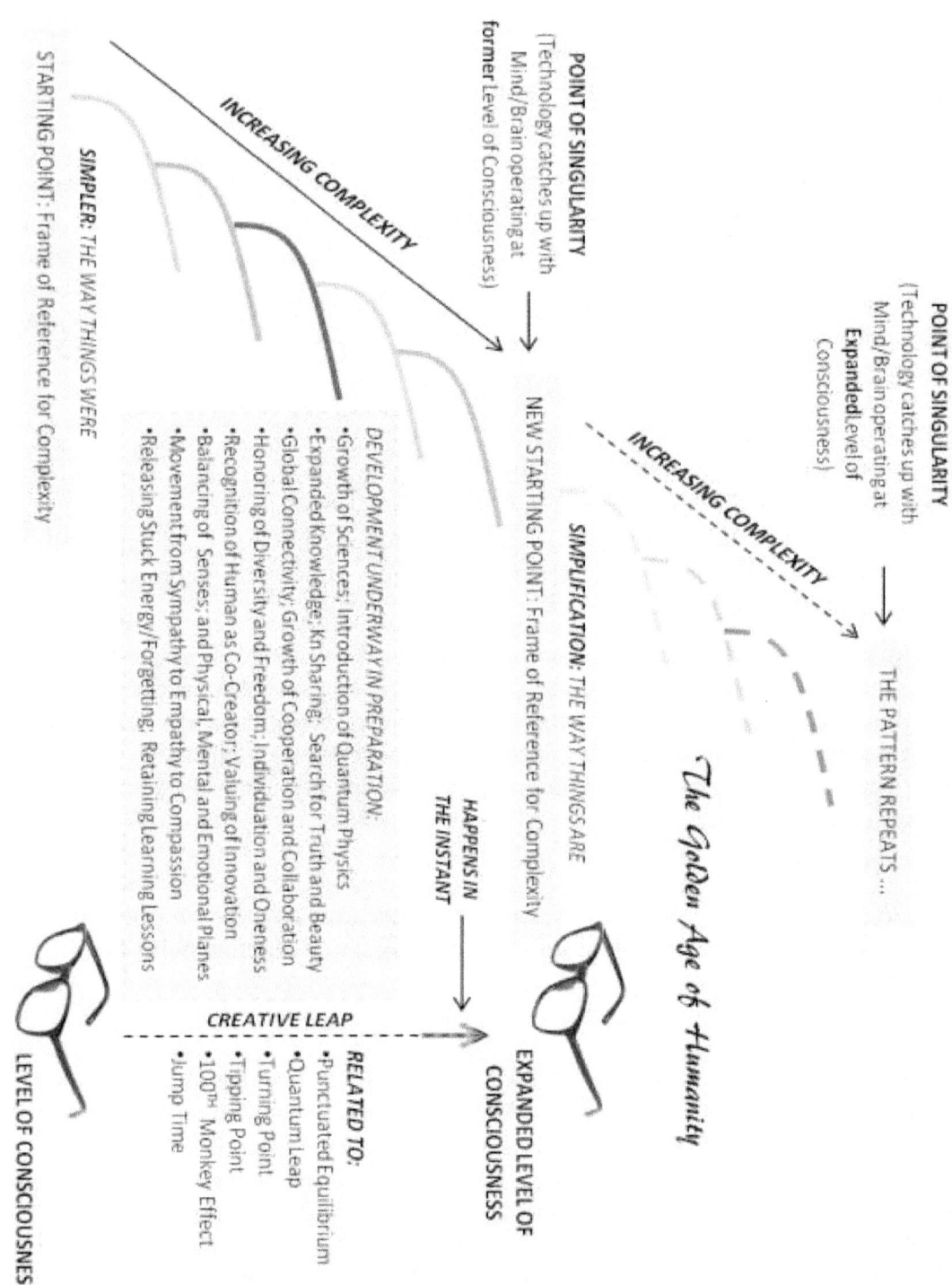

Figure 38-3. *Complexity begets complexity, from which emerges simplicity.*

opening the door, what is behind that door is potential, and once the door is open our frame of reference has shifted such that "all that is possible" after the door is open can be quite different than "all that is possible" before the door is open. This is the realm of *incluessence*, that which is beyond our ability to imagine or dream.

The Singularity will most likely occur in concert with our consciousness shift, and indeed this is part of our human journey, the instant where we surpass our current level of thinking, whether expressed through technology or through the expansion of our consciousness and mastering of our mind/brain. Focusing and creating from this *new place of learning and expansion*, there is a new point of Singularity to move towards.

Are we ready to take this creative leap?

Houston contends there is only one path we can choose. Her words ring true to our minds and hearts, and so we choose to share them here.

Though the forces of entropy and fear seek to contain or regress us, we know there is no going back. Our complex time requires a wiser use of our capacities, a richer music from the instrument we have been given. The world will thrive only if we can grow. The possible society will become a reality only if we learn to be the possible humans we are capable of being. (Houston, 2000, p. 32)

Can we become the possible humans we are capable of becoming? We, as individuals and a humanity, have a choice, with that choice informed by the mental faculties we have developed in this round-trip journey of change. Choice empowers change, enabling us to embrace the future as the co-creators that we are.

Closing Thoughts

In the Alchemical cycle, we have been in the Fermentation stage facing the Shadow and Dark Night of the Soul, representing the further breakdown of hidden impurities and the final death of the old structure. What is in front of us is the sixth stage of Distillation, where we harness the subtle energies and *infuse consciousness into our very substance*, elevating to higher realms and anchoring those subtle energies back into tangible form as we head toward Coagulation, a crystallization into final perfection. Such are the possibilities for humanity.

Relationship Network Management and social theory teach us that the conversations we have today directly impact the decisions we make tomorrow. From neuroscience we know that the thoughts of today become the reality of tomorrow.

As we tie the thoughts within this book together and bound it in order to share it with you, we wonder:

How will these conversations influence the choices before us? Have we integrated the pieces sufficiently for understanding to emerge?

As organizations, and as individuals, can we overcome the arrogance that has resulted from escalation of our mental faculties? Can we balance our physical, mental and emotional planes with the spiritual essence of who we are? Can we find our humility and humanity?

Will we stay in the safety of the known and keep repeating the past? Are we content to live in Plato's shadows on the wall of the cave, or will be move out into the light of consciousness?

Are we ready to embrace this future as One, honoring diversity and valuing individuation and each unique journey in our search for truth?

And, repeating the question that keeps emerging into thought:

Are we as a humanity ready to take the creative leap?

The Bifurcation by Cindy Taylor (2017)

ADDENDUM
Manifesting Our Choice

After many years of diligent research into atomic theory and nature, physicist Niels Bohr (1961, p. 119) concluded, "We are both onlookers and actors in the great drama of existence." In Chapter 23/Part IV we took the stance that we are co-creators of our reality, and, pursuing a consilience approach, presented different frames of reference for considering our role in life as co-creators.

Emerging from the work of Jahn and Dunne (2011, 2009, 1987), and others, was laboratory proof that somehow the unconscious mind was communicating with the subtangible physical world, a world of Quantum possibilities, and, somehow, "this marriage of unformed mind and matter would then assemble itself into something tangible in the manifest world" (McTaggart, 2002, p. 121). This is the world of implicate order described by Bohm (1980) and the cobweb of Puthoff (1981, 1989, 1990), Popp (2000, 2002), Beneveniste (1996, 1998, 1999) and Pribram (1991, 1993, 1998).

This amazing connection between mind and matter is what unfolded in the work of William Tiller of Standard University, who proved through repeated experimentation that it is possible to significantly change the properties of physical substance by holding a clear intention to do so (Tiller, 2007, 1997; Tiller et al., 2001). As with the authors referenced above, Tiller's work has mind-shifting and potentially world-changing results. He began with using intent to change the acid/alkaline balance in purified water; then moved on to experiment with liver enzymes and the life cycle of the fruit fly. Using his terminology, what Tiller discovered is that there are two unique levels of physical reality. The "normal level" of substance is the electric atom molecule level, what until the last century most of us perceived as the only physical reality. However, a second level of substance exists that is at the magnetic information level. While these two levels always interpenetrate each other, under "normal" conditions they do not interact; they are "uncoupled." Intention changes this condition, causing these two levels to interact, or move into a "coupled" state.

Where humans are concerned, Tiller states that *what an individual intends for himself with a strong sustained desire is what that individual will eventually become.* As introduced in Chapter 25/Part IV, intention is the source with which we are doing something, the act or instance of mentally setting some course of action or result, a determination to act in some specific way. It can take the form of a declaration (often in the form of action), an assertion, a prayer, a cry for help, a wish, a visualization, a thought or an affirmation.

The ramifications of the research cited above—and the past and present work of so many other researchers exploring related areas—has the potential to impact every aspect of human life. Perhaps the most mind-boggling thought is that all of this already exists. It is only the limits of our minds that remain to expand so that we can fully engage the world as the co-creators we are.

How can that occur? How can we break through our limits, open to our birthright and move down that road heretofore less traveled? The personal answer the Universe offered to us came through experience. The only way to share this experience is in the voicing of the authors written shortly afterwards, so we will do so.

[Excerpts taken from Bennet & Bennet (2012) *The Journey into the Myst*]

The Miracle

Alex

What we are about to tell you would have been quite unbelievable to me before this journey began. It is not a story of the reality either of us has known for well over our 60 and 70 years of age, but rather, the reality of dreams and fairytales.

From my viewpoint, my life's journey has moved through a myriad of bumps and breaks, always somehow mending itself and moving through new and interesting turns and twists. I've had the opportunity to sing on the outdoor stage of the Metropolitan Opera, live and work abroad, serve as the Chief Knowledge Officer of the U.S. Department of the Navy, and research and publish books with my partner. We've written a myriad of material focused around knowledge, learning and change. Oh, yes, I've been on the internal journey—an exploration of the inner self, the unconscious—for many years as well. But that journey has always been tucked safely away from the outside world. Although no doubt the inner journey has significantly influenced my thoughts and feelings, it has not visibly danced around the events of my external world … until now!

This story we write is perhaps even more difficult for my partner to put into words. David is by education a nuclear physicist and mathematician, teaching many years ago at the U.S. Navy Nuclear Power School under the legendary Admiral

Rickover. David is an incessant learner, collecting knowledges with every breath along the way, with many degrees and credentials punctuating an active business life.

Our journey into the *Myst*[A-1] came with the Summer of 2010. In these latter years, like many in our generation, we are becoming more sensitive to our physical health. So, after various friends and colleagues mentioned the value of a colonoscopy as a preventive measure for cancer, David decided to have it done. The procedure occurred on a Friday without any surprises. He was in; he was out … quick and relatively painless, sort of a "check the list" kind of thing in terms of preventative medicine.

It was quite a surprise when he woke me the following Tuesday, early in the morning, a matter-of-factly reporting that he was heavily bleeding. Indeed, he was. The hospital of choice is 62 miles away from our country inn and farm; that's about an hour and thirty minutes through winding two-lane country roads. We decided not to wait for the doctor's office to open but to leave immediately heading towards the emergency room. To pull up the memory of this is as if it is again happening, now.

In the driver's seat as the sun is rising, I weave my way through the turns and curves, around trees and cow pastures occasionally dotted by a farmhouse. We make it about half way to the hospital. In the front passenger seat, David is experiencing considerable pressure and pain, and says he cannot control it; he feels like he is exploding and insists on my pulling the car over to the side of the road. It is early in the morning, with no houses nearby. No cars. No people. I pull over. David gets out of the car and goes about 10 feet into tall grass. As a liter of blood and tissue explode out of him, he passes out and falls to the ground.

Watching from the car, I quickly jump out and run to him, shaking him, yelling at him to wake up. David is white and clammy, in shock. I grab his arm and start pulling him up, then reach under his shoulders and drag him toward the car. As I attempt to get him in the front seat of the car, he regains consciousness. He tries to help, pulling up on the lever to the right of the seat, releasing the seat backwards and down. His head is leaning back against the head rest as fluids start gurgling up into his throat, falling out of his mouth. There is blood, and I am afraid he will drown in his own juices. "No!" I yell, reaching across to pull the seat back up. As his head rises with the seat it lolls to the side, losing consciousness.

I jump into the driver's seat of the still-idling car, purring as if nothing was happening, as if my world wasn't falling apart. I talk to David as I release the brake and move forward, "Stay with me." I know he cannot hear me. His head is lolling to the right; and blood is dripping out onto the seat of the car. I see the moisture on his white face vividly, and the hospital is still 30 miles away. We will not make it. We are at a critical life/death point.

I press my foot to the gas and **scream to my guides and guardian angels with every cell in my body, demanding, "I need help! I need help now!"**

I focus on the road ahead, speeding, swinging around an S curve. My only thoughts are to move, to drive toward help. And there, as I come out of the S curve, waiting on the right side of the road, sits an ambulance, a rescue squad vehicle, and a fire engine. As I pull over, I see a tow truck sitting on the left, with three or four men standing in a circle chatting, watching the tow truck pull an abandoned car out of a ditch.

The tableau is surreal; I cannot fathom it. Now on automatic response, I throw the driver's door open, hopping out and waving my hands, screaming for help. Three men race across the road and pull David out of the car onto a magically appearing gurney. Within minutes he is stabilized, and awake. The ambulance driver leans toward me as the attendant inside the ambulance prepares David for transport. "I didn't know why we were here," he shares softly. "But now I know." He then asks, "Can you follow the ambulance?" "Yes," I respond, and the race to the hospital continues.

David

Have you ever been a patient in an intensive care unit (ICU)? I have. Once, for a fibrillating heart that was fixed by an easy operation, and the second from the loss of blood that Alex just described. I was lucky—or helped by outside forces—or both. Lying in a hospital bed where you can do nothing but what you are told leads you to either rebel or succumb to patience. Without realizing it, I was trained by the daily commute in the rush hour traffic of Washington, D.C. Given two choices—(1) to rebel and try to change the world and fail, or (2) to not worry about what you cannot change—the latter choice is almost always the best. Simply redirect your thoughts to something more productive.

Back to the ICU. I was weak, relaxed and conscious, with nothing to do but lie there and think about things that seemed important. (I had to sign that I wouldn't attempt to sit up.) Clearly, this experience had been a close call, but was it luck, fate or synchronicity that chose to put me in the ICU instead of underground and perhaps in the spiritual world? This was not the first time I'd had a close call with a life/death outcome. As I reflect, I can remember a number of situations where, if things had been a little bit different, I wouldn't be sharing this story. Luck, chance, destiny, help from above—I'm a scientist. I just don't know.

For the past decade Alex and I have defined and studied, given workshops and lectures, written books and published papers, on knowledge and its sources, meaning and application. Our focus has been on the ability to take effective action, that is, given current situation "A" and a desired situation "B", having the knowledge such that the decisions you make and actions you take move situation "A" toward situation "B". Since we can only influence the world by our actions, our definition of knowledge as the capacity to take effective action becomes critical to surviving in a changing, uncertain and complex world.

One thing we have learned is that "absolute" knowledge is not something we humans are likely to possess. We simply do not live long enough in time, nor travel far enough in space, to validate any knowledge as "absolute." This is a very important conclusion to me, because it means that it is **wiser** to keep an **open** and **inquisitive** mind when we run across events and phenomena that appear to conflict with, or contradict, our past experiences and/or current beliefs.

When I was 12 years old I read a book called *The Rise of the New Physics* by Albert Einstein and Leopold Enfield. I understood only a small part of it, but was fascinated by everything I read. I decided then and there that I wanted to be a physicist when I grew up so that I could understand how the world worked (so I thought). It was more than 24 years before I graduated with a Bachelors in Math and a Bachelors and Masters in Physics from the University of Texas, my first degrees along my learning journey.

What I have learned about physics is that as beautiful, valuable, and insightful as it is—from Newtonian Mechanics to Quantum Mechanics and Einstein's two ingenious relativity theories—*there are many things in our Universe that are still incomprehensible*. Our limitations of understanding become clear when we ask questions about foundational concepts such as time, space, energy or even the meaning of our theories, experiments or actions.

All too often we form beliefs—from learning and from our experience, goals and fears—that tend to solidify in our brains and become absolutes, even "who we are" and, often subconsciously, which we must defend at all costs. Where it applies, the scientific method is excellent for those phenomena. But yes, science has boundaries in terms of its knowledge and applications. It also has limits in terms of its understanding and methodology, and contradictions within its findings, such that scientists have to live, at least temporarily, with some incomprehensible results.

The challenge arises, however, when we discover aspects of our Universe that do not succumb to the methods of scientific validation, things that lie beyond the boundaries of current scientific understanding and capabilities for validation. An example is the phenomenon of meditation. How does one validate that the process and results of meditation are what the meditator says they are? One can never exactly "repeat" the results, and there can be no objectivity to the outcome. The scientific method is simply not applicable … yet. However, as the Dali Lama has offered: "If 10,000 monks can meditate over 3,000 years and all of them say that they get similar results, one should give these results some credibility." As distinct from scientific truth, the Dali Lama calls this *rational inference*.

All of these thoughts were on my mind while I was in the ICU. And my thoughts just kept rambling. So many of us tend to take a stand of egotism that says "I am right" or even arrogance, "I am right, you are wrong, and I'm not listening." I have found very few things that support these dichotomies. Things are never—or rarely—either right or wrong, yes or no, good or bad, black or white, true or false. The Universe isn't so simple, or perhaps it is and we have yet to understand the underlying rules. As we delve down into understanding knowledge, we discover that, from the level at which we use it, knowledge is context sensitive and situation dependent. Simplification can be very valuable—or it can be disastrous.

Why did all of these thoughts keep moving through my mind? It clearly had something to do with the remarkable events that brought me to the ICU.

Of the unusual occurrences in my life, until recently the main one was a precognition of an automobile accident that actually occurred 10 minutes later. As a motorcyclist came off of a short pier in Newport Rhode Island, the motorcycle fell over and the driver's body was thrown into the brick wall of a restaurant 10 feet in front of my car. While the outcome is in the police records, my sensing the accident remains a personal experience and cannot be verified externally. But "I" vividly remember that ten minutes before the accident, when I touched the door handle of the car sitting in a parking lot four miles from the scene of the accident, my gut said "there is going to be an automobile accident." This could sound crazy if we knew what time was; but, in fact, even today we do not fully understand what time, space, energy or even a vacuum are. We can only speculate.

In a sense, we as humans have done ourselves a huge disfavor by separating our world into areas of knowledge such as science, psychology, philosophy, religion and spirituality. While specialization certainly guides research, it also labels people and tends to limit our thinking, thereby sometimes creating walls or stovepipes that result in languages, beliefs and ownerships that make interactions, combinations and synergistic thinking difficult, if not impossible. Am I repeating myself? Am I getting ahead of the story?

As I lay on the hospital bed getting blood transfusions and wondering how long I would need to be here, I thought about the road not taken. I would very much like to stay here on planet Earth and continue to achieve what Alex and I consider our purpose for being, that is, learning, understanding and contributing where we can to the forward march and quality of human development. I could perhaps live another 20 years, and share with others our lessons learned, our thoughts, ideas and experiences. Or perhaps I could slide quietly into the night, my atoms continuing on their 13 billion year life history by separating and once again going out into space and wondering around until the Universe reaches its end.

Or perhaps there is another road, a non-physical part of our world that is compatible with us, yet exists under different "rules and laws" than our material world has provided. Do souls live forever? Are angels real? Are psychics really psychic? I do not know the answers to these questions, but I do know that sometimes this world demonstrates amazing things that appear impossible from a purely material viewpoint.

Perhaps the appearance of the ambulance was luck, perhaps it was a Cosmic determination, who knows? In any case, after three days of deep reflection I was able to leave the ICU. But I left with the dramatic memories of my close call floating in my awareness, and a deeper feeling of how little I know about our world. Do you realize how many things and happenings lay right in front of us, yet we have so much trouble seeing, feeling, sensing and comprehending them? The easy path invites our direction. The safest stand makes us feel good. Any new direction on "the path not taken" scares us. Perhaps the light of the unknown is so low that many of us choose the better-known, common path that we can easily see, understand and follow. Or do we dare to grow, run risks, question the unquestionable and keep an open but cautious and learning mind.

Clearly, the Universe recognized that both Alex and I needed time to consider these events. I had fallen in a Poison Oak patch, and Alex had pulled me out of that patch. As if that wasn't enough, I caught a Staph infection during those three days in ICU and Alex, who was with me sleeping in a chair beside my bed, had a spot emerge on her left forearm. The next few weeks, we were forced to slow down and focus on helping each other heal our bodies. And during these weeks we asked over and over again: What just happened?

The Aftermath

There is no end to the wonder and diversity of the Universe, and the learning and expansion available to each and every person. We now *know*, from experience, that through our thoughts, feelings and actions *we* are indeed co-creating every instant of our lives *with a collective higher consciousness that is out there*. We are part of a larger intelligent field, whether you call it the Quantum field, the Noosphere, the Zero Point, the Akashic or the God Field.

And the final sharing: **Find beauty and joy in the everyday moments of your life. It is inside of you, waiting to be summoned. You are co-creator of your experience.**

In Co-Service, *Alex and David Bennet*

Appendix A: The Overarching ISCJ Model

The Intelligent Social Change Journey (ISCJ)

NOTE: Each model builds on the understanding gained from experiencing the previous phase

Phase 1: LEARNING FROM THE PAST
CHARACTERISTICS: Linear and Sequential; Repeatable; Engaging past learning; Starting from current state; Cause and effect relationships.

Phase 2: LEARNING IN THE PRESENT
CHARACTERISTICS: Recognition of patterns; Social interaction; Co-evolving with environment through continuous learning, quick response, robustness, flexibility, adaptability, alignment.

Phase 3: CO-CREATING OUR FUTURE
CHARACTERISTICS: Creative imagination; Recognition of global Oneness; Mental in service to the intuitive; Balancing senses; Bringing together past, present and future; Knowing; Beauty; Wisdom.

SYMPATHY → **SOCIAL STATE (Depth of Connection)** → **EMPATHY** → **COMPASSION**

MOVEMENT

NATURE:
- Product of the past
- Context sensitive, situation dependent
- Partial, incomplete

EXPANDED CONSCIOUSNESS

REDUCTION OF FORCES (Engage forces by choice)

INCREASED INTELLIGENT ACTIVITY (Growth of wisdom)

FORCES occur when one type of energy affects another type of energy in a way where they are moving in different directions. Bounded (inward focused) and/or limited knowledge creates forces.

(Open to the Spiritual)

REFLECTION:
- Review of interactions, feedback
- Determination of cause and effect (logic)
- (Inward focus) Questioning decisions and actions: What did I intend? What really happened? Why were there differences? What would I do the same? What would I do differently?

KNOWLEDGE (The capacity (potential or actual) to take effective action)
- Expanded knowledge sharing, social learning, cooperation, collaboration
- Questioning of why?
- Pursuit of truth
- Deeper development of conceptual thinking (higher mental thought)
- Connecting power of diversity and individuation to whole (Moving toward outward focus)
- Recognition of different world views; the exploration of information from different perspectives
- Expanded knowledge capacities.

CONSCIOUSNESS is considered a state of awareness and a private, selective and continuously changing process, a sequential set of ideas, thoughts, images, feelings and perceptions and an understanding of the connections and relationships among them and our self.

INTELLIGENT ACTIVITY represents a perfect state of interaction where intent, purpose, direction, values and expected outcomes are clearly understood and communicated among all parties, reflecting wisdom and achieving a higher truth.

- Recognition that with knowledge comes responsibility
- Conscious pursuit of larger truth
- Knowledge selectively used as a measure of effectiveness
- Valuing of creative ideas. Asking larger questions: How does this idea serve humanity? Are there any negative consequences?
- (Outward focus) Openness to other's ideas with humility: What if this idea is right? Are my beliefs or other mental models limiting my thought? Are hidden assumptions or feelings interfering with intelligent activity?
- Sense and knowing of Oneness
- Development of both lower (feels) and upper (conceptual) mental faculties, which work in concert with the emotional guidance system
- Application of patterns across knowledge domains for greater good
- Recognition of self as a co-creator of reality
- Ability to engage in intelligent activity
- Developing the ability to tap into the intuitional plane at will

COGNITIVE SHIFTS:
- Recognition of importance of feedback
- Ability to recognize systems; impact of external forces
- Recognition and location of "me" in the larger picture (conscious awareness)
- Early pattern recognition and concept development
- Ability to recognize and apply patterns at all levels within a domain of knowledge to predict outcomes
- Growing understanding of complexity
- Increased connectedness of choices; recognition of direction you are heading; expanded meaning-making
- Expanded ability to bisociate ideas; increased creativity

Taken from: Bennet, et al. (2017) *The Profundity and Bifurcation of Change, Parts I through V.* Frost, WV: MQIPress.

Developed by Mountain Quest Institute. Contact alex@mountainquestinstitute.com for permissions.

Appendix B
Table of Contents for Full Book

The Profundity and Bifurcation of Change
The Intelligent Social Change Journey

[This book is published in five separate Parts]

Cover
Title Page
Quote from *The Kybalion*
Table of Contents
Tables and Figures
Appreciation

Preface

Introduction to the Intelligent Social Change Journey

Part I: LAYING THE GROUNDWORK

Part I Introduction

Chapter 1: Change is Natural
    CHANGE AS A VERB...OUR CHANGING THOUGHTS...FINAL THOUGHT
Chapter 2: Knowledge to Action
    KNOWLEDGE (INFORMING) AND KNOWLEDGE (PROCEEDING)...LEVELS OF KNOWLEDGE...FROM KNOWLEDGE TO ACTION...THE NATURE OF KNOWLEDGE...LEVELS OF COMPREHENSION...FINAL THOUGHTS
Chapter 3: Forces We Act Upon
    AMPLITUDE, FREQUENCY AND DURATION...FROM THE VIEWPOINT OF THE INDIVIDUAL...CONTROL AS FORCE...REDUCING FORCES...THE SELF AND FORCES...FROM THE SPIRITUAL VIEWPOINT...STRATEGIC FORCES IN ORGANIZATIONS...THE CORRELATION OF FORCES...FINAL THOUGHTS
Chapter 4: The Ever-Expanding Self
    THE SUBJECT/OBJECT RELATIONSHIP...THE PERSONALITY...CHARACTERISTICS OF PERSONALITY...DEVELOPMENT OF SELF...THE HEALTHY SELF...THE CONNECTED SELF...INDIVIDUATION...THE POWER OF HUMILITY...FINAL THOUGHTS
Chapter 5: The Window of Consciousness
    PROPERTIES OF CONSCIOUSNESS...THE THRESHOLD OF CONSCIOUSNESS...LEVELS OF CONSCIOUSNESS...MEANING AND PURPOSE...CONSCIOUSNESS AS A QUANTUM FIELD...FLOW AS THE OPTIMAL EXPERIENCE...CONSCIOUSLY ACCESSING THE UNCONSCIOUS...FINAL THOUGHTS

Chapter 6: The Individual Change Model
   THE HUMAN AS A COMPLEX ADAPTIVE SYSTEM...THE ENVIRONMENT AND THE KNOWLEDGE
   WORKER...THE MODEL...APPLYING THE MODEL...FINAL THOUGHTS

Part II: LEARNING FROM THE PAST

Part II Introduction

Chapter 7: Looking for Cause and Effect
   CAUSES AND CONDITIONS...MOTIVES...LINKING CAUSE AND EFFECT...WHY CAUSE AND EFFECT
   IS NOT ENOUGH...FINAL THOUGHTS
Chapter 8: A Kaleidoscope of Models
   THEORIES OF CHANGE... WE BEGIN A FEW YEARS EARLIER...THE NEW CENTURY...FINAL
   THOUGHTS
Chapter 9: Modalities of Change
   EXPERIENCING, LEARNING AND
   ENGAGING...VISIONING...IMAGINING...CONCEPTUALIZING...POSITIVE THINKING...WEAVING IN
   DESIRE, DRIVE AND COURAGE
Chapter 10: Grounding Change
   HIERARCHY AS A GROUNDING STRUCTURE...GROUNDING THROUGH
   RELATIONSHIPS...GROUNDING THROUGH IDEAS...GROUNDING THROUGH BELIEFS AND
   FAITH...FINAL THOUGHTS
Chapter 11: Assessing Readiness
   A STARTING POINT...ASSESSING READINESS...PRIMING THE PUMP...THE STATEMENTS...PART
   I...PART II...PART III... PART IV... PART V...SCORING
Chapter 12: The Change Agent's Strategy
   THE GROWTH PATH OF KNOWLEDGE SHARING...CREATE A SHARED VISION...BUILD THE
   BUSINESS CASE...DEMONSTRATE LEADERSHIP COMMITMENT...FACILITATE A COMMON
   UNDERSTANDING...SET LIMITS...SHARE NEW IDEAS, WORDS AND BEHAVIORS...IDENTIFY THE
   STRATEGIC APPROACH...DEVELOP THE INFRASTRUCTURE...MEASURE AND
   INCENTIVIZE...PROVIDE TOOLS...PROMOTE LEARNING...ENVISION AN EVEN GREATER FUTURE

Part III: LEARNING IN THE PRESENT

Part III Introduction
   MOVING TOWARD CO-EVOLVING...PHASE 2 OF THE INTELLIGENT SOCIAL CHANGE JOURNEY
Chapter 13: The New Reality
   OUR WORLD IS CUCA...META-PRAXIS...SOCIAL REALITY (AN ANALOGY WRITTEN FROM THE
   VIEWPOINT OF THE MIND/BRAIN)...INTERACTING WITH THE NEW WELTANSCHAUUNG... THE ROLE
   OF TRUST...SELF EFFICACY...OPTIMUM AROUSAL...FINAL THOUGHTS
Chapter 14: "Co-ing" and Evolving
   CO-EVOLVING...JOURNEY INTO COOPERATION AND COLLABORATION...THREE-WAY
   COOPERATION AND COLLABORATION...CO-EVOLVING IN A CUCA
   WORLD...SUSTAINABILITY...ICAS AND SUSTAINABILITY...SUSTAINABLE KNOWLEDGE...A NEW
   GENERATION OF CO-CREATORS...THE DISCOVERY OF COMMUNITY
Chapter 15: Managing Change in a Knowledge Organization
   THE ORGANIZATION AS A COMPLEX ADAPTIVE SYSTEM...THE INTERNAL KNOWLEDGE
   ENVIRONMENT...THE CHANGE APPROACH...THE ADIIEA MODEL...THE CHANGE PROCESS...THE

ELEMENTS OF CHANGE...EMERGENT CHARACTERISTICS...THE STRATEGIC INITIATIVE PULSE...FINAL THOUGHTS

Chapter 16: Time and Space
THE USEFULNESS OF TIME...PAST, PRESENT AND FUTURE...THE GIFT OF PLANNING...EXPLORING TIME: BUILDING CONCEPTUAL RELATIONSHIPS...THE RHYTHM OF CHANGE...TAKING ADVANTAGE OF TIME AND SPACE

Chapter 17: Connections as Patterns
INFORMATION INCOMING...PATTERNS OF THE PAST...EXPLORING ENERGY PATTERNS IN THE MYST ... PATTERNS AS STORY...THE STORY OF SELF...THE RHYTHMS OF LIFE...FINAL THOUGHT

Chapter 18: Easing into the Flow
LIFE FORCE...THE ENERGY CENTERS...INFORMATION AS ENERGY...ENERGY ENTANGLEMENT...THE FLOW OF LIFE...THE OPTIMAL HUMAN EXPERIENCE...FINAL THOUGHTS

Chapter 19: Emotions as a Guidance System
EMOTIONS AS ENERGY...PRINCIPLES OF EMOTION...COGNITIVE CONVEYORS...LISTENING TO THE WHISPERS...EMOTIONAL INTELLIGENCE...THE WONDER OF LOVE...INTO THE FLOW WITH PASSION...FINAL THOUGHTS

Chapter 20: Stuck Energy: Limiting and Accelerating
MENTAL MODELS...STRESS...FORGETTING... LETTING GO... MENTAL CHATTER...WEBS OF ENERGY...FINAL THOUGHTS

Chapter 21: Knowledge Capacities
EXPLORING KNOWLEDGE CAPACITIES...SOME QUICK EXAMPLES...*LEARNING HOW TO LEARN...SHIFTING FRAMES OF REFERENCE...REVERSAL...COMPREHENDING DIVERSITY... ORCHESTRATING DRIVE... SYMBOLIC REPRESENTATION*...A WORKING EXAMPLE: *INSTINCTUAL HARNESSING*...WHY IS INSTINCTUAL HARNESSING EFFECTIVE AS A KNOWLEDGE CAPACITY?

Part IV: CO-CREATING THE FUTURE

Part IV Introduction
Chapter 22: Learning Points Along the Path
CONSILIENCE...DIVINATION, PREDICTION AND FORECASTING...EMPATHY...GIVINGNESS... HAPPINESS...HARMONY...INCLUSIVENESS...NOBILITY...PRESENCE...SERENDIPITY...SYMMETRY AND SYMBIOTIC THINKING... SYNCHRONICITY...SYNERGY...THOUGHT FORMS...FINAL THOUGHTS

Chapter 23: Co-Creation Frames of Reference
OUR GREATEST CO-CREATION...WHAT DOES IT MEAN TO CO-CREATE OUR REALITY?...MULTIPLE PERSPECTIVES ON SELF CO-CREATING REALITY...*FROM THE LITERARY PERSPECTIVE...FROM A LIVING SYSTEM PERSPECTIVE...FROM A CONSCIOUSNESS PERSPECTIVE...FROM A SCIENTIFIC PERSPECTIVE...FROM A SPIRITUAL PERSPECTIVE*...FINAL THOUGHTS

Chapter 24: Knowledge and the Search for Truth
SURFACE, SHALLOW, DEEP...TRUTH AND CONSCIOUSNESS...MISINFORMATION AND DISINFORMATION...PERCEPTION AND PROPAGANDA...FORMS OF PROPAGANDA...BRAINWASHING...FINAL THOUGHTS

Chapter 25: Attention and Intention
EXPLORING ATTENTION...EXPLORING INTENTION...THE POWER OF INTENTION...BRINGING THEM TOGETHER

Chapter 26: The Mental Fabric
CRITICAL THINKING...THOUGHT...CONCEPTUAL THINKING...CONNECTING TO THEORY...FROM RELATIVISM TO HEURISTICS

Chapter 27: Moving into Wisdom
   INTELLIGENT ACTIVITY...CONNECTING KNOWLEDGE AND WISDOM...THE WISDOM OF MENTAL DISCIPLINE...FINAL THOUGHTS
Chapter 28: Tapping into the Intuitional
   EARNED INTUITION...REVEALED INTUITION...CONTROLLED INTUITION...MIRROR NEURONS...THEY ALL WORK TOGETHER...THE FIELD OF IDEAS...A FEW FINAL THOUGHTS
Chapter 29: Exploring Creativity
   FROM WHENCE DOES CREATIVITY COME?...IS EVERYONE CREATIVE?...KNOWLEDGE AS THE ACTION LEVER FOR CREATIVITY...NEUROSCIENCE FINDINGS...EXTRAORDINARY CREATIVITY...FINAL THOUGHTS
Chapter 30: The Creative Leap
   EXPANDING OUR CREATIVE CAPACITY...BEYOND CONTEXT AND SITUATION...FROM THE QUANTUM PERSPECTIVE...AN IN-DEPTH LOOK...ARE YOU READY TO LEAP?...IN SUMMARY

Part V: LIVING THE FUTURE

Part V Introduction
   A REFLECTIVE MOMENT...THE LARGER JOURNEY
Chapter 31: The Alchemy of Change
   THE SEVEN STEPS OF TRANSFORMATION...THE METAMORPHOSIS...OUR CURRENT CYCLE OF CHANGE...WHERE CAN WE GO FROM HERE AS WE LIVE THE FUTURE?
Chapter 32: Balancing and Sensing
   THE SENSE OF BALANCE...SELF BALANCING...BALANCING THE SENSES... DYNAMIC BALANCING...FINAL THOUGHTS
Chapter 33: The Harmony of Beauty
   SENSING BEAUTY...BEAUTY IN OUR THINKING...BEAUTY IN ART...HEALTH AS A WORK OF ART...SHARING BEAUTY...BEAUTY AS TRANSCENDENCE...FINAL THOUGHTS
Chapter 34: Virtues for Living the Future
   BEAUTY, GOODNESS AND TRUTH...GOOD CHARACTER...GOOD CHARACTER IS ACTIONABLE...EXPLORING GOOD CHARACTER THROUGH CORE VALUES...ALL PEOPLE ARE NOT CREATED EQUAL...FINAL THOUGHTS
Chapter 35: Conscious Compassion
   TOWARDS A GLOBAL ETHIC...MOVING INTO COMPASSION... JUDGING AND COMPASSION...DEVELOPING CONSCIOUS COMPASSION...COMPASSION AS A TOOL FOR CHANGE...FINAL THOUGHTS
Chapter 36: The Changing Nature of Knowledge
   KNOWLEDGE AS A MEASURE OF SELF GROWTH...SPREADING THE KNOWLEDGE MOVEMENT...IT'S GLOBAL...THE SPIRITUAL NATURE OF KNOWLEDGE...KNOWING...ONENESS
Chapter 37: Consciousness Rising
   INFORMATION FIELDS AS CONSCIOUSNESS FIELDS...EXTRAORDINARY CONSCIOUSNESS...NEW ROLE FOR PERSONALITY... BEYOND ASSOCIATIVE PATTERNING...ASSOCIATIVE ATTRACTING...THE HOLOGRAPHIC UNIVERSE...FINAL THOUGHTS
Chapter 38: The Bifurcation
   FREEDOM AND CHOICE...CHOOSING BEYOND DUALITY...THE SPLIT IN THE ROAD...IS HUMANITY READY FOR THE CREATIVE LEAP?..CLOSING THOUGHTS

ADDENDUM: Manifesting Our Choice *by David and Alex Bennet*

APPENDICES:
Appendix A: The Overarching ISCJ Model
Appendix B: The Table of Contents for All Parts
Appendix C: *An Infinite Story*
Appendix D: Engaging Tacit Knowledge
Appendix E: Knowing
Appendix F: Values for Creativity

ENDNOTES

REFERENCES

About Mountain Quest
About the Authors

TOOLS

Part I: Introduction
3-1. Force Field Analysis
4-1. Self Belief Assessment
4-2. Humility
5-1. Engaging Tacit Knowledge (See Appendix D.)

Part II: Learning From the Past
7-1. Personal Plane-ing Process
7-2. The Five Whys
9-1. Engaging Outside Worldviews
9-2. Practicing Mental Imagining
10-1. Grounding through Nature
10-2. Relationship Network Management
11-1. Co-Creating Conversations that Matter

Part III: Learning in the Present
13-1. Trust Mapping
14-1. Building Mental Sustainability
16-1. Integrating Time into the Self Experience
16-2. Scenario Building
17-1. Thinking Patterns
18-1. Connecting through the Heart
18-2. Discovering Flow.

19-1. Mood Shifting
19-2. Releasing Emotions Technique
19-3. Focusing
20-1. Letting Go
21-1. Focused Trait Transference

Part IV: Co-Creating the Future
22-1. Predicting through Pattern Discovery
22-2. Choosing Happiness
24-1. Truth Searching
24-2. Rhythm Disruptor
26-1. Situational Backtalk
26-2. Activating New Resources
27-1. Learning from Your Inner Self
28-1. Redirecting the Mind
28-2. Sleep on It
28-3. Transmuting Negative Thought Forms
29-1. Quieting the Mind
30-1. Honoring Mistakes

Part V: Living the Future
32-1. The Lokahi Triangle and The Life Triangle
32-2. Holding Neurovascular Reflect Points
33-1. Choosing Beauty
34-1. Developing a Good Character Action Set
35-1. Discerning Judgment
35-2: Achieving Zero Limits through *Ho'oponopono*

Appendix D
Engaging Tacit Knowledge

[Detail for the Tool "Engaging Tacit Knowledge" introduced in Chapter 5/Part I. Skip to the subtitle "Accessing Tacit Knowledge" below if you already understand the concepts of "knowledge", "tacit" and the four types of tacit knowledges: embodied, intuitive, affective and spiritual.]

Background

Knowledge—the capacity (potential or actual) to take effective action—was introduced in Chapter 3/Part I. Our focus in this Part Is on that knowledge residing in the unconscious, that is, tacit knowledge (Item 1-E). Tacit knowledge is the descriptive term for those connections among thoughts that cannot be pulled up in words, a knowing of what decision to make or how to do something that cannot be clearly voiced in a manner such that another person could extract and re-create that knowledge (understanding, meaning, etc.). An individual may or may not know they have tacit knowledge in relationship to something or someone; but even when it is known, the individual is unable to put it into words or visuals that can convey that knowledge. We all know things, or know what to do, yet may be unable to articulate why we know them, why they are true, or even exactly what they are. To "convey" is to cause something to be known or understood or, in this usage, to transfer information from which the receiver is able to create knowledge.

As a point of contrast, explicit knowledge is information (patterns) and processes (patterns in time) that can be called up from memory and described accurately in words and/or visuals (representations) such that another person can comprehend the knowledge that is expressed through this exchange of information. This has historically been called declarative knowledge (Anderson, 1983). Implicit knowledge is a more complicated concept, and a term not unanimously agreed-upon in the literature. This is understandable since even simple dictionary definitions—which are generally unbiased and powerful indicators of collective preference and understanding—show a considerable overlap between the terms "implicit" and "tacit," making it difficult to differentiate the two. We propose that a useful interpretation of implicit knowledge is knowledge stored in memory of which the individual is not immediately aware which, while not readily accessible, may be pulled up when triggered (associated). Triggering can occur through questions, dialogue or reflective thought, or happen as a result of an external event. In other words, implicit knowledge is knowledge that the individual does not know they have, but is self-discoverable! However, once this knowledge is surfaced, the individual may or may not have the ability to adequately describe it such that another individual could create the same knowledge; and the "why and how" may remain tacit.

A number of published psychologists have used the term implicit interchangeably with our usage of tacit, that is, with implicit representing knowledge that once acquired can be shown to effect behavior but is not available for conscious retrieval (Reber, 1993; Kirsner et al, 1998). As described in the above discussion of implicit knowledge, what is forwarded here is that the concept of implicit knowledge serves as a middle ground between that which can be made explicit and that which cannot easily, if at all, be made explicit. By moving beyond the dualistic approach of explicit and tacit—that which can be declared versus that which can't be declared, and that which can be remembered versus that which can't be remembered—we posit implicit as representing the knowledge spectrum between explicit and tacit. While explicit refers to easily available, some knowledge requires a higher stimulus for association to occur but is not buried so deeply as to prevent access. This understanding opens the domain of implicit knowledge.

Tacit and explicit knowledge can be thought of as residing in "places," specifically, the unconscious and the conscious, respectively, although both are differentiated patterns spread throughout the neuronal system, that is, the volume of the brain and other parts of the central nervous system. On the other hand, implicit knowledge may reside in either the unconscious (prior to triggering, or tacit) or the conscious (when triggered, or explicit). Note there is no clean break between these three types of knowledge (tacit, implicit and explicit); rather, this is a continuum.

Calling them interactive components of cooperative processes, Reber agrees that there is no clear boundary between that which is explicit and that which is implicit (our tacit): "There is ... no reason for presuming that there exists a clean boundary between conscious and unconscious processes or a sharp division between implicit and explicit epistemic systems ..." (Reber, 1993, p. 23). Reber describes the urge to treat explicit and implicit (our tacit) as altogether different processes the "polarity fallacy" (Reber, 1993). Similarly, Matthews says that the unconscious and conscious processes are engaged in what he likes to call a "synergistic" relationship (Matthews, 1991). What this means is that the boundary between the conscious and the unconscious is somewhat porous and flexible.

Knowledge starts as tacit knowledge, that is, the initial movement of knowledge is from its origins within the self (in the unconscious) to an outward expression (albeit driving effective action). What does that mean? Michael Polanyi, a professor of chemistry and the social sciences, wrote in The Tacit Dimension that, "We start from the fact that we can know more than we can tell" (Polanyi, 1967, p 108). He called this pre-logical phase of knowing tacit knowledge, that is, knowledge that cannot be articulated (Polanyi, 1958).

The Types of Tacit Knowledge

Tacit knowledge can be thought of in terms of four aspects: embodied, intuitive, affective and spiritual (Bennet & Bennet, 2008c). While all of these aspects are part of Self, each represents different sources of tacit knowledge whose applicability, reliability and efficacy may vary greatly depending on the individual, the situation and the knowledge needed to take effective action. They are represented in Figure D-1 along with explicit and implicit knowledge on the continuum of awareness.

Embodied tacit knowledge is also referred to as somatic knowledge. Both kinesthetic and sensory, it can be represented in neuronal patterns stored within the body. Kinesthetic is related to the movement of the body and, while important to every individual every day of our lives, it is a primary focus for athletes, artists, dancers, kids and assembly-line workers. A commonly used example of tacit knowledge is knowledge of riding a bicycle. Sensory, by definition, is related to the five human senses through which information enters the body (sight, smell, hearing, touch and taste). An example is the smell of burning rubber from your car brakes while driving or the smell of hay in a barn. These odors can convey knowledge of whether the car brakes may need replacing (get them checked immediately), or whether the hay is mildewing (dangerous to feed horses, but fine for cows). These responses would be overt, bringing to conscious awareness the need to take effective action and driving that action to occur.

Intuitive tacit knowledge is the sense of knowing coming from inside an individual that may influence decisions and actions; yet the decision-maker or actor cannot explain how or why the action taken is the right one. The unconscious works around the clock with a processing capability many times greater than that at the conscious level. This is why as the world grows more complex, decision-makers will depend more and more on their intuitive tacit knowledge, a combination of life lessons. But in order to use it, decision-makers must first be able to tap into their unconscious.

Affective tacit knowledge is connected to emotions and feelings, with emotions representing the external expression of some feelings. Feelings expressed as emotions become explicit (Damasio, 1994). Feelings that are not expressed—perhaps not even recognized—are those that fall into the area of affective tacit knowledge. Feelings as a form of knowledge have different characteristics than

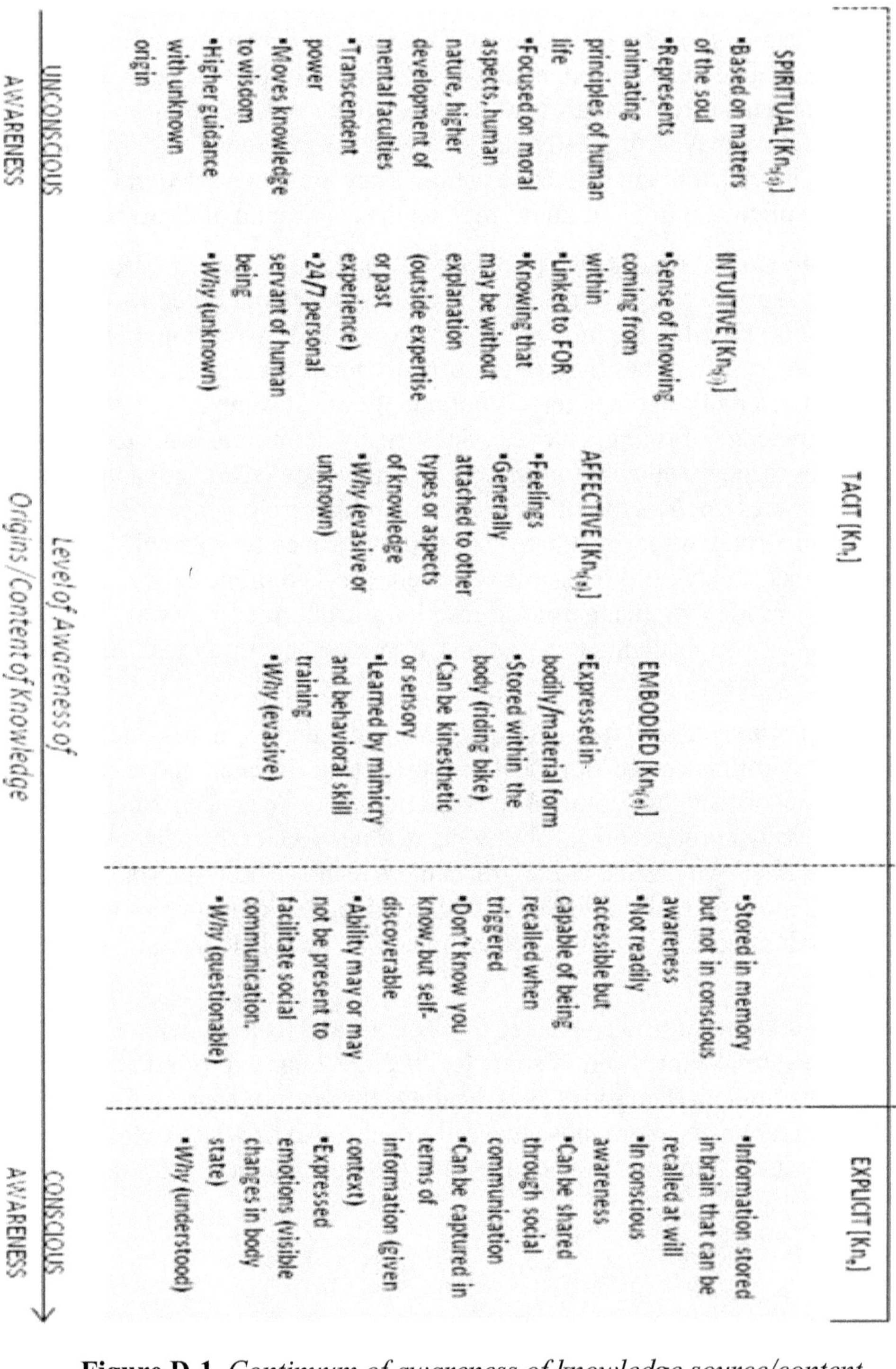

	TACIT [Kn_t]			IMPLICIT [Kn_i]	EXPLICIT [Kn_e]
SPIRITUAL [Kn_{sp}]	**INTUITIVE [Kn_{in}]**	**AFFECTIVE [Kn_{af}]**	**EMBODIED [Kn_{el}]**		
•Based on matters of the soul	•Sense of knowing coming from within	•Feelings	•Expressed in-bodily/material form	•Stored in memory but not in conscious awareness	•Information stored in brain that can be recalled at will
•Represents animating principles of human life	•Linked to FOR	•Generally attached to other types or aspects of knowledge	•Stored within the body (riding bike)	•Not readily accessible but capable of being recalled when triggered	•In conscious awareness
•Focused on moral aspects, human nature, higher development of mental faculties	•Knowing that may be without explanation (outside expertise or past experience)	•Why (evasive or unknown)	•Can be kinesthetic or sensory	•Don't know you know, but self-discoverable	•Can be shared through social communication
•Transcendent power	•24/7 personal servant of human being		•Learned by mimicry and behavioral skill training	•Ability may or may not be present to facilitate social communication.	•Can be captured in terms of information (given context)
•Moves knowledge to wisdom	•Why (unknown)		•Why (evasive)	•Why (questionable)	•Expressed emotions (visible changes in body state)
•Higher guidance with unknown origin					•Why (understood)

UNCONSCIOUS AWARENESS ← *Level of Awareness of Origins/Content of Knowledge* → CONSCIOUS AWARENESS

Figure D-1. *Continuum of awareness of knowledge source/content.*

language or ideas, but they may lead to effective action because they can influence actions by their existence and connections with consciousness. When feelings come into conscious awareness, they can play an informing role in decision-making, providing insights in a non-linguistic manner and thereby influencing decisions and actions. For example, a feeling (such as fear or an upset stomach) may occur every time a particular action is started which could prevent the decision-maker from taking that action.

Spiritual tacit knowledge can be described in terms of knowledge based on matters of the soul. The soul represents the animating principles of human life in terms of thought and action, specifically focused on its moral aspects, the emotional part of human nature, and higher development of the mental faculties (Bennet & Bennet, 2007c). While there is a "knowing" related to spiritual knowledge similar to intuition, this knowing does not include the experiential base of intuition, and it may or may not have emotional tags. The current state of the evolution of our understanding of spiritual knowledge is such that there are insufficient words to relate its transcendent power, or to define the role it plays in relationship to other tacit knowledge. Nonetheless, this area represents a form of higher guidance with unknown origin. Spiritual knowledge may be the guiding purpose, vision and values behind the creation and application of tacit knowledge. It may also be the road to moving information to knowledge and knowledge to wisdom (Bennet & Bennet, 2008d). In the context of this book, spiritual tacit knowledge represents the source of higher learning, helping decision-makers create and implement knowledge that has greater meaning and value for the common good.

Whether embodied, affective, intuitive or spiritual, *tacit knowledge represents the bank account of the Self.* The larger our deposits, the greater the interest, and the more we are prepared for co-evolving in a changing, uncertain and complex environment.

Accessing Tacit Knowledge

There are many ways to bring our tacit resources into our consciousness. For example, we propose a four-fold action model with nominal curves for building what we call extraordinary consciousness, that is, expanding our consciousness through accessing tacit resources. The four approaches to accessing include surfacing, embedding, sharing and inducing resonance. (See Figure D-2 below.)

Surfacing Tacit Knowledge. As individuals observe, experience, study and learn throughout life they generate a huge amount of information and knowledge that becomes stored in their unconscious mind. Surfacing tacit knowledge is focused on accessing the benefit of that which is tacit by moving knowledge from the unconscious to conscious awareness. Three ways that tacit knowledge can be surfaced are through external triggering, self-collaboration and nurturing.

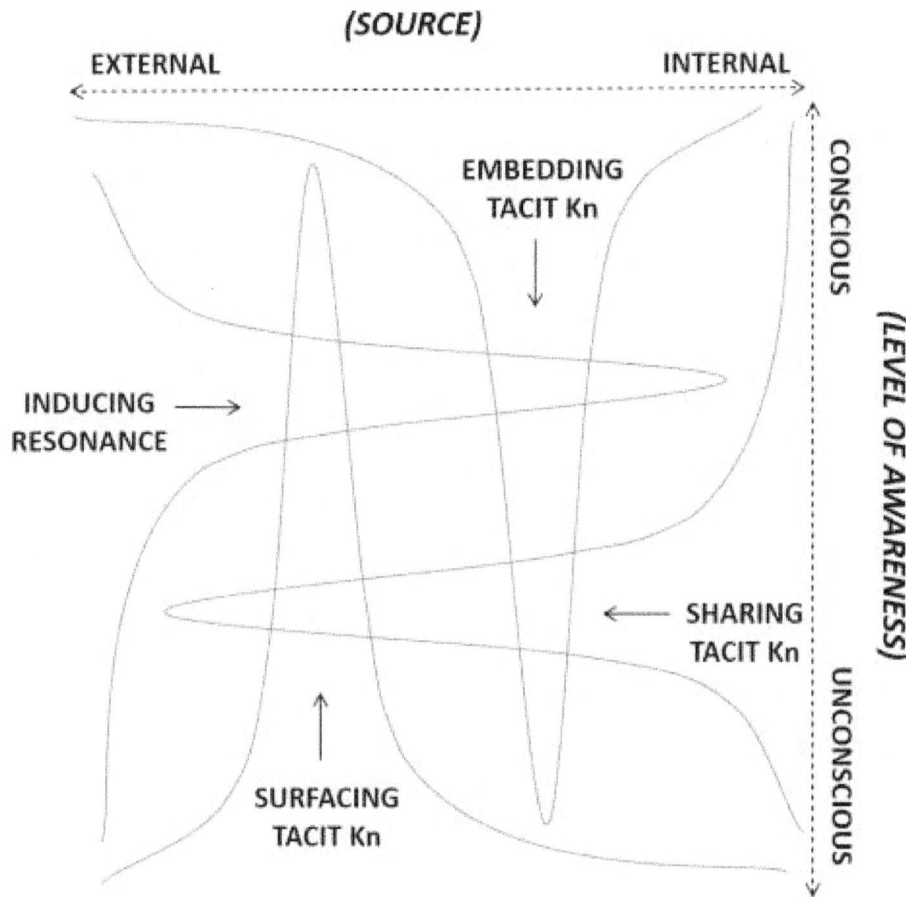

Figure D-2. *Accessing Tacit Knowledge.*

The process of triggering is primarily externally driven with internal participation. For example, conversation, dialogue, questions, or an external situation with specific incoming information may trigger the surfacing of tacit knowledge needed to respond. Triggering is often the phenomenon that occurs in "sink or swim" situations, where an immediate decision must be made that will have significant consequences.

Although collaboration is generally thought about as interactions among individuals and/or groups, a type of collaboration that is less understood is the process of *individuals consciously collaborating with themselves*. What this means is the conscious mind learning to communicate with, listen to, and trust its own unconscious based on a relationship built over time between the self and the personality. With the self in charge, the selection process and semantic complexing of all the experiences, learning, thoughts and feelings throughout life is consistent with the focus and purpose of the self. One way to collaborate with your self is through creating an internal dialogue. For example, accepting the authenticity of, and listening deeply to, a continuous stream of conscious thought while following the tenets of dialogue. Those tenets would include: withholding quick judgment, not demanding quick answers, and exploring underlying assumptions (Ellinor & Gerard, 1998, p. 26), *then* looking for collaborative meaning between what you consciously think and what you feel. A second approach is to ask yourself a lot of questions related to the task at hand. Even if you don't think you know the answers, reflect carefully on the questions, and be patient. Sleeping on a question will often yield an answer the following morning. Your unconscious mind processes information 24/7; it is not a figment of your imagination, or your enemy. To paraphrase the Nobel Laureate Neuroscientist Dr. Eric Kandel, your unconscious is a part of you. It works 24 hours a day processing incoming information on your behalf. So when it tells you something via intuition, lucid dreaming, etc., you should listen carefully (but it may not always be right) (Kandel, 2006).

Although requiring time, openness and commitment, there are a number of approaches readily available for those who choose to nurture their sensitivity to tacit knowledge. These include (among others) meditation, inner tasking, lucid dreaming, and hemispheric synchronization. Meditation practices have the ability to quiet the conscious mind, thus allowing greater access to the unconscious (Rock, 2004). Inner tasking is a wide-spread and often used approach to engaging your unconscious. Tell yourself, as you fall asleep at night, to work on a problem or question. The next morning when you wake up, but before you get up, lie in bed and listen to your own, quiet, passive thoughts. Frequently, but not always, the answer will appear, although it must be written down quickly before it is lost from the conscious mind. Like meditation, the efficacy of this approach takes time and practice to develop (Bennet and Bennet, 2008e).

Lucid dreaming is a particularly powerful way to access tacit knowledge. The psychotherapist Kenneth Kelzer wrote of one of his lucid dreams:

> In this dream I experienced a lucidity that was so vastly different and beyond the range of anything I had previously encountered. At this point I prefer to apply the concept of the spectrum of consciousness to the lucid dream and assert that within the lucid state a person may have access to a spectrum or range of psychic energy that is so vast, so broad and so unique as to defy classification. (Kelzer, 1987)

Another way to achieve sensitivity to the unconscious is *through the use of sound*. For example, listening to a special song in your life can draw out deep feelings and memories buried in your unconscious. Sound and its relationship to humans has been studied by philosophers throughout recorded history; extensive treatments appear in the work of Plato, Kant and Nietzsche. Through the last century scientists have delved into studies focused on acoustics (the science of sound), psychoacoustics (the study of how our minds perceive sound) and musical psychoacoustics (the discipline that involves every aspect of musical perception and performance). As do all patterns in the mind, sound has the ability to change and shape the physiological structure of the brain.

For example, hemispheric synchronization (bringing both hemispheres of the brain into coherence) can be accomplished through the use of sound coupled with a binaural beat. (See Bullard and Bennet, 2013 or Bennet et al., 2015b for in-depth treatment of hemispheric synchronization.) Inter-hemispheric communication is the setting for brain-wave coherence which facilitates whole-brain cognition, assuming an elevated status in subjective experience (Ritchey, 2003). What can occur during hemispheric synchronization is a physiologically reduced state of arousal, quieting the body *while maintaining conscious awareness* (Mavromatis, 1991; Atwater, 2004; Fischer, 1971; West, 1980; Delmonte, 1984; Goleman, 1988; Jevning et al., 1992), thus providing a doorway into the unconscious. It is difficult to imagine the amount of learning and insights that might reside therein—and the expanded mental capabilities such access may provide—much less the depth and breadth of experience and emotion that has been hidden there, perhaps making such access a mixed blessing

Embedding Tacit Knowledge. Every experience and conversation is *embedding* potential knowledge (information) in the unconscious as it is associated with previously stored information to create new patterns. Thinking about embedding as a process for improving our tacit knowledge can lead to new approaches to learning. Embedding is both externally and internally driven, with knowledge moving from the conscious to the unconscious through exposure or immersion, by accident or by choice. Examples include travel, regularly attending church on Sunday, or listening to opera and imitating what you've heard in the shower every day. Practice moves beyond exposure to include repeated participation in some skill or process, thus strengthening the patterns in the mind. For example, after many years of imitation (practice) look at what Paul Potts, an opera singer and winner of the *Britain's Got Talent* competition in 2007, accomplished!

Creating tacit knowledge occurs naturally through diverse experiences in the course of life as individuals become more proficient at some activity (such as public speaking) or cognitive competency (such as problem solving). When the scope of experience widens, the number of relevant neuronal patterns increases. As an individual becomes more proficient in a specific focus area through effortful practice, the pattern gradually becomes embedded in the unconscious, ergo it becomes tacit knowledge. When this happens, the reasons and context within which the knowledge was created often lose their connections with consciousness.

Embodied tacit knowledge requires new pattern embedding for change to occur. This might take the form of repetition in physical training or in mental thinking. For example, embodied tacit knowledge might be embedded through mimicry, practice, competence development or visual imagery coupled with practice. An example of this would be when an athlete training to become a pole vaulter reviews a video of his perfect pole vault to increase his athletic capability. This is a result of the fact that when the pole vaulter performs his perfect vault, the patterns going through his brain while he is doing it are the same patterns that go through his brain when he is watching himself do it. When he is watching the video he is repeating the desired brain patterns and this repetition strengthens these patterns in unconscious memory. When "doing" the pole vault, he cannot think about his actions, nor try to control them. Doing so would degrade his performance because his conscious thoughts would interfere with his tacit ability.

In the late 1990's, neuroscience research identified what are referred to as mirror neurons. As Dobb's explains,

> These neurons are scattered throughout key parts of the brain—the premotor cortex and centers for language, empathy and pain—and fire not only as we perform a certain action, but also when we watch someone else perform that action. (Dobbs, 2007, p. 22)

Watching a video is a cognitive form of mimicry that transfers actions, behaviors and most likely other cultural norms. Thus when we *see* something being enacted, our mind creates the same patterns that we would use to enact that "something" ourselves. As these patterns fade into long-term memory, they would represent tacit knowledge—both Knowledge (Informing) and Knowledge (Proceeding). While mirror neurons are a subject of current research, it would appear that they represent a mechanism for the transfer of tacit knowledge between individuals or throughout a culture. For more information on mirror neurons, see Gazzaniga, 2004.

Intuitive tacit knowledge can be nurtured and developed through exposure, learning, and practice. Knowledge (Informing) might be embedded through experience, contemplation, developing a case history for learning purposes, developing a sensitivity to your own intuition, and effortful practice. Effortful study moves beyond practice to include identifying challenges just beyond an individual's competence and focusing on meeting those challenges one at a time (Ericsson, 2006). The way people become experts involves the chunking of ideas and concepts and creating understanding through the development of significant patterns useful for solving problems and anticipating future behavior within their area of focus. In the study of chess players introduced earlier, it was concluded that "effortful practice" was the difference between people who played chess for many years while maintaining an average skill and those who became master players in shorter periods of time. The master players, or experts, examined the chessboard patterns over and over again, studying them, looking at nuances, trying small changes to perturb the outcome (sense and response), generally "playing with" and studying these *patterns* (Ross, 2006b). In other words, they use *long-term working memory, pattern recognition and chunking* rather than logic as a means of understanding and decision-making. This indicates that by exerting mental effort and emotion while exploring complex situations, knowledge—often problem-solving expertise and what some call wisdom—becomes embedded in the unconscious mind. For additional information on the development of expertise see Ericsson (2006). An important insight from this discussion is the recognition that when facing complex problems which do not allow reasoning or cause and effect analysis because of their complexity, the solution will most likely lie in studying patterns and chunking those patterns to enable a tacit capacity to anticipate and develop solutions. For more on the reference to wisdom see Goldberg (2005).

Affective tacit knowledge requires nurturing and the development of emotional intelligence. Affective tacit knowledge might be embedded through digging deeply into a situation—building self-awareness and developing a sensitivity to your own emotions—and having intense emotional experiences. How much of an experience is kept as tacit knowledge depends upon the mode of incoming information and the emotional tag we (unconsciously) put on it. The stronger the emotion attached to the experience, the longer it will be remembered and the easier it will be to recall. Subtle patterns that occur during any experience may slip quietly into our unconscious and become affective tacit knowledge. For a good explanation of Emotional Intelligence see Goleman (1998).

Spiritual tacit knowledge can be facilitated by encouraging holistic representation of the individual and respect for a higher purpose. Spiritual tacit knowledge might be embedded through dialogue, learning from practice and reflection, and developing a sensitivity to your own spirit, living with it over time and exploring your feelings regarding the larger aspects of values, purpose and meaning. Any individual who, or organization which, demonstrates—and acts upon—their deep concerns for humanity and the planet is embedding spiritual tacit knowledge.

Sharing Tacit Knowledge. In our discussion above on surfacing tacit knowledge, it became clear that surfaced knowledge is new knowledge, a different shading of that which was in the unconscious. If knowledge can be described in words and visuals, then this would be by definition explicit; understanding can only be symbolized and to some extent conveyed through words. Yet the subject of this paragraph is sharing tacit knowledge. The key is that **it is not necessary to make knowledge explicit in order to share it**.

Sharing tacit knowledge occurs both consciously and unconsciously, although the knowledge shared remains tacit in nature. *There is no substitute for experience.* The power of this process has been recognized in organizations for years, and tapped into through the use of mentoring and shadowing programs to facilitate imitation and mimicry. More recently, it has become the focus of group learning, where communities and teams engage in dialogue focused on specific issues and experiences mentally and, over time, develop a common frame of reference, language and understanding that can create solutions to complex problems. The words that are exchanged serve as a tool of creative expression rather than limiting the scope of exchange.

The solution set agreed upon may retain "tacitness" in terms of understanding the complexity of the issues (where it is impossible to identify all the contributing factors much less a cause and effect relationship among them). Hence these solutions in terms of understanding would not be explainable in words and visuals to individuals outside the team or community. When this occurs, the team (having arrived at the "tacit" decision) will often create a rational, but limited, explanation for purposes of communication of why the decision makes sense.

Inducing Resonance. Through exposure to diverse, and specifically opposing, concepts that are well-grounded, it is possible to create a resonance within the receiver's mind that amplifies the meaning of the incoming information, increasing its emotional content and receptivity. Inducing resonance is a result of external stimuli resonating with internal information to bring into conscious awareness. While it is words that trigger this resonance, it is the current of truth flowing under that linguistically centered thought that brings about connections. When this resonance occurs, the incoming information is consistent with the frame of reference and belief systems within the receiving individual. This resonance amplifies feelings connected to the incoming information, bringing about the emergence of deeper perceptions and validating the re-creation of externally-triggered knowledge in the receiver.

Further, this process results in the amplification and transformation of internal affective, embodied, intuitive or spiritual knowledge from tacit to implicit (or explicit). Since deep knowledge is now accessible at the conscious level, this process also creates a sense of ownership within the listener. The speakers are not telling the listener what to believe; rather, when the tacit knowledge of the receiver resonates with what the speaker is saying (and how it is said), a natural reinforcement and expansion of understanding occurs within the listener. This accelerates the creation of deeper tacit knowledge and a stronger affection associated with this area of focus.

An example of inducing resonance can be seen in the movie, *The Debaters*. We would even go so far as to say that the purpose of a debate is to transfer tacit knowledge. Well-researched and well-grounded external information is communicated (explicit knowledge) tied to emotional tags (explicitly expressed). The beauty of this process is that this occurs on *both sides* of a question such that the active listener who has an interest in the area of the debate is pulled into one side or another. An eloquent speaker will try to speak from the audience's frame of reference to tap into their intuition. Such a speaker will come across as confident, likeable and positive to transfer embodied tacit knowledge, and may well refer to higher order purpose, etc. to connect with the listener's spiritual tacit knowledge. An example can be seen in litigation, particularly in the closing arguments, where for opposing sides of an issue emotional tags are tied to a specific frame of reference regarding what has been presented.

[Excerpted from Bennet et al. (2015)]

Appendix E
The Art of Knowing

[We explore knowing from a more pragmatic viewpoint inclusive of brief exercises to expand our external sensing capabilities. To this end, a Knowing Framework developed for the U.S. Department of the Navy is utilized. For purposes of this discussion, Knowing is poetically defined as **seeing beyond images, hearing beyond words, sensing beyond appearances, and feeling beyond emotions**. *In this treatment, it is considered a sense that emerges from our collective tacit knowledge.]*

Every decision and the actions that decision drives is a learning experience that builds on its predecessors by broadening the sources of knowledge creation and the capacity to create knowledge in different ways. For example, as an individual engages in more and more conversations across the Internet in search of meaning, thought connections occur that cause an expansion of shallow knowledge. As we are aware, *knowledge begets knowledge.* In a global interactive environment, the more that is understood, the more that can be created and understood. This is how our personal learning system works. As we tap into our internal resources, *knowledge enables knowing, and knowing inspires the creation of knowledge.*

The concept of "knowing" is not easy to define, since the word and concept are used in so many different ways. We consider Knowing as a *sense* that is supported by our tacit knowledge. In this appendix, we provide a Knowing Framework (published as a chapter in Bennet & Bennet, 2013) that focuses on methods to increase individual sensory capabilities. This Framework specifically refers to our five external senses and to the increase of the ability to consciously integrate these sensory inputs *with our tacit knowledge*, that knowledge created by past learning experiences that is *entangled with* the flow of spiritual tacit knowledge continuously available to each of us. In other words, knowing—**driven by the unconscious as an integrated unit**—is the *sense* gained from experience that resides in the *subconscious* part of the mind, *and* the energetic connection our mind enjoys with the *superconscious*.

The subconscious and superconscious are both part of our unconscious resources, with the subconscious directly supporting the embodied mind/brain and the superconscious focused on tacit resources involving larger moral aspects, the emotional part of human nature and the higher development of our mental faculties. When engaged by an intelligent mind which has moved beyond logic into conscious processing based on trust and recognition of the connectedness and interdependence of humanity, these resources are immeasurable.

In Figure E-1 below, the superconscious is described with the terms spiritual learning, higher guidance, values and morality, and love. It is also characterized as "pre-personality" to emphasize that there are no personal translators such as beliefs and mental models attached to this form of knowing. In Chapter 26/Part IV, the flow of information from the superconscious is very much focused on the moment at hand and does not bring with it any awareness patterns that could cloud the decision-makers full field of perception.

In contrast, the memories stored in the subconscious are very much a part of the personality of the decision-maker, and may be heavily influenced by an individual's perceptions and feelings at the time they were formed. Embodied tacit knowledge would be based on the physical preferences of personality expression while affective tacit knowledge would be based on the feelings connected with the personality of the decision-maker. For example, if there was a traumatic event that occurred in childhood that produced a feeling of "helplessness," later in life there might be neuronal patterns that are triggered that reproduce this feeling when the adult encounters a similar situation. While these feelings may have been appropriate for the child, they would rarely be of service to a seasoned, intelligent decision-maker.

Descriptive terms for the subconscious include life learning, memory, associative patterning, and material intellect. The subconscious in an autonomic system serving a life-support function (see the discussion of personality in Chapter 4/Part I). We all must realize that **the human *subconscious* is in service to the conscious mind**. It is not intended to dominate decision-making. The subconscious expands as it integrates and connects (complexes) all that we put into it through our five external-connected senses. *It is at the conscious mind level that we develop our intellect and make choices that serve as the framework for our subconscious processing.*

Figure E-1 is a nominal graphic showing the continuous feedback loops between knowledge and knowing. Thinking about (potential) and experiencing (actual) effective action (knowledge) supports development of embodied, intuitive and affective tacit knowledges. When we recognize and use our sense of knowing—regardless of its origin—we are tapping into our tacit knowledge to inform our decisions and actions. These decisions and actions, and the feedback from taking those actions, in turn expand our knowledge base, much of which over time will become future tacit resources. Since our internal sense of knowing draws collectively from all areas of our tacit knowledge, the more we open to this inner sense, respond accordingly, and observe and reflect on feedback, the more our inner resources move beyond limited perceptions which may be connected to embedded childhood memories.

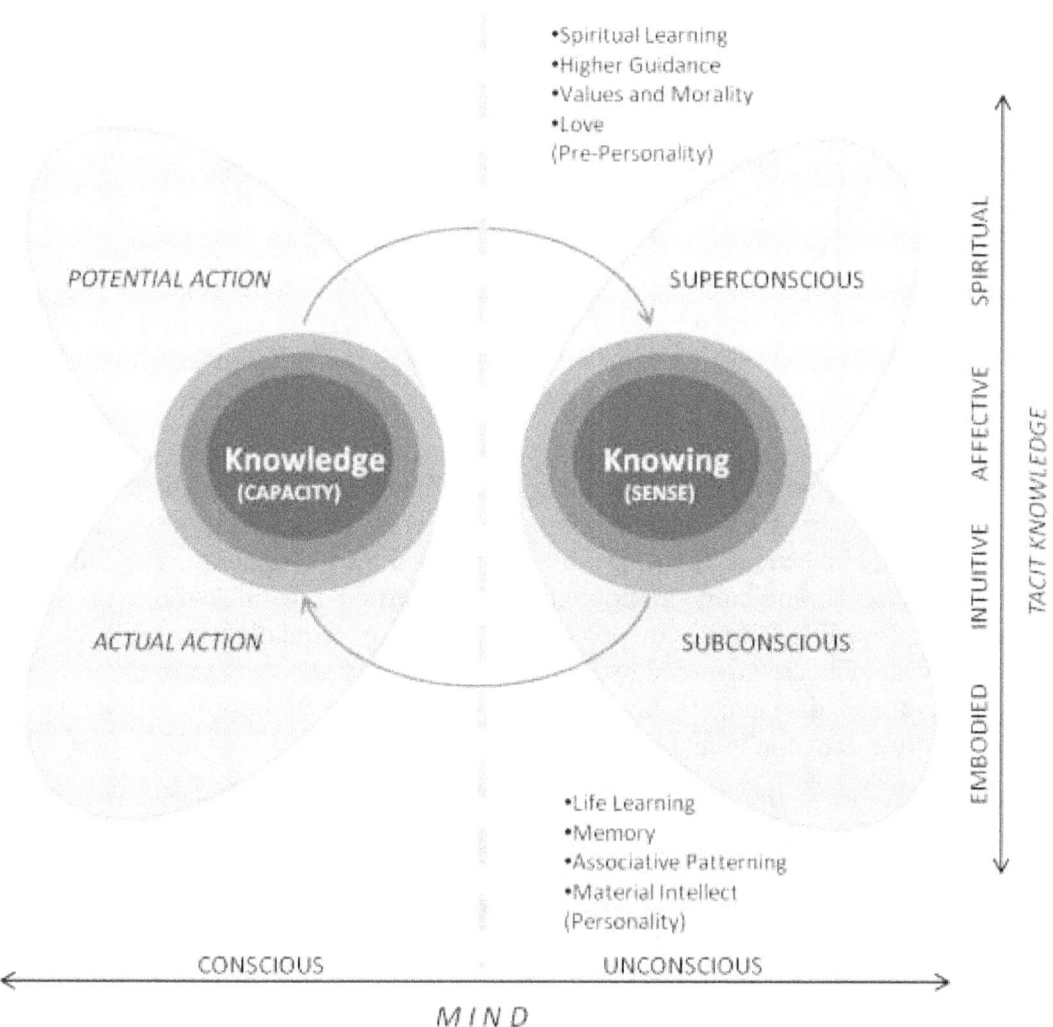

Figure E-1. *The Eternal Loop of Knowledge and Knowing*

Critical Areas of Knowing

The Knowing Framework encompasses three critical areas. The first is "knowing our self," learning to love and trust ourselves. This includes deep reflection on our self in terms of beliefs, values, dreams and purpose for being, and appreciation for the unique beings that we are. It includes understanding of our goals, objectives, strengths and weaknesses in thought and action, and internal defenses and limitations. By knowing ourselves we learn to work within and around our limitations and to support our strengths, thus ensuring that the data, information, and knowledge informing our system is properly identified and interpreted. Further, knowing our self means recognizing that we are a social being, part of the large ecosystem we call Gaia and inextricably connected to other social beings around the world, which brings us to the second critical element: knowing others.

We live in a connected world, spending most of our waking life with other people, and often continuing that interaction in our dreams! There is amazing diversity in the world, so much to learn and share with others. Whether in love or at war, people are always in relationships and must grapple with the sense of "other" in accordance with their beliefs, values and dreams.

The third critical area is that of "knowing" the situation in as objective and realistic a manner as possible, understanding the situation, problem, or challenge in context. In the military this is called situational awareness and includes areas such as culture, goals and objectives, thinking patterns, internal inconsistencies, capabilities, strategies and tactics, and political motivations. The current dynamics of our environment, the multiple forces involved, the complexity of relationships, the many aspects of events that are governed by human emotion, and the unprecedented amount of available data and information make situational awareness a challenging but essential phenomenon in many aspects of our daily lives.

As we move away from predictable patterns susceptible to logic, decision-makers must become increasingly reliant on their "gut" instinct, an internal sense of knowing combined with high situational awareness. Knowing then becomes key to decision-making. The mental skills honed in knowing help decision-makers identify, interpret, make decisions, and take appropriate action in response to current situational assessments.

This construct of knowing can be elevated to the organizational level by using and combining the insights and experiences of individuals through dialogue and collaboration within teams, groups, and communities, both face-to-face and virtual. Such efforts significantly improve the quality of understanding and responsiveness of actions of the organization. They also greatly expand the scope of complex situations that can be handled through knowing because of the greater resources brought to bear—all of this significantly supported by technological interoperability.

Organizational knowing is an aspect of *organizational intelligence*, the capacity of an organization as a whole to gather information, generate knowledge, innovate, and to take effective action. This capacity is the foundation for effective response in a fast-changing and complex world. Increasing our sensory and mental processes contributes to the "positioning" understood by the great strategist Sun Tzu in the year 500 B.C. when he wrote his famous dictum for victory: *Position yourself so there is no battle* (Clavell, 1983). Today in our world of organizations and complex challenges we could say "Position ourselves so there is no confusion."

By exploring our sense of knowing we expand our understanding of ourselves, improve our awareness of the external world, learn how to tap into internal resources, and increase our skills to affect internal and external change. The Knowing Framework provides ideas for developing deep knowledge within the self and sharing that knowledge with others to create new perceptions and levels of understanding. Since each situation and each individual is unique, this Framework does not provide specific answers. Rather, it suggests questions and paths to follow to find those answers.

Principles of Knowing

In response to a changing environment, the Knowing Framework presented below in its expanded form was first developed at the turn of the century for the U.S. Department of the Navy. There are a number of recognized basic truths that drove its development. These truths became the principles upon which the Knowing Framework is based.

(1) Making decisions in an increasingly complex environment requires new ways of thinking.

(2) All the information in the world is useless if the decision-maker who needs it cannot process it and connect it to their own internal values, knowledge, and wisdom.

(3) We don't know all that we know.

(4) Each of us has knowledge far beyond that which is in our conscious mind. Put another way, we know more than we know we know. (Much of our experience and knowledge resides in the unconscious mind.)

(5) By exercising our mental and sensory capabilities we can increase those capabilities.

(6) Support capabilities of organizational knowing include organizational learning, knowledge centricity, common values and language, coherent vision, whole-brain learning, openness of communications, effective collaboration, and the free flow of ideas.

The concept of knowing focuses on the cognitive capabilities of observing and perceiving a situation; the cognitive processing that must occur to understand the external world and make maximum use of our internal cognitive capabilities; and the mechanism for creating deep knowledge and acting on that knowledge via the self as an agent of change. Each of these core areas will be discussed below in more detail.

The Cognitive Capabilities

The cognitive capabilities include observing, collecting and interpreting data and information, and building knowledge relative to the situation. The six areas we will address are: listening, noticing, scanning, sensing, patterning, and integrating. These areas represent means by which we perceive the external world and begin to make sense of it.

Listening

The first area, listening, sets the stage for the other five cognitive capabilities. Listening involves more than hearing; it is a sensing greater than sound. It is a neurological cognitive process involving stimuli received by the auditory system. The linguist Roland Barthes distinguished the difference between hearing and listening when he says: "Hearing is a physiological phenomenon; listening is a psychological act." What this means is that there is a choice involved in listening in terms of the listener choosing to interpret sound waves to potentially create understanding and meaning (Barthes, 1985).There are three levels of listening: alerting, deciphering and understanding. Alerting is picking up on environmental sound cues. Deciphering is relating the sound cues to meaning. Understanding is focused on the impact of the sound on another person. Active listening is intentionally focusing on who is speaking in order to take full advantage of verbal and non-verbal cues.

In developing active listening, imagine how you can use all your senses to focus on what is being said. One way to do this is to role-play, imagining you are in their shoes and feeling the words. Active listening means fully participating, acknowledging the thoughts you are hearing with your body, encouraging the train of thought, actively asking questions when the timing is appropriate. The childhood game of pass the word is an example of a fun way to improve listening skills. A group sits in a circle and whispers a message one to the next until it comes back to the originator. A variation on this theme is Chinese Whispers where a group makes a line and starts a different message from each end, crossing somewhere in the middle and making it to the opposite end before sharing the messages back with the originators. Another good group exercise is a "your turn" exercise, where one individual begins speaking, and another person picks up the topic, and so forth. Not knowing whether you are next in line to speak develops some good listening skills.

The bottom line is that what we don't hear cannot trigger our knowing. Awareness of our environment is not enough. We must listen to the flow of sound and search out meaning, understanding and implications.

Noticing

The second area, noticing, represents the ability to observe around us and recognize, i.e., identify those things that are relevant to our immediate or future needs. We are all familiar with the phenomenon of buying a new car and for the next six months recognizing the large number of similar cars that are on the streets. This is an example of a cognitive process of which we are frequently unaware. We notice those things that are recently in our memory or of emotional or intellectual importance to us. We miss many aspects of our environment if we are not focusing directly on them. Thus the art of noticing can be considered the art of "knowing" which areas of the environment are important and relevant to us at the moment, and focusing in on those elements and the relationships among those elements. It is also embedding a recall capability of those things not necessarily of immediate importance but representing closely related context factors. *This noticing is a first step in building deep knowledge, developing a thorough understanding and a systems context awareness of those areas of anticipated interest.* This is the start of becoming an expert in a given field of endeavor, or situation.

A classic example of mental exercises aimed at developing latent noticing skills is repetitive observation and recall. For example, think about a room that you are often in, perhaps a colleague's office or a friend's living room. Try to write down everything you can remember about this room. You will discover that despite the fact you've been in this room often, you can't remember exactly where furniture is located, or what's in the corners or on the walls. When you've completed this exercise, visit the room and write down everything you see, everything you've missed. What pictures are on the walls? Do you like them? What personal things in the room tell you something about your colleague or friend? How does the layout of furniture help define the room? (These kinds of questions build relationships with feelings and other thinking patterns.) Write a detailed map and remember it. A few days later repeat this exercise from the beginning. If you make any mistakes, go back to the room again, and as many times as it takes to get it right. Don't let yourself off the hook. You're telling yourself that when details are important you know how to bring them into your memory. As your ability to recall improves, repeat this exercise focusing on a street, a building, or a city you visit often.

Scanning

The third area, scanning, represents the ability to review and survey a large amount of data and information and selectively identify those areas that may be relevant. Because of the exponential increase in data and information, this ability becomes more and more important as time progresses. In a very real sense, scanning represents the ability to reduce the complexity of a situation or environment by objectively filtering out the irrelevant aspects, or environmental noise. By developing your own system of environmental "speed reading," scanning can provide early indicators of change.

Scanning exercises push the mind to pick up details and, more importantly, patterns of data and information, *in a short timeframe*. This is an important skill that law enforcement officers and investigators nurture. For example, when you visit an office or room that you've never been in before, take a quick look around and record your first strong impressions. What feelings are you getting? Count stuff. Look at patterns, look at contrasts, look at colors. Try to pick up everything in one or two glances around the room. Make a mental snapshot of the room and spend a few minutes impressing it in your memory. As you leave, remember the mental picture you've made of the room, the way you feel. Impress upon yourself the importance of remembering this. This picture can last for days, or years, despite the shortness of your visit. Your memory can literally retain an integrated *gestalt* of the room. Realize that what you can recall is only a small part of what went into your mind.

Sensing

The fourth area, sensing, represents the ability to take inputs from the external world through our five external senses and ensure the translation of those inputs into our mind to represent as accurate a transduction process (the transfer of energy from one form to another) as possible. The human ability to collect information through our external sensors is limited because of our physiological limitations. For example, we only see a very small part of the electromagnetic spectrum in terms of light, yet with technology we can tremendously expand the sensing capability. As humans we often take our senses for granted, yet they are highly-sensitized complex detection systems that cause immediate response without conscious thought! An example most everyone has experienced or observed is a mother's sensitivity to any discomfort of her young child. The relevance to "knowing" is, recognizing the importance of our sensory inputs, to learn how to fine tune these inputs to the highest possible level, then use discernment and discretion to interpret them.

Exercise examples cited above to increase noticing, scanning, and patterning skills will also enhance the sense of sight, which is far more than just looking at things. It includes locating yourself in position to things. For example, when you're away from city lights look up on a starry night and explore your way around the heavens. Try to identify the main constellations. By knowing their relative position, you know where you are, what month it is, and can even approximate the time of day. The stars provide context for positioning yourself on the earth.

Here are a few exercise examples for other senses. Hearing relates to comprehension. Sit on a park bench, close your eyes and relax, quieting your mind. Start by listening to what is going on around you---conversations of passersby, cars on a nearby causeway, the birds chattering, the wind rustling leaves, water trickling down a nearby drain. Now stretch beyond these nearby sounds. Imagine you have the hearing of a panther, only multidirectional, because you can move your ears every direction and search for sounds. Focus on a faint sound in the distance, then ask your auditory systems to bring it closer. Drag that sound toward you mentally. It gets louder. If you cup one hand behind one ear and cup the other hand in front of the opposite ear, you can actually improve your hearing, focusing on noises from the back with one ear and noises from the front with the other. How does that change what you are hearing?

Next time you are in a conversation with someone, focus your eyes and concentrate on the tip of their nose or the point of their chin. Listen carefully to every word they say, to the pause between their words, to their breathing and sighs, the rise and fall of their voice. Search for the inflections and subtle feelings being communicated behind what is actually being said. When people are talking, much of the meaning behind the information they impart is in their feelings. The words they say are only a representation, a descriptive code that communicates thought, interacting electrical pulses and flows influenced by an emotion or subtle feeling. By listening in this way, with your visual focus not distracting your auditory focus, you can build greater understanding of the subtleties behind the words.

There are many games that accentuate the sense of touch. An old favorite is blind man's bluff; more current is the use of blindfolding and walking through the woods used in outdoor management programs. Try this at home by spending three or four hours blindfolded, going about your regular home activities. At first you'll stumble and bump, maybe even become frustrated. But as you continue, your ability to manage your movements and meet your needs using your sense of touch will quickly improve. You will be able to move about your home alone with relative little effort, and you'll know where things are, especially things that are alive, such as plants and pets. You will develop the ability to *feel* their energy. Such exercises as these force your unconscious mind to create, re-create, and surface the imagined physical world. It activates the mind to bring out into the open its sensitivity to the physical context in which we live.

Patterning

The fifth area, patterning, represents the ability to review, study, and interpret large amounts of data/events/information and identify causal or correlative connections that are relatively stable over time or space and may represent patterns driven by underlying phenomena. These hidden drivers can become crucial to understanding the situation or the enemy behavior. This would also include an understanding of rhythm and randomness, flows and trends. Recall the importance of structure, relationships, and culture in creating emergent phenomena (patterns) and in influencing complex systems.

A well-known example of the use of patterning is that of professional card players and successful gamblers, who have trained themselves to repeatedly recall complicated patterns found in randomly drawn cards. To learn this skill, and improve your patterning skills, take a deck of cards and quickly flip through the deck three or four at a time. During this process, make a mental picture of the cards that are in your hand, pause, then turn over three or four more. After doing this several times, recall the mental picture of the first set of cards. What were they? Then try to recall the second set, then the third.

The secret is not to try and remember the actual cards, but to close your eyes and recall the mental picture of the cards. Patterns will emerge. After practicing for awhile, you will discover your ability to recall the patterns---as well as your ability to recall larger numbers of patterns---will steadily increase. As you increase the number of groups of cards you can recall, and increase the number of cards within each group, you are increasing your ability to recall complex patterns.

Study many patterns found in nature, art, science, and other areas of human endeavor. These patterns will provide you with a "mental reference library" that your mind can use to detect patterns in new situations. Chess experts win games on pattern recognition and pattern creation, not on individual pieces

Integrating

The last area in the cognitive capabilities is integration. This represents the top-level capacity to take large amounts of data and information and pull them together to create meaning; this is frequently called sense-making. This capability, to pull together the major aspects of a complex situation and create patterns, relationships, models, and meaning that represent reality is what enables us to make decisions. This capability also applies to the ability to integrate internal organization capabilities and systems.

While we have used the word "integrating" to describe this capability, recall that the human mind is an associative patterner that is continuously complexing (mixing) incoming information from the external environment with all that is stored in memory. Thus, while the decision-maker has an awareness of integrating, the unconscious is doing much of the work and providing nudges in terms of feelings and speculative thought. Our unconscious is forever our partner, working 24/7 for us.

These five ways of observing represent the front line of cognitive capabilities needed to assist all of us in creative and accurate situational awareness and building a valid understanding of situations. To support these cognitive capabilities, we then need processes that transform these observations and this first-level knowledge into a deeper level of comprehension and understanding.

The Cognitive Processes

Internal cognitive processes that support the capabilities discussed above include visualizing, intuiting, valuing, choosing, and setting intent. These five internal cognitive processes greatly improve our power to understand the external world and to make maximum use of our internal thinking capabilities, transforming our observations into understanding.

Visualizing

The first of these processes, visualizing, represents the methodology of focusing attention on a given area and through imagination and logic creating an internal vision and scenario for success. In developing a successful vision, one must frequently take several different perspectives of the situation, play with a number of assumptions underlying these perspectives, and through a playful trial-and-error, come up with potential visions. This process is more creative than logical, more intuitive than rational, and wherever possible should be challenged, filtered, and constructed in collaboration with other competent individuals. Often this is done between two trusting colleagues or perhaps with a small team. While there is never absolute assurance that visualizing accurately represents reality, there are probabilities or degrees of success that can be recognized and developed

Intuiting

The second supporting area is that of intuiting. By this we mean the art of making maximum use of our own intuition developed through experience, trial-and-error, and deliberate internal questioning and application. There are standard processes available for training oneself to surface intuition. Recognize that intuition is typically understood as being the ability to access our unconscious mind and thereby make effective use of its very large storeroom of observations, experiences, and information. In our framework, intuition is one of the four ways tacit knowledge expresses.

Empathy represents another aspect of intuition. Empathy is interpreted as the ability to take oneself out of oneself and put oneself into another person's world. In other words, as the old Native American saying goes, "Until you walk a mile in his moccasins, you will never understand the person." The ability to empathize permits us to translate our personal perspective into that of another, thereby understanding their interpretation of the situation and intuiting their actions. A tool that can be used to trigger ideas and dig deeper into one's intuitive capability, bringing out additional insights, is "mind mapping." Mind mapping is a tool to visually display and recognize relationships from discrete and diverse pieces of information and data (Wycoff, 1991).

Valuing

Valuing represents the capacity to observe situations and recognize the values that underly their various aspects and concomitantly be fully aware of your own values and beliefs. A major part of valuing is the ability to align your vision, mission, and goals to focus attention on the immediate situation at hand. A second aspect represents the ability to identify the relevant but unknown aspects of a situation or competitor's behavior. Of course, the problem of unknown unknowns always exists in a turbulent environment and, while logically they are impossible to identify because by definition they are unknown, there are techniques available that help one reduce the area of known unknowns and hence reduce the probability of them adversely affecting the organization.

A third aspect of valuing is that of meaning, that is, understanding the important aspects of the situation and being able to prioritize them to anticipate potential consequences. Meaning is contingent upon the goals and aspirations of the individual. It also relies on the history of both the individual's experience and the context of the situation. Determining the meaning of a situation allows us to understand its impact on our own objectives and those of our organization. Knowing the meaning of something lets us prioritize our actions and estimate the resources we may need to deal with it.

Choosing

The fourth supporting area is that of choosing. Choosing involves making judgments, that is, conclusions and interpretations developed through the use of rules-of-thumb, facts, knowledge, experiences, emotions and intuition. While not necessarily widely recognized, judgments are used far more than logic or rational thinking in making decisions. This is because all but the simplest decisions occur in a context in which there is insufficient, noisy, or perhaps too much information to make rational conclusions. Judgment makes maximum use of heuristics, meta-knowing, and verication.

Heuristics represent the rules-of-thumb developed over time and through experience in a given field. They are shortcuts to thinking that are applicable to specific situations. Their value is speed of conclusions and their usefulness rests on consistency of the environment and repeatability of situations. Thus, they are both powerful and dangerous. Dangerous because the situation or environment, when changing, may quickly invalidate former reliable heuristics and historically create the phenomenon of always solving the last problem; yet powerful because they represent efficient and rapid ways of making decisions where the situation is known and the heuristics apply.

Meta-knowing is knowing about knowing, that is, understanding how we know things and how we go about knowing things. With this knowledge, one can more effectively go about learning and knowing in new situations as they evolve over time. Such power and flexibility greatly improves the quality of our choices. Meta-knowing is closely tied to our natural internal processes of learning and behaving as well as knowing how to make the most effective use of available external data, information, and knowledge and intuit that which is not available. An interesting aspect of meta-knowing is the way that certain errors in judgment are common to many people. Just being aware of these mistakes can reduce their occurrence. For example, we tend to give much more weight to specific, concrete information than to conceptual or abstract information. (See Kahneman et al., 1982, for details.)

Verication is the process by which we can improve the probability of making good choices by working with trusted others and using *their* experience and knowing to validate and improve the level of our judgmental effectiveness. Again, this could be done via a trusted colleague or through effective team creativity and decision-making.

Setting Intent

Intent is a powerful internal process that can be harnessed by every human being. Intention is the source with which we are doing something, the act or instance of mentally setting some course of action or result, a determination to act in some specific way. It can take the form of a declaration (often in the form of action), an assertion, a prayer, a cry for help, a wish, visualization, a thought or an affirmation. Perhaps the most in-depth and focused experimentation on the effects of human intention on the properties of materials and what we call physical reality has been that pursued for the past 40 years by Dr. William Tiller of Stanford University. Tiller has proven through repeated experimentation that it is possible to significantly change the properties (ph) of water by holding a clear intention to do so. His mind-shifting and potentially world-changing results began with using intent to change the acid/alkaline balance in purified water. The ramifications of this experiment have the potential to impact every aspect of human life.

What Tiller has discovered is that there are two unique levels of physical reality. The "normal level" of substance is the electric/atom/molecule level, what most of us think of and perceive as the only physical reality. However, a second level of substance exists that is the magnetic information level. While these two levels always interpenetrate each other, under "normal" conditions they do not interact; they are "uncoupled." Intention changes this condition, causing these two levels to interact, or move into a "coupled" state. Where humans are concerned, Tiller says that what an individual intends for himself with a strong sustained desire is what that individual will eventually become (Tiller, 2007).

While informed by Spiritual, the Embodied, Intuitive and Affective tacit knowledges are *local expressions of knowledge*, that is, directly related to our expression in physical reality in a specific situation and context. Connecting Tiller's model of intention with our model of tacit knowledge, it begins to become clear that effective intent relates to an alignment of the conscious mind with the tacit components of the mind and body, that is Embodied, Intuitive, and Affective tacit knowledge. We have to *know* it, *feel* it, and *believe* it to achieve the coupling of the electric/atom/molecule level and magnetic information level of physical reality.

As we use our power of intent to co-create our future, it is necessary to focus from outcome to intention, not worrying about what gets done but staying focused on what you are doing and how you "feel" about what you are doing. Are we in alignment with the direction our decisions are taking us? If not, back to the drawing board—that's looking closer at you, the decision-maker, and ensuring that your vision is clear and your intent is aligned with that vision.

In summary, the five internal cognitive processes—visualizing, intuiting, valuing, choosing and setting intent—work with the six cognitive capabilities—listening, noticing, scanning, patterning, sensing, and integrating—to process data and information and create knowledge within the context of the environment and the situation. However, this knowledge must always be suspect because of our own self-limitations, internal inconsistencies, historical biases, and emotional distortions, all of which are discussed in the third area of knowing: the Self as an Agent of Change.

The Self as an Agent of Change

The third area of the knowing framework—the self as an agent of change—is the mechanism for creating deep knowledge, a level of understanding consistent with the external world and our internal framework. As the unconscious continuously associates information, the self as an agent of change takes the emergent deep knowledge and uses it for the dual purpose of our personal learning and growth, and for making changes in the external world.

Recall that deep knowledge consists of beliefs, facts, truths, assumptions, and understanding of an area that is so thoroughly embedded in the mind that we are often not consciously aware of the knowledge. To create deep knowledge an individual has to "live" with it, continuously interacting, thinking, learning, and experiencing that part of the world until the knowledge truly becomes a natural part of the inner being. An example would be that a person who has a good knowledge of a foreign language can speak it fluently; a person with a deep knowledge would be able to think in the language without any internal translation and would not need their native language to understand that internal thinking.

In the discussion of self as an agent of change, there are ten elements that will be presented. Five of these elements are internal: know thyself, mental models, emotional intelligence, learning and forgetting, and mental defenses; and five of these elements are external: modeling behaviors, knowledge sharing, dialogue, storytelling, and the art of persuasion

Internal Elements

Alexander Pope, in his essay on man (1732-3/1994), noted that: "Know then thyself, presume not God to scan; the proper study of mankind is man." We often think we know ourselves, but we rarely do. To really understand our own biases, perceptions, capabilities, etc., each of us must look inside and, as objectively as possible, ask ourselves, who are we, what are our limitations, what are our strengths, and what jewels and baggage do we carry from our years of experience. Rarely do we *take ourselves out of ourselves and look at ourselves*. But without an objective understanding of our own values, beliefs, and biases, we are continually in danger of misunderstanding the interpretations we apply to the external world. Our motives, expectations, decisions, and beliefs are frequently driven by internal forces of which we are completely unaware. For example, our emotional state plays a strong role in determining how we make decisions and what we decide.

The first step in knowing ourselves is awareness of the fact that we cannot assume we are what our conscious mind thinks we are. Two examples that most of us have experienced come to mind. The first is that we frequently do not know what we think until we hear what we say. The second example is the recognition that every act of writing is an act of creativity. Our biases, prejudices, and even brilliant ideas frequently remain unknown to us until pointed out by others or through conversations. Consciousness is our window to the world, but it is clouded by an internal history, experiences, feelings, memories, and desires.

After awareness comes the need to constantly monitor ourselves for undesirable traits or biases in our thinking, feeling, and processing. Seeking observations from others and carefully analyzing our individual experiences are both useful in understanding ourselves. We all have limitations and strengths, and even agendas hidden from our conscious mind that we must be aware of and build upon or control.

Part of knowing ourselves is the understanding of what mental models we have formed in specific areas of the external world. Mental models are the models we use to represent our own picture of reality. They are built up over time and through experience and represent our beliefs, assumptions, and ways of interpreting the outside world. They are efficient in that they allow us to react quickly to changing conditions and make rapid decisions based upon our presupposed model. Concomitantly, they are dangerous if the model is inaccurate or misleading.

Because we exist in a rapidly changing environment, many of our models quickly become outdated. We then must recognize the importance of continuously reviewing our perceptions and assumptions of the external world and questioning our own mental models to ensure they are consistent with reality (Senge, 1990). Since this is done continuously in our subconscious, we must always question ourselves as to our real, versus stated, motives, goals and feelings. *Only then can we know who we are, only then can we change to who we want to be.*

The art of knowing not only includes understanding our own mental models, but the ability to recognize and deal with the mental models of others. Mental models frequently serve as drivers for our actions as well as our interpretations. When creating deep knowledge or taking action, the use of small groups, dialogue, etc. to normalize mental models with respected colleagues provides somewhat of a safeguard against the use of incomplete or erroneous mental models.

A subtle but powerful factor underlying mental models is the role of emotions in influencing our perception of reality. This has been extensively explored by Daniel Goleman (1995) in his seminal book *Emotional Intelligence*. Emotional intelligence is the ability to sense, understand, and effectively apply the power and acumen of emotions as a source of human energy, information, connection, and influence. It includes self-control, zeal and persistence, and the ability to motivate oneself. To understand emotional intelligence, we study how emotions affect behavior, influence decisions, motivate people to action, and impact their ability to interrelate. Emotions play a much larger role in our lives than previously understood, including a strong role in decision-making. For years it was widely held that rationality was the way of the executive. Now it is becoming clear that the rational and the emotional parts of the mind must be used together to get the best performance in organizations.

Much of emotional life is unconscious. Awareness of emotions occurs when the emotions enter the frontal cortex. As affective tacit knowledge, emotions in the subconscious play a powerful role in how we perceive and act, and hence in our decision-making. Feelings come from the limbic part of the brain and often come forth before the related experiences occur. *They represent a signal* that a given potential action may be wrong, or right, or that an external event may be dangerous. Emotions assign values to options or alternatives, sometimes without our knowing it. There is growing evidence that fundamental ethical stances in life stem from underlying emotional capacities. These stances create the basic belief system, the values, and often the underlying assumptions that we use to see the world—our mental model. From this short treatment of the concept, it is clear that emotional intelligence is interwoven across the ten elements of the self as an agent of change. (See Goleman, 1995 and 1998.)

Creating the deep knowledge of knowing through the effective use of emotional intelligence opens the door to two other equally important factors: learning and forgetting. Learning and letting go—in terms of "filing" away or putting away on the bookshelf—are critical elements of the self as an agent of change because they are the primary processes through which we change and grow. They are also the prerequisite for continuous learning, so essential for developing competencies representing all of the processes and capabilities discussed previously. Because the environment is highly dynamic and will continue to become more complex, continuous learning will be more and more essential and critical in keeping up with the world.

Since humans have limited processing capability and the mind is easily overloaded and tends to cling to its past experiences and knowledge, "letting go" becomes as important as learning. Letting go is the art of being able to let go of what was known and true in the past. Being able to recognize the limitations and inappropriateness of past assumptions, beliefs, and knowledge is essential before creating new mental models and for understanding ourselves as we grow. It is *one of the hardest acts of the human mind* because it threatens our self-image and may shake even our core belief systems.

The biggest barrier to learning and letting go arises from our own individual ability to develop invisible defenses against changing our beliefs. These self-imposed mental defenses have been eloquently described by Chris Argyris (1990). The essence of his conclusion is that the mind creates built-in defense mechanisms to support belief systems and experience. These defense mechanisms are invisible to the individual and may be quite difficult to expose in a real-world situation. They are a widespread example of not knowing what we know, thus representing invisible barriers to change. Several authors have estimated that information and knowledge double approximately every nine months. If this estimate is even close, the problems of saturation will continue to make our ability to acquire deep knowledge even more challenging. We must learn how to filter data and information through vision, values, experiences, goals, and purposes using an open mind, intuition and judgment as our tools. This discernment and discretion within the deepest level of our minds provides a proactive aspect of filtering, thereby setting up purposeful mental defenses that reduce complexity and provide conditional safeguards to an otherwise open system. This is a fundamental way in which the self can simplify a situation by eliminating extraneous and undesirable information and knowledge coming from the external world.

The above discussion has identified a number of factors that can help us achieve an appropriate balance between change and our resistance to change. This is an important attribute: not all change is for the best, yet rigidity begets antiquity. This balance is situational and comes only from experience, learning, and a deep sense of knowing when to change and when not to change the self.

This section has addressed the self as an agent of change through internal recognition of certain factors that can influence self-change. Another aspect of change is the ability of the self to influence or change the external world. This is the active part of knowing. Once the self has attained deep knowledge and understanding of the situation and external environment, this must be shared with others, accompanied by the right actions to achieve success. We live in a connected world.

External Elements

The challenge becomes that of translating knowledge into behavior, thus creating the ability to model that behavior and influence others toward taking requisite actions. Role-modeling has always been a prime responsibility of leadership in the government as well as the civilian world. Having deep knowledge of the situation the individual must then translate that into personal behavior that becomes a role model for others to follow and become motivated and knowledgeable about how to act. Effective role-modeling does not require the learner to have the same deep knowledge as the role model, yet the actions and behaviors that result may reflect the equivalent deep knowledge and over time creates deep knowledge in the learner—

but only in specific situations. This is how you share the effectiveness from learning and thereby transfer implicit knowledge.

Wherever possible, of course, it is preferable to develop and share as much knowledge as possible so that others can act independently and develop their own internally and situation-driven behavior. This is the reason Knowledge Management and communities of practice and interest require management attention. Since most deep knowledge is tacit, knowledge sharing can become a real challenge.

A third technique for orchestrating external change is through the use of dialogue. Dialogue is a process described by David Bohm (1992) to create a situation in which a group participates as coequals in inquiring and learning about some specific topic. In essence, the group creates a common understanding and shared perception of a given situation or topic. Dialogue is frequently viewed as the collaborative sharing and development of understanding. It can include both inquiry and discussions, but all participants must suspend judgment and not seek specific outcomes and answers. The process stresses the examination of underlying assumptions and listening deeply to the self and others to develop a collective meaning. This collective meaning is perhaps the best way in which a common understanding of a situation may be developed as a group and understood by others.

Another way of creating change and sharing understanding is through the effective use of the time-honored process of storytelling. Storytelling is a valuable tool in helping to build a common understanding of our current situation in anticipating possible futures and preparing to act on those possible futures. Stories tap into a universal consciousness that is natural to all human communities. Repetition of common story forms carries a subliminal message, a subtext that can help convey a deep level of complex meaning. Since common values enable consistent action, Story in this sense provides a framework that aids decision-making under conditions of uncertainty.

Modeling behavior, knowledge sharing, dialogue, and storytelling are all forms of building understanding and knowledge. Persuasion, our fifth technique, serves to communicate and share understanding with others who have a specific conviction or belief and/or to get them to act upon it. To change the external environment we need to be persuasive and to communicate the importance and need for others to take appropriate action. The question arises: When you have deep knowledge, what aspects of this can be used to effectively influence other's behavior? Since deep knowledge is tacit knowledge, we must learn how to transfer this to explicit knowledge. Nonaka and Tageuchi (1995) and Polyani (1958) have done seminal work in this area. Persuasion, as seen from the perspective of the self, gets us back to the importance of using all of our fundamental values, such as personal example, integrity, honesty, and openness to help transfer our knowing to others.

As can be seen in the discussion above, **all four forms of tacit knowledge inform knowing**. The Knowing Framework seeks to engage our senses and hone our internal processing mechanisms to take full advantage of our minds/brains/bodies. By bringing our focus on knowing, we have the opportunity to move through relational, experiential, and cultural barriers that somewhere along the course of our lives have been constructed, and sometimes self imposed. This, however, is not the case for many of the young decision-makers moving into the workplace.

[Excerpted from Bennet and Bennet (2013)].

Endnotes

32-1. CUCA refers to the increasing complexity and uncertainty, and the personal anxiety resulting from those. CUCA was introduced in Chapter 13/Part III.

36-1. See http://www.sciencealeert.com/are-we-all-really-connected-by-just-six-degrees-of-separation

37-1. This is a reference to Chapter 33, where we quoted Nicholas Gage, as the hero of the move *Next* (2007) as saying: "There's an Italian painter named Carlotti, and he defined beauty. He said it was the summation of the parts working together in such a way that nothing needed to be added, taken away or altered." While to our knowledge there was no such painter, the quote is representative of how we perceive beauty.

References

Amen, D. G. (2005). *Making a Good Brain Great*. New York: Harmony Books.
Anderson, J.R. (1983). *The Architecture of Cognition*. Cambridge, MA: Harvard University.
Argüelles, J. (2009). "Afterword: WorldShift 2012—A New Beginning" in Laszlo, E., *WorldShift 2012*. Rochester, VT: Inner Traditions.
Argyris, C. (1990). *Overcoming Organizational Defenses: Facilitating Organizational Learning*. Englewood Cliffs, NJ: Prentice Hall.
Argyris, C. and Schon, D. (1978). *Organizational Learning: A Theory of Action Perspective*. Reading, MA: Addison-Wesley.
Aristotle (1962/4th cent. BCE). *Nichomachean Ethics* (M. Oswald, Trans.). Indianapolis, IN: Hobbs-eMrrill.
Asplund, C., Fougnie, D., Zughini, S., Martin, J.W. and Marois, R. (2014). "The Attentional Blink Reveals the Probabilistic Nature of Discrete Conscious Perception" in *Psychological Science*, 25, 824-831.
Assagioli, R. (1975), *Psychosynthesis: A Manual of Principles and Techniques*, Turnstone Press, London.
Atwater, F.H. (2004). *The Hemi-Sync Process*. Faber, VA: The Monroe Institute.
Bateson, G. (1972). *Steps to an Ecology of the Mind*. New York: Ballantine.
Beck, D. E. (2002). *Spiral Dynamics: Integral Level 1 Certification Course*. Spiral Dynamics.
Begley, S., (2007). *Train Your Mind Change Your Brain: How a New Science Reveals Our Extraordinary Potential to Transform Ourselves*. New York: Ballantine Books.
Beneveniste, J. et al. (1996). "Digital Recording/Transmission of the Cholinergic Signal" in *FASEB Journal* 10, A1479.
Beneveniste, J. et al. (1998). "Digital Biology: Specificity of the Digitized Molecular Signal" in *FASEB Journal* 12, A412.
Beneveniste, J. et al. (1999). "A Simple and Fast Method for in vivo Demonstration of Electromagnetic Molecular Signaling (EMS) vis High Dilution or Computer Recording" in *FASEB Journal* 13, A163.
Beneveniste, J. et al. (1999). "The Molecular Signal is not Functioning in the Absence of 'Informed' Water" in *FASEB Journal* 13, A163.
Bennet, A. (2005). *Exploring Aspects of Knowledge Management that Contribute to the Passion Expressed by Its Thought Leaders*. Frost, WV: Self-published.
Bennet, A. and Bennet, D. (2012). *Journey into the Myst*. Frost, WV: MQIPress.
Bennet, A. and Bennet, D. (2008c). "The Fallacy of Knowledge Reuse" in *Journal of Knowledge Management*, 12(5), 21-33.

Bennet, A. and Bennet, D. (2008d). "Moving from Knowledge to Wisdom, from Ordinary Consciousness to Extraordinary Consciousness" in *VINE: Journal of Information and Knowledge Systems*, Vol. 38, No. 1, 7-15.

Bennet, A. and Bennet, D. (2007b). *Knowledge Mobilization in the Social Sciences and Humanities: Moving From Research To Action*. MQIPress, Frost, WV.

Bennet, A. and Bennet, D. (2007c). "The Knowledge and Knowing of Spiritual Learning" in *VINE: The Journal of Information and Knowledge Management Systems*, 37 (2), 150-168.

Bennet, A., Bennet, D. and Avedisian, J. (2015a). *The Course of Knowledge: A 21st Century Theory*. Frost, WV: MQIPress.

Bennet, D. (2001). "Loosening the World Knot", unpublished paper available at www.mountainquestinstitute.com

Bennet, D. and Bennet, A. (2008e). "Engaging Tacit Knowledge in Support of Organizational Learning" in *VINE: Journal of Information and Knowledge Systems,* 38(1), 72-94.

Bennet, D., Bennet, A. and Turner, R. (2015b). *Expanding the Self: The Intelligent Complex Adaptive Learning System*. Frost, WV: MQI Press.

Berman, M. (1981). *The Reenchantment of the World*. Ithaca, NY: Cornell University Press.

Besant, A. and Leadbeater, C.W. (1999). *Thought-Forms*. Wheaton, IL: Quest Books.

Beversluis, J. (2000). *Cross-Examining Socrates: A Defense of the Interlocutors in Plato's Early Dialogues*. Cambridge: Cambridge University Press.

Beversluis, J. (Ed.) (1993). "The Declaration of a Global Ethic", signed by 143 respected leaders from the world's major faiths at the 1993 Parliament of the World's Religions held in Chicago, IL on September 4, 1993. Retrieved 11/20/16 from http://www.religioustolerance.org/parliame.htm

Bohm, D. (1980). *Wholeness and the Implicate Order*. London: Routledge & Kegal.

Bohm, D. (1992). *Thought as a System*. New York: Routledge.

Brown, M.Y. (1979), *The Art of Guiding: the Psychosynthesis Approach to Individual Counselling and Psychology*, Johnson College, University of Redlands, Redlands, CA.

Bucke, R.M. (Ed.) (2010). *Cosmic Consciousness: A Study in the Evolution of the Human Mind*. Mansfield Centre, CT: Martino Publishing.

Bullard, B. and Bennet, A. (2013). *REMEMBRANCE: Pathways to Expanded Learning with Music and Metamusic®*. Frost, WV: MQIPress.

Bullard, T. (2013). *The Game Changers: Social Alchemists of the 21st Century*. Self-Published.

Buzsaki, G. (2006). *Rhythms of the Brain*. New York: Oxford University Press.

Caprara, G.V. & Cervone, D. (2000), *Personality: Determinants, Dynamics, and Potentials*, Cambridge University Press, Cambridge, UK.

Carroll, G.D. (1986). "Brain Hemisphere Synchronization and Musical Learning." Reprint of paper. Greensboro, NC: University of North Carolina.

Carroll, S. (2016). *The Big Picture: On the Origins of Life, Meaning, and the Universe Itself.* New York: Dutton.

Chodron, P. (2002). *The Places that Scare You: A Guide to Fearlessness in Difficult Times.* Boston: Shambhala.

Clavell, J. (Ed.) (1983). *The Art of War: Sun Tzu. New York:* Dell Publishing.

Cooper, J.M. (1999). *Reason and Emotion: Essays on Ancient Moral Psychology and Ethical Theory.* Princeton, NJ: Princeton University Press.

Copeland, L., Lamm, L.W. and McKenna, S.J. (1999). *The World's Great Speeches.* Mineola, NY: Dover Publications.

Cozolino, L. J. (2006). *The Neuroscience of Human Relationships: Attachment and the Developing Social Brain.* New York: W.W. Norton.

Damasio, A. R. (1994). *Descartes' Error: Emotion, Reason, and the Human Brain.* New York: G.P. Putnam's Sons.

Damon, W. (1997). *The Youth Charter: How Communities Can Work Together to Raise Standards for All Our Children.* New York: Free Press.

Davis, S. (1996). *Future Perfect.* Reading, MA: Addison-Wesley Publishing Company, Inc.

Dearlove, D. (2003). *The Ultimate Book of Business Thinking: Harnessing the Power of the World's Greatest Business Ideas.* Oxford: Capstone Books.

de Chardin, P. Teilhard (1959). *The Phenomenon of Man.* St James Palace, London: Collins.

Dehaene, S., Changeux, J.P., Naccache, L., Sackur, J. and Sergent, C. (2006). "Conscious, Preconscious, and Subliminal Processing: A Testable Taxonomy" in *Trends in Cognitive Sciences*, 10: 204-211.

Delmonte, M.M. (1984). "Electrocortical Activity and Related Phenomena Associated with Meditation Practice: A Literature Review" in *International Journal of Neuroscience*, 24: 217-231.

Dictionary.com (2016). Retrieved 07/18/16
http://www.dictionary.com/browse/harmony

Dilts, R. (2003). *From Coach to Awakener.* Capitola, CA: Meta Publications.

Dirac, P.A.M. (1964). *Lectures on Quantum Mechanics.* New York: Belfer Graduate School of Science, Yeshiva University.

Dobbs, D. (2007). "Turning Off Depression" in F. E. Bloom (Ed.), *Best of the Brain from Scientific American: Mind, Matter, and Tomorrow's Brain.* New York: Dana Press, 169-178.

Dunning, J. (2014). Discussion of consciousness via the Internet on December 13.

Durham, M. (2004). "Three Critical Roles for Knowledge Management Workspaces: Moderators, Thought Leaders, and Managers" in E. Koenig & T. Srikantaiah, *Knowledge Management Lessons Learned: What Works and What Doesn't.* Medford, NJ: Information Today.

Eden, D. (2008). *Energy Medicine: Balancing Your Body's Energies for Optimal Health, Joy, and Vitality*. New York: Penguin Group.

Elgin, D. (1993). *Awakening Earth: Exploring the Evolution of Human Culture and Consciousness*. New York: William Morrow.

Ellinor, L. and Gerard, G. (1998). *Dialogue: Rediscover the Transforming Power of Conversation*. New York: John Wiley & Sons, Inc.

Encarta World English Dictionary (1999). New York: St Martin's Press.

English, L.M. and Gillen, M.A. (2000). Addressing Spiritual Dimensions of Adult Learning. San Francisco, CA: JoseyBass.

Ericsson, K.A., Charness, N., Feltovich, P.J. & Hoffman, R.R. (Eds.) (2006). *The Cambridge Handbook of Expertise and Expert Performance*. New York: Cambridge University Press.

Fazekas, P. and Overgaard, M. (2016b). "A Multi-Factor Account of Degrees of Awareness" Draft paper retrieved 11/17/16 from ResearchGate https://www.academia.edu/29703924/A_Multi-Factor_Account_of_Degrees_of_Awareness?auto=download&campaign=weekly_digest

Fischer, R. (1971). "A Cartography of Ecstatic and Meditative States" in *Science*, 174 (4012), 897-904.

Frankl, V. E. (1969/1988). *The Will to Meaning: Foundations and Applications of Logotherapy*. Middlesex, England: Penguin Books.

Frankl, V. E. (1948/1975). *The Unconscious God: Psychotherapy and Theology*. New York: Simon and Schuster.

Frankl, V. E. (1939/1963). *Man's Search for Meaning: An Introduction of Logotherapy*. New York: Pocket Books.

Freud, S. (1938), "Splitting of the ego in the process of defence" in *Standard edition Vol. 23*, Hogarth Press, London.

Gardner, H. (2011a). *Truth, Beauty, and Goodness Reframed: Educating for the Virtues in the Age of Truthiness and Twitter*. New York: Basic Books.

Gazzaniga, M.S. (Ed.) (2004). *The Cognitive Neurosciences III*. Cambridge, MA: The MIT Press.

Gell-Mann, M. (1994). *The Quark and the Jaguar: Adventures in the Simple and the Complex*. NY: W.H.Freeman and Company.

Goffman, E. (1959), *The Presentation of Self in Everyday Life*, Anchor, New York.

Goleman, D. (2015). *A Force for Good: The Dalai Lama's Vision for Our World*. New York: Bantam Books.

Goleman, G.M. (1988). *Meditative Mind: The Varieties of Meditative Experience*. New York: G.P. Putnam.

Goldberg, E. (2005). *The Wisdom Paradox: How Your Mind Can Grow Stronger as Your Brain Grows Older*. New York: Gotham Books.

Goleman, D. (1998). "What Makes a Leader?" in *Harvard Business Review*, 93-102.

Goleman, D. (1995). *Emotional Intelligence*. New York: Bantam Books.

Google (2016). Synonyms for "virtue" retrieved 09/30/16 from
https://www.google.com/webhp?sourceid=chrome-instant&rlz=1C1SKPL_enUS425&ion=1&espv=2&ie=UTF-8#q=virtue%20definition

Greenwald, A.G., Draine, S.C. and Abrams, R.L. (1996). "Three Cognitive Markers of Unconscious Semantic Activation" in *Science*, 273, 1699-1702.

Gyatso, T. (The Fourteenth Dalai Lama) (1992). *The Meaning of Life: Buddhist Perspectives on Cause and Effect*. Boston: Wisdom Publications.

Haidt, J. (2006). *The Happiness Hypothesis: Finding Modern Truth in Ancient Wisdom*. New York: Basic Books.

Harvey, R. (2013). "The Ancient Thread of Authenticity" (An interview on Sacred Attention Therapy), 2013. Retrieved 06/13/15 from www.sacredattentiontherapy.com/Articles.html

Hauck, D.W. (1999). *The Emerald Tablet: Alchemy for Personal Transformation*. New York: Penguin Group.

Hawkins, D.R. (2002). *Power VS Force: The Hidden Determinants of Human Behavior*. Carlsbad, CA: Hay House.

Hink, R.F., Kodera, K., Yamada, O., Kaga, K. and Suzuki, J. (1980). "Binaural Interaction of a Beating Frequency Following response" in *Audiology*, 19: 36-43.

Hodgkin, R. (1991). "Michael Polanyi—Profit of Life, the Universe, and Everything" in *Times Higher Educational Supplement*, September 27, 15.

Houston, J. (2000). *Jump Time: Shaping Your Future in a World of Radical Change*. New York: Penguin Putnam Inc.

Hubbard, B.M. (2015). The Eolutionary Testament of Co-Creation: The Promised Will Be Kept. Los Angeles, CA: Muse Harbor Publishing.

Hunter, J.D. (2000). *The Death of Character: Moral Education in an Age Without Good and Evil*. New York: Basic Books.

Inner World, Outer World (2012). Documentary by Daniel Schmidt. Creative Direction by Barbara Dimetto. REM Publishing Ltd. (Responsible Earth Media).

Jahn, R.G. and Dunne, B.J. (2011). *Consciousness and the Source of Reality: The PEAR Odyssey*. Princeton, NJ: ICRL Press.

Jahn, R.G. and Dunne, B.J. (2009). *Margins of Reality: The Role of Consciousness in the Physical World*. New York: Harcourt Brace & Company.

Jahn, R.G. and Dunne, B. (1987). *Margins of Reality: The Role of Consciousness in the Physical World*. New York: Harcourt Brace Jovanovich.

James, J. (1996). *Thinking in the Future Tense: A Workout for the Mind*. New York: Touchstone.

Jevning, R., Wallace, R.K., and Beidenbach, M. (1992). "The Physiology of Meditation: A Review" in *Neuroscience and Behavioral Reviews*, 16, 415-424.

Jung, C.J. (Trans. By Hull, R.F.C.) (1990), *The Archetypes and the Collective Unconscious* (10th Ed.), Princeton University, Princeton, NJ.

Kahneman, D., P. Slovic and Tversky, A. (1982). *Judgment Under Uncertainty: Heuristics and Biases*. New York: Cambridge University Press.

Kandel, E. R. (2006). *In Search of Memory: The Emergence of a New Science of Mind*. New York: W.W. Norton & Company.

Kauffman, D.L. (1980). *Systems 1: An Introduction to Systems Thinking*. Minneapolis, MN: S.A. Carlton, Publisher.

Kelzer, K. (1987). *The Sun and the Shadow: My Experiment with Lucid Dreaming*. Virginia Beach, VA: ARE Press.

Kiefer, M., Ansorge, U., Haynes, J-D., Hamker, F., Mattler, U., Verleger, R., and Niedeggen, M. (2011). "Neuro-Cognitive Mechanisms of Conscious and Unconscious Visual Perception: From a Plethora of Phenomena to General Principles" in *Advances in Cognitive Psychology*, 7, 55-67.

Kihlstrom, J.F. & Cantor, N. (1984), "Mental representations of the self" in L. Berkowitz (Ed.), *Advances in Experimental Social Psychology 17*, Academic Press, New York.

Klein, G. (2003). *Intuition at Work: Why Developing Your Gut Instincts Will Make You Better at What You Do*. New York: Doubleday.

Kohut, H. (1984). *How Does Analysis Cure?* Ed. A. Goldberg & P. Stepansky. Chicago: University of Chicago Press.

Kolb, D. A. (1984). *Experiential Learning: Experience as the Source of Learning and Development*. New Jersey: Prentice-Hall.

Kornfield, J. (2008). *Meditation for Beginners*. Boulder, CO: Sounds True, Inc.

Kuek, COA LG Desmond (2006). "Leading Soldiers While Leading Change". Speech made at Distinguished Speakers' Programme, 37th SCSC, Singapore Armed Forces, January 17.

Kurtzman, J. (Ed.). (1998). *Thought Leaders: Insights on the Future of Business*. San Francisco: Jossey-Bass.

Kurzweil, R. (2005). *The Singularity is Near: When Humans Transcend Biology*. New York: Viking.

The Kybalion (1940/1912). *The Kybalion: A Study of Hermetic Philosophy of ancient Egypt and Greece*. Yogi Pub. Society.

Laszlo, E. (2009). *WorldShift 2012: Making Green Business, New Politics & Higher Consciousness Work Together*. Rochester, VT: Inner Traditions.

Laszlo, E. (2004). *Science and the Akashic Field: An Integral Theory of Everything*. Rochester, Vermont: Inner Traditions.

Laszlo, E. (1995). *The Interconnected Universe: Conceptual Foundations of Transdisciplinary Unified Theory*. Singapore: World Scientific.

LeDoux, J. (1996). *The Emotional Brain: The Mysterious Underpinnings of Emotional Life*. New York: Touchstone.

Leonard-Barton, D. (1995). *Wellsprings of Knowledge: Building and Sustaining the Sources of Innovation*. Boston, MA: Harvard Business School Press.

Levey, J. and Levey, M. (2014). *Living Balance: A Mindful Guide for Thriving in a Complex World*. Studio City, CA: Divine Arts.

Lewin, K. (1936), *Topological Psychology*, McGraw-Hill, New York.

Lewis, J. (2013). *The Explanation Age (3rd Edition)*. Charleston: Amazon Create Space.

Linden, S.J. (2003). *The Alchemy Reader: From Hermes Trismegistus to Isaac Newton*. Cambridge, UK: Cambridge University Press.

Lipton, B. (2005). *The Biology of Belief: Unleashing the Power of Consciousness*. Carlsbad, CA: Hay House.

Lipton, B. and Bhaerman, S. (2009). *Spontaneous Evolution: Out Positive Future (And a Way to Get There from Here)*. Carlsbad, CA: Hay House.

MacFlouer, Niles (2004-16). *Why Life Is...* Weekly radio shows: BBSRadio.com (#1-#480) and KXAM (#1-#143). Retrieved from http://www.agelesswisdom.com/archives_of_radio_shows.htm

Mahoney, D. and Restak, R. (1998). *The Longevity Strategy: How to Live to 100 Using the Brain-Body Connection*. New York: John Wiley & Sons, Inc.

Martin, R. (2000). "Breaking the Code of Change: Observations and Critique" in Beer, M. and Nohria, N. (Eds.) (2000). *Breaking the Code of Change*. Boston, MA: Harvard Business School Press, 394-415.

Matthews, R.C. (1991). "The Forgetting Algorithm: How Fragmentary Knowledge of Exemplars Can Yield Abstract Knowledge" in *Journal of Experimental Psychology: General*, 120, 117-119.

Mavromatis, A. (1991). *Hypnagogia*. Routledge, New York, NY.

May, Rollo (1975). *The Courage to Create*. New York: Bantam.

McHale, J. (1977). "Futures Problems or Problems in Futures Studies" in Linstone, H.A. and Simmonds, W.H.C. (Eds.), *Futures Research: New Directions*. Reading, MA: Addison-Wesley Publishing Company, Inc.

McIntosh, S. (2013). *Integral Consciousness and the Future of Evolution*. St. Paul, MN: Paragon House.

McTaggart, L. (2002). *The Field: The Quest for the Secret Force of the Universe*. New York: Harper Perennial.

McWhinney, W. (1997). *Paths of Change: Strategic Choices for Organizations and Society*. Thousand Oaks, CA: SAGE Publications, Inc.

Medina, J. (2008). *Brain Rules: 12 Principles for Surviving and Thriving at Work, Home, and School*. Seattle, WA: Pear Press.

Merriam-Webster (2016). Retrieved 07/06/16 http://www.merriam-webster.com/dictionary/personality ; Retrieved 08/27/16 http://www.webster-dictionary.org/definition/Agape ; Retrieved 08/28/16 http://www.merriam-webster.com/dictionary/Quantum%20leap ; Retrieved

09/30/16 http://www.merriam-webster.com/dictionary/virtue ; Retrieved 10/01/16 http://www.merriam-webster.com/dictionary/sympathy

Metcalf, B. (2016). "Field Effect Audio Technology™ (F.E.A.T.™) FAQ" shared with author by Metcalf on 11/05/2016.

Mulhall, D. (2002). *Our Molecular Future: How Nanotechnology, Robotics, Genetics, and Artificial Intelligence will Transform Our World*. Amherst, NY: Prometheus Books.

Mulford, P. (2007). *Thoughts Are Things*. New York: Barnes & Noble.

Murray, P. (2012). *Giving Myself Permission: Putting Fear and Doubt in Their Place*. Little Elm, TX: GMP Publishing.

Nonaka, I. and Takeuchi, H. (1995). *The Knowledge-Creating Company: How Japanese Companies Create the Dynamics of Innovation*. New York: Oxford University Press.

Oster, G. (1973). "Auditory Beats in the Brain" in *Scientific American*, 229, 94-102.

Oxford English Dictionary (5th Ed) (2002). Volumes 1 and 2. Oxford: Oxford University Press.

Peccei, A. (1977). *The Human Quality*. Oxford: Pergamon Press.

Pert, C. B. (1997). *Molecules of Emotion: A Science Behind Mind-Body Medicine*. New York: Touchstone.

Peterson, C. and Seligman, M.E.P. (2004). *Character Strengths, Character Virtues Handbook*. New York: Oxford University Press.

Polanyi, M. (1958). *Personal Knowledge: Towards a Post-Critical Philosophy*. Chicago: University of Chicago Press.

Popp, F.A. and Chang, JJ. (2000). "Mechanism of Interaction Between Electromagnetic Fields and Living Systems" in *Science in China* (Series C), 43, 507-18.

Popp, F.A. (2002). "Biophotonics: A Powerful Tool for Investigating and Understanding Life" in Durr, H.P., Popp, F.A. and Schommers, W. (Eds.), *What is Life? Scientific Approaches and Philosophical Positions* (Series on the Foundations of Natural Science and Technology). Singapore: World Scientific.

Polanyi, M. (1958). *Personal Knowledge: Towards a Post-Critical Philosophy*. Chicago: University of Chicago Press.

Polanyi, M. (1967). *The Tacit Dimension*. New York: Anchor Books.

Polkinghorne, J. (1996). *Beyond Science: The Wider Human Context*. New York: Press Syndicate of the University of Cambridge.

Pribram, K.H. (1991). *Brain and Perception: Holonomy and Structure in Figural Processing*. Hillsdale, NJ: Lawrence Erlbaum.

Pribram, K.H. (Ed.) (1993). *Rethinking Neural Networks: Quantum Fields and Biological Data*, Proceedings of the First Appalachian Conference on Behavioral Neurodynamics. Hillsdale, NJ: Lawrence Erlbaum.

Pribram, K.H. (1998). "Autobiography in Anecdote: The Founding of Experimental Neuropsychology" in Bilder, R. (Ed.), *The History of Neuroscience in Autobiography*. San Diego: California Academic Press, 306-49.

Puthoff, H.E. (1981). "Experimental PSI Research: Implication for Physics" in Jahn, R. (Ed.), *The Role of Consciousness in the Physical World*, AAA Selected Symposia Series. Boulder, CO: Westview Press.

Puthoff, H.E. (1989). "Source of Vacuum Electromagnetic Zero-Point Energy" in *Physical Review A* 40: 4857-62.

Puthoff, H. (1989). "Where Does the Zero-Point Energy Come From?" in *New Scientist* (December 2), 36.

Puthoff, H. (1990). "Everything for Nothing" in *New Scientist* (July 28), 52-5.

Quinn, R.E. (1996). *Deep Change: Discovering the Leader Within*. San Francisco: Jossey-Bass Publishing.

Reber, A.S. (1993). *Implicit Learning and Tacit Knowledge: An Essay on the Cognitive Unconscious*. New York: Oxford University Press.

Redfearn, J.W.T. (1985), *My Self, My Many Selves*, Academic Press, London.

Reynolds, J.H. and Chelazzi, L. (2004). "Attentional Modulation of Visual Processing" in *Annual Review Neuroscience 27*, 611-647.

Riggio, R.E. (2015). "Are You Empathic? 3 Types of Empathy and What They Mean". Retrieved 09/14/15 from https://www.psychologytoday.com/blog/cutting-edge-leadership/201108/are-you-empathic-3-types-empathy-and-what-they-mean

Ritchey, D. (2003). *The H.I.S.S. of the A.S.P.: Understanding the Anomalously Sensitive Person*. Terra Alta, WV: Headline Books, Inc.

Rock, A. (2004). *The Mind at Night: The New Science of How and Why We Dream*. New York: Perseus Books Group.

Ross, P. E. (2006b). "The Expert Mind" in *Scientific American*, (August), 64-71.

Rowan, J. (1990), *Subpersonalities: The People Within Us*. New York: Routledge.

Russell, P. (2007). *The Awakening Earth: The Global Brain*. Edinburgh: Floris Books.

Russell, P. (1982). *The Awakening Earth: The Global Brain*. London: Routledge & Kegan Paul.

Salk, J. (1973). *The Survival of the Wisest*. New York: Harper & Row.

Schempp, W. (1993). "Cortical Linking Neural Network Models and Quantum Holographic Neural Technology" in Pribram, K.H. (Ed.), *Rethinking Neural Networks: Quantum Fields and Biological Data,* Proceedings of the First Appalachian conference on Behavioral Neurodynammics. Hillsdale, NJ: Lawrence Erlbaum.

Schlar, G. and Freeman, R.D. (1982). "Orientation Selectivity in the Cat's Striate Cortex is Invariant with Stimulus Contrast" in *Experimental Brain Research*, 46, 457-461.

Schrödinger, E. (1983). *My View of the World*. Oxford, England: Ox Bow Publishers.
Scott, C. (2016a). *Life Bites*. Frost, WV: MQIPress.
Seife, C. (2006). *Decoding the Universe: How the New Science of Information is Explaining Everything in the Cosmos, from our Brains to Black Holes*. New York: Penguin Group.
Senge, Peter (1990). *The Fifth Discipline*. New York: Doubleday.
Sheldrake, R. (1995). *The Presence of the Past: Morphic Resonance and the Habits of Nature*. (2nd Ed.) Bethel, Maine: Park Street Press.
Sheldrake, R. (1989). *The Presence of the Past: Morphic Resonance and the Habits of Nature*. New York: Vintage Books.
Smith, M.K. (2003). "Michael Polanyi and Tacit Knowledge" in *The Encyclopedia of Informal Education*, 2, www.infed.org/thinkers/Polanyi.htm
Stanford School of Medicine (2016). Ethnogeriatrics. "Traditional Health Beliefs: Native Hawaiian Values." Dowloaded 09/28/2016 from
Statista (2016). Live theater visitors. Retrieved 10/8/2016 from https://www.statista.com/statistics/227494/live-theater-visitors-usa/
Stewart, W.J. (1985). *The Runkles—A Manual of Wisdom and Wit for All Ages*. Mill Valley, CA: Self published.
Suttie, J. (2015). "Can Compassion Change the World" (Interview of Daniel Goleman re his book *A Force for Good: The Dalai Lama's Vision for Our World*). Retrieved 101716 from http://greatergood.berkeley.edu/article/item/can_compassion_change_the_world
Swann, R.S., Bosanko, R., Cohen, R., Midgley, R. and Seed, K.M. (1982). *The Brain: A User's Manual*. New York: G.P Putnam & Sons.
Tapscott, D. (2009). *Grown up Digital*. McGraw Hill, New York.
Tart, C.T. (1975), "Science, states of consciousness and spiritual experiences: the need for state-specific sciences" in C.T. Tart (Ed.), *Transpersonal Psychologies*, Routledge & Kegan Paul, London.
Templeton, Sir John (2002). *Wisdom from World Religions: Pathways Toward Heaven on Earth*. Philadelphia, PA: Templeton Foundation Press.
Tiller, W.A. (1997). *Science and Human Transformation: Subtle Energies, Intentionality and Consciousness*. Walnut Creek, CA: Pavior Publishing.
Tiller, W.A., Dibble, W.E. and Kohane, M.J. (2001). *Conscious Acts of Creation: The Emergence of a New Physics*. Walnut Creek, CA: Pavior Publishing.
Tiller, W. (2007). *Psychoenergetic Science: A Second Copernican-Scale Revolution*. DVD from www.tillerfoundation.com
Tolle, E. (2004). *The Power of Now: A Guide to Spiritual Enlightenment*. Vancouver, BC, Canada: Namaste Publishing.
Urbanovic, J. (2017). "Beauty". Personal email to alex@moountainquestinstitute dated January 03.

Vernadsky, V. I. (1998). *The Biosphere*. New York: Copernicus, Springer-Verlag.

Vitale, J. and Len, I.H. (2007). *Zero Limits: The Secret Hawaiian System to Wealth, Health, Peace & More*. New Jersey: John Wiley & Sons, Inc.

Wagner, Roy (1975). *The Invention of Culture*. Chicago: University of Chicago.

Walsch, N.D. (2009). When Everything Changes, Change Everything: In a Time of Turmoil, A Pathway to Peace. Ashland, OR: EmNin Books.

Watzlawick, P. (1974). *How Real is Real?* New York: Random House.

Wenger (2000). *Communities of Practice: Learning, Meaning, and Identity (Learning in Doing: Social, Cognitive and Computational Perspectives)*. Cambridge: Cambridge University Press.

Wenger, E., McDermott, R.A., and Snyder, W. (2002). *Cultivating Communities of Practice: From Idea to Execution*. Boston: Harvard Business School Press.

West, M.A. (1980). "Meditation and the EEG" in *Psychological Medicine*, 10: 369-375.

Wilber, K. (2000). *Integral Psychology: Consciousness, Spirit, Psychology, Therapy*. Boston: Shambhala Publications.

Wilber, K. (1999). *The Collected Works of Ken Wilber*, Vols. 1-8. Boston: Shambhala

Willis, A. (2012). *Achieving Balance*. Great Britain: Manicboy Publishing.

Wilrieke, (2016). "Judging Others Is About You" from Pure Wilrieke web log. Retrieved 09/30/16 from http://www.purewilrieke.com/judging-others-is-about-you

Wing, R.L. (Trans) (1986). *The Tao of Power: Lao Tzu's Classic Guide to Leadership, Influence, and Excellence*. New York: Doubleday.

Wlodkowski, R.J. (1998). Enhancing Adult Motivation to Learn: A Comprehensive Guide for Teaching All Adults. San Francisco, CA: Jossey-Bass.

World Transhumanist Association (July 7, 2001). Definition of transhumanism. Retrieved 08/14/16 from www.Transhumanist.org/index.html#transhumanism

Index

affirmations 17
alchemy 22-39, 131-136
  cycle of change, current 31-36
  (def) 22
  ego 132-133, 134
  field of 23
  imaginal cells 27, (photo) 27
  metamorphosis 27-30
  personality, and (def) 131, 131-136
  process of 22
  science, relationship with 22
  self, true 133
  symbols, language of 23
    Caduceus 23
  transformation 24-26
    calcination 24, 27, 31
    coagulation 26, 30, 39
    conjunction 25, 28
    dissolution 25, 27, 31-32
    distillation 26, 30, 39
    fermentation 25, 29-30, 37-38
    separation 25, 28, 32-33
    seven steps 24-26
art
  artists
    Crouse, Corbie 62-63, (art) 63
    Schneider, Reefka 60-61, (art) 61
    Taylor, Cindy 62, (art) 62
    Urbanovic, Jackie 63-64, (art) 64, 65-66
  beauty in 59-64
  beliefs, relationship with 59
  health as 64-67
  language as 60
associative attracting 141-142
associative patterning x, 99, 119, 136, 138, 142, 196, 205
assumptions ix-x

balancing and sensing 40-53, (graphic) 52, 81, 110, 121, 128, 142, 146, 153, 159
  alchemy, in 25, 28, 30, 39
  imbalances 36, 37
  "Balancing the Heart and Mind" (poem) 158
  conscious compassion, relationship with 53
  counterbalance 101, 103, 135
    humility, as 40
    spiritual energy, as 40, 108, 109, 143, 158
  creates beauty 57
  dynamic balancing 52-53
  equal, does not mean 44
  Feng Shui 57
  forces of Nature 42
  freedom and control/security 49-50, (graphic) 50, 152
  imbalance 40, 42, 123
  inner balance
    Field Effect Audio Technology 46
    hemispheric synchronization 45
    meditation 45
  inner and outer worlds, of 40, 45
  past, present, future 48-49
  physical and emotional, of 41
  physical, mental, emotional 42
  point between spiritual and material 158, 159, (poem) 158
  potential and actions 49
  rhythm of rest 50-51
  self balancing 44-51
  senses 3, 5, (table) 7, (table) 10, 51-52, 58, 59, 71, 89, (table) 122, 132, 136, 149
  stress, managing for balance 46-47
  thoughts and emotions 47

(tool) Holding Neurovascular Reflect Points 47-48
time 74-75
tools
  Lokahi Triangle 43-44
  Life Triangle 43-44
virtue as 49
yin and yang 42
beauty ix, 5, (table) 7, (table) 10, 30, 37, 51-52, 54-72, 77, (table) 122, 125, 149, 153
balance, created via 57
Choosing Beauty (tool) 66-67
conflict, relationship to 55
environment of, creating 67, 68, (picture) 69
experience, in 68
fractals, relationship with 54-55
gifting for others to enjoy, of 70
harmony, relationship with 54
health, relationship with 64-65
learning from each other, of 70
love, of 58, 61
mathematical equations, in 58
multiplier, as 67, 68
natural setting, in 68
negative forces as catalyst 55-56
peace, relationship with 56
property of experiences, as 55
sensing beauty 56-57
  unifies senses 56, 71
sharing 67-71
thinking, of 57-58, 68
transcendence, as 71-72
virtue, as 73-75
bifurcation 147-165
  (def) vii-viii
  painting by Cindy Taylor 167
  (see conscious evolution)
biosphere 15, 44, 150, 152
change (throughout)
  Bateson's levels of learning 8-10

Table 10
need to viii
choice ix, x, (table) 7, (table) 10, 15, 19
  beyond duality 154-156, (figure) 157
  contrast, intensity of 155
  facing humanity today 152
  (see bifurcation)
  human journey of choice (graphic) 153
  "Manifesting our Choice" 169-175
  openness to new 9
  split in road 156-159
co-evolving 51, 89, 99, 100, 115, (table) 122, 125, 152
cognitive-based ordering of change 8-11
  levels of learning 8-9
collaborative entanglement 103, 138-139
compassion 86-98
  Achieving Zero Limits (tool) 86, 94-95
  Assembly of Religious and Spiritual Leaders 86-87
  change, as tool for 97
  conscious 53, 86-98, 160
    developing 95-97
    (table) 96
  (def) 86, 88
  judging and 90-94
    decisions, in 90-91
    discernment and discretion 92-93
    Discerning Judging (tool) 86, 92
    judging others 91
    negative emotions, relationship with 93
    responsibility, comes with 92-93
  muscular compassion 97
  selfless service, giving 88
  social connection continuum 86, 89-90, (figure) 90

universal 94
complexity 102, 132, 148, 162, 163, 192, 193, 202, 212, 215
  begets complexity (figure) 164
  ISCJ, as part of 6, (table) 7
  optimum level 44
connectedness of choices 6, (table) 7, 49
conscious evolution 148-149
  beyond duality 154-156, (figure) 157
  conventionalizing 149
  creative leap 149-150, 159-165
  differentiating 149
  freedom and choice 151-153
  Golden Age of Humanity 149
  split in the road 156-159
  transformation 147-151
  transhumanism 150
consciousness 118-146, 147-167
  expansion through beauty 51-52
  extraordinary (def) 128, 127-130
  fields 120-121
  focused attention and 123-125
  form, expresses through 120-121
  global 149
  information fields as 119-127
  levels of 16, 121-122, 133, 142
    ISCJ, and phase of (table) 122
  process, not state 121
  resonance as quality of (figure) 140
  rising (figure) 137
  superconscious 111, 112
  tacit knowledge, relationship with 127-128, 129, (figure) 129
  threshold of 122-123
  unconscious 111
consilience approach vii
creative imagination ix, 5, (table) 7, (table) 10, 66, 100, 122, 124, 142
creative leap 3, (table) 7, (table) 10, 11, 22, 24, 30, 89, (table) 122, 125

NOW, needed 37
readiness for 21, 159-165
creativity ix, 6, (table) 7, 29, 30, 37, 48-49, 56, 61, 82, 98, 100, 108, 114, 140, 143, 146, 150, 210
  assumption x
  bisociation of ideas, as 149
  creation of beauty 67
  team 207
  types of 67
CUCA 53, 163, 215
dynamic balancing 52-53
  co-ordination 52
  equalization 52
  harmonization 52
  integration 52
  symmetrization 52
emotions 15, 96, 121, 123-125, 128, 142-143, 150, 207
  affective tacit knowledge 185, (table) 186, 192
  balancing 41, 42, 47, 48
  Emotional Intelligence 210-211
  empathy, in 80, 89
  fueling alchemical cycle 25, 31, 33, 37
  guidance system, as 41-42, 125
  negative 93
  response to beauty 55, 59
  role in mind/brain 41-42
ethics 73, 77
  core value, as 82
  ethical stances in life 211
  toward a global 76, 86-88
  unethical 81
forces ix, 4, 5, (table) 7, 18, 31, 44, 49, 52, 55, 89, 93, 118, 139, 165. 198, 209
  alchemy, in 31, 37, 38
  humanity, pushing 154, 161, 162
  knowledge as x, 99, 127
  nature, in 19, 42

reducing 56, 58, 114
separation of time and space 33
geosphere 15, 152
global world 59, 74, 113, 138, 152
  knowledge as 106-108
  (see Oneness)
health 64-67, 82, 171
  aging 65
  beauty, relationship with 64-65
  consistency of choices 65
  superhealth 150
  thoughts, relationship with 64
  work of art, as 64-67
hemispheric synchronization 45-46, 128, 189, 190
holographic universe 126, 144-146
  implicate order 144
  memory stored in 145
humility 6, (table) 7, 40, 77, 145, 166
  tool for balancing 40, 42, 43
incluessence 9, 165
ideas, resonance of 138
  field, in 119, 120, 140
information (def) 120
  shared accumulation in field 140
innovation 20, 29, 38, 82, 101, 104, 106, 107-108, 114, 117, 143, 148, 160
  in service to others 143
intelligent activity 1, 4, 6, (table) 7, 11, 19, 20, 49, 73-74, 97, 101, 105, 113, 143, 146
  (def) 5, 49, 73, 76
  knowledge in service to 101
intuitional field
  ability to tape into, understand and act 3, 89, 102, 103
  controlled intuition 11, 103, 119, 128, 135
  earned ix, 119
  revealed ix 102

ISCJ (Intelligent Social Change Journey) 53, 86, 88-89, 99-100, 115, 118-119, 121, 125, 136, 143, 152-153, (figure) 153
  baseline model (fig) 2
  Co-Creating the Future 3
  growing through change (firgure) 116
  introduction to 1-12
  journey, the 15
  Learning from the Past 1
  Learning in the Present 3
  levels of consciousness, and 122
  life as a geological force 15
  overarching model 4-7
  phases 1-6
    Table 7
  relationship of parts/phases 11-12
  similarity to alchemical cycle 24
judging 86, 121
  compassion, and 90-94, (figure) 93
  Discerning Judging (tool) 92
knowing xii, 5, 6, (table) 7, (table) 10, 66, 72, 92, 101, 119, (table) 122, 183
  art of knowing 195-214
  extraordinary consciousness, as 127
  (def) 111
  knowledge, and (graphic) 197
  sense, as a 111-113, 185
  spiritual tacit knowledge, as 187
  together 107
knowledge (throughout text)
  connections 101
  conceptual thinking, knowledge as tool for 6, (table) 7, 100-101, 112, 125
  consciousness, relationship with 127-129, (figure) 129
  context sensitive and situation dependent x, 5, (table) 7, 99, 174
  (def) 99

explosion 40-41
incomplete x, 5, (table) 7, 99, 119-120
intelligent activity, in service to 101
knowing, and (graphic) 197
measure of effectiveness, as 102
measure of self-growth, as 101-103
self as light of 130
shifting perception 99 (figure) 99
sub-personalities, and 130-131
tacit x-xi, 80, 111, 119, 138, 161, (figure) 186
  accessing 187-194, (figure) 188
  engaging tacit knowledge 183-194,
  extraordinary consciousness, as part of 127-130, (graphic) 129
  knowing, as part of 195-214
  types of 185-187
Knowledge Management 103-104, 158, 213
  spreading the movement 103-106
  thought leader research study 104-105
  thought leaders on:
    changing the world 106-109, (figure) 110
    contactivity 106
    KM field 105-106
    spiritual nature of knowledge 108-111
knowledge sharing 6, (table) 7, 32, 60, 80, 102, 104, 116, 118, 209, 213
  connective tissue for Oneness 116
learning (throughout text)
  beauty of learning from each other 70
  capacity 151
  chunking 11
  duality, role in 56
  levels of 8-10
meditation 28, 45, 128, 173, 189

memory 41, 48, 55, 92, 113, 120, 128, 145, 154, 171, 183, 191, 192, 196, 201, 202, 205
  collective 139
  stored in field 145
mind/brain 112
  associative attracting 119, 141-143
  associative patterning x, 99, 119, 142, 196, 205
    beyond ap 136-141
  beautification of the mind 51-52, 57-58, 68
  emotions, role of 41-42
  exercise and 41
  intuitive thinking 58
  neurogenesis 41
  pattern creation 41
  rhythm of rest 50-51
  thought forms 57, 58
  use it or lose it 41
Mountain Quest 60-63, 68, (picture) 69, (About) 234
Myst-Art 68-69, (picture) 70
Thought leader research study 104-105 *(see Knowledge Management)*
natural setting, beauty in 68
Noosphere 15, 119, 126, 135, 145, 150, 153, 162, 175
Oneness 5, 6, (table) 7, (table) 10, 51, 74, 76, (poem) 79, 111, 112, 113-117, 121, (table) 122, 133, 135, 140, 150, 153, 159
  energy field, emersion in 113-114
  knowledge sharing as connective tissue 116
  non-dual space, as 114
  state of being, as 116
personality 75, 103, 118, 124, 136, 138, 162, 189, 196
  alchemy, from viewpoint of 132-136
  (def) 130

new role for 130-136, 142
self, relationship with 131-132, 134
sub-personalities 130-131
surrendering 134
traits imprinted at birth 130
planes 40, 42, 65, 87, 102, 123, 124, 128, 131, 135, 136, 152
  balancing of 52, (figure) 52, 89
  mental 135, 166
  mental and emotional 76, 84, 138
  physical and emotional 41
  physical and mental 41
Principle of Correspondence 37
profundity
  (def) viii
Relationship Network Management 165-166
resonance (def) 139, (figure) 140, 115, 138-139
  field, with larger xi, 46, 139, 140, (figure) 140
  ideas, of 138, 139
  inducing resonance of tacit knowledge 187, 193-194
  morphic resonance 139, 141
  people, among 138-139
  thought 136, 142
  values, with 138
self 3, 28, 73, 75, 76, 78, 94, 118, 121-122, 125, 130-132, 138, 142, 160, 162, 184, 189
  agent of change, as an 200, 209-214
  balancing, self 48
  (see balancing)
  beauty of 65
  co-creator, as 6, (table) 7
  consciousness, light of 130
  (see consciousness)
  fusion, point of 142
  good character 75-78
    actionable 78-80
  individuation 114

knowing, relationship with 111, 197-199
knowledge as measure of self-growth 101-103
merging of higher and lower 135-136
permission, giving yourself 16-17, (def) 16
(see personality)
reflective moment (story) 17-19
senses
  balancing of 51-52, 71
  senses of self, created 76
  seventh sense 112
  sixth sense 112
true self 133-134
truth 49
value and valued 124
sensing *(see balancing and sensing)*
Singapore Armed Forces 80-82
singularity
  point of 163-165, (figure) 164
spiritual 43, 53, 78, 101, 103, 114-115, 119, 120, 121, (table) 122, 125, 142, 143, 146, 150, 152, 158, (poem) 158, 162, 166, 172
  alchemy, as part of 26, 29, 30
  Assembly of Religious and Spiritual Leaders 86-88
  balance, as 40, 135
  connectedness, as 115
    see Oneness
  (def) 87-88, 135
  energy, as 15, 40, 42, 102
  knowledge, nature of 108-111, (graphic) 109
  learning 112
  plane 133, 135
  tacit knowledge 111, 119, 128, 161
  wisdom 159
spirituality ix, 22, 42, 78, 86-88, 108, 110, 114-115, 174

universal spirituality 76, 87
stress viii, 46-47, 64, 65
  Holding Neurovascular Reflect Points (tool) 47-48
  learning, optimal for 44
  managing for balance 46-47
thought forms 37, 57, 58, 140-142, 146
  associative attracting, as 141-142
transcendence
  beauty as 71-72, 77
truth ix, 31, 48, 54, 58, 74, (poem) 79, 82, 84, 100, 112, 147, 193, 200, 209
  balancing past, present, future 48-49,
  balancing senses 58
  discerning 32, 40, 43
  level of 48, 51, 100
  scientific 173
  search for higher ix, 3, 5, 6, (table) 7, 17, 19, 49, 51, 83, 116, 124, 142, 146, 160, 166
  self 19, 49, 133
  untruth 35
  virtue, as 73-75
values 5, (table) 10, 29, 49, 67, 75-76, 92, 103, 105, 112, 138, 148, 151, 154, 187, 192, 196-199, 206, 209, 211, 212, 213
  core values 80-82
  (see ethics)
  hierarchy of 8
  intelligent activity, part of 5, 19, 49, 73, 146
  Singapore Armed Forces 80-82
valuing 206

virtues ix, 73-85, 116, 118, 152-153
  balance, equals 49
  beauty, goodness, truth 73-75
  character, as part of good 75-78
    actionable, is 78-80
  compassion as 86
  core values, relationship with 80-83
  created, is 76
  (def) 73-74
  Developing a Good Character Action Set (tool) 82-83
  highest on planes 73
  living the future, for 73-85
  unconditional love as highest virtue 86
  understanding patterns of goodness 84
  created equal, people not 83-84
  (def) 73, 74
  spirit in form, as 73
wisdom 5, (table) 7, (table) 10, 44, 58, 65, 74, 77, 80, 96, 98, 107, (table) 122, 130, 132, 135, 146, 187, 192, 199
  alchemy, as part of 23, 26
  balancing of opposites 43
  emergence from balancing of opposites 43
  Hermes, god of 23
  humility as a tool for 43
  intelligent activity, part of 5, 19, 49, 73, 146
  spiritual 159
wisdom circle movement 104

About The Mountain Quest Institute

MQI is a research, retreat and learning center dedicated to helping individuals achieve personal and professional growth and organizations create and sustain high performance in a rapidly changing, uncertain, and increasingly complex world. Drs. David and Alex Bennet are co-founders of MQI. They may be contacted at alex@mountainquestinstitute.com

Current research is focused on Human and Organizational Systems, Change, Complexity, Sustainability, Knowledge, Learning, Consciousness, and the nexus of Science and Spirituality. MQI has three questions: The Quest for Knowledge, The Quest for Consciousness, and The Quest for Meaning. **MQI is scientific, humanistic and spiritual and finds no contradiction in this combination**. See www.mountainquestinstitute.com

MQI is the birthplace of Organizational Survival in the New World: The Intelligent Complex Adaptive System (Elsevier, 2004), a new theory of the firm that turns the living system metaphor into a reality for organizations. Based on research in complexity and neuroscience—and incorporating networking theory and knowledge management—this book is filled with new ideas married to practical advice, all embedded within a thorough description of the new organization in terms of structure, culture, strategy, leadership, knowledge workers and integrative competencies.

Mountain Quest Institute, situated four hours from Washington, D.C. in the Monongahela Forest of the Allegheny Mountains, is part of the Mountain Quest complex which includes a Retreat Center, Inn, and the old Farm House, Outbuildings and mountain trails and farmland. See www.mountainquestinn.com The Retreat Center is designed to provide full learning experiences, including hosting training, workshops, retreats and business meetings for professional and executive groups of 25 people or less. The Center includes a 26,000 volume research library, a conference room, community center, computer room, 12 themed bedrooms, a workout and hot tub area, and a four-story tower with a glass ceiling for enjoying the magnificent view of the valley during the day and the stars at night. Situated on a 430 acres farm, there is a labyrinth, creeks, four miles of mountain trails, and horses, Longhorn cattle, Llamas and a myriad of wild neighbors. Other neighbors include the Snowshoe Ski Resort, the National Radio Astronomy Observatory and the CASS Railroad.

About The Organizational Zoo Ambassadors Network

The Organizational Zoo Ambassadors Network (OZAN) is an international group of professionals interested in using The Organizational Zoo concepts as part of their capability development programs. Zoo Ambassadors have been trained in the application of OZAN Tools and approaches. They freely share their experiences through an international network which interacts primarily through a wiki supplemented by occasional face to face events and some on-line learning modules. See http://www.organizationalzoo.com/ambassadors/

About Quantra Leadership Academy

Quantra Leadership Academy (aka QLA Consulting) is a transformational leadership and personal development training company run by Dr. Theresa Bullard**. QLA is dedicated to helping individuals and organizations innovate their way of thinking to achieve breakthrough results.** There is one question that lies at the foundation of QLA: *What is your potential?* When you tap into your potential, greatness happens, you experience breakthroughs, "Ah-ha" moments occur, and you get into "The Zone" of peak performance. It is our passion to help you access your full potential, sustain what you achieve, and be able to refuel whenever you want. When you get to the point where you can do this on demand that is when you become a self-transforming agent of change. QLA shows you how to get there and gives you tools to accelerate your progress. By blending science, consciousness studies, and mental alchemy, or the art and science of transforming your mindset, we help you **reach your potential** and become more successful in essential areas of your work and life. *To help you* **access more of your potential,** *we offer a progression of transformative tools and trainings that integrate quantum principles, cutting-edge methods, and ancient wisdom for using your mind more creatively and effectively.* For more info: www.QLAconsulting.com

About Blue Ray of Hope

Blue Ray of Hope is an organization dedicated to empowering humanity in the realization of their ability to *heal themselves and live a life filled with joy and abundance.* Our mission is to provide practical tools and techniques that open the doors to understanding our true human potential. Educational programs, holistic retreats, spiritual counseling and alternative wellness guidance are offered to assist humanity in their quest for a healthy and joy-filled life. See http://www.bluerayofhope.com

About the Authors

Dr. Alex Bennet, a Professor at the Bangkok University Institute for Knowledge and Innovation Management, is internationally recognized as an expert in knowledge management and an agent for organizational change. Prior to founding the Mountain Quest Institute, she served as the Chief Knowledge Officer and Deputy Chief Information Officer for Enterprise Integration for the U.S. Department of the Navy, and was co-chair of the Federal Knowledge Management Working Group. Dr. Bennet is the recipient of the Distinguished and Superior Public Service Awards from the U.S. government for her work in the Federal Sector. She is a Delta Epsilon Sigma and Golden Key National Honor Society graduate with a Ph.D. in Human and Organizational Systems; degrees in Management for Organizational Effectiveness, Human Development, English and Marketing; and certificates in Total Quality Management, System Dynamics and Defense Acquisition Management. Alex believes in the multidimensionality of humanity as we move out of infancy into full consciousness.

Dr. David Bennet's experience spans many years of service in the Military, Civil Service and Private Industry, including fundamental research in underwater acoustics and nuclear physics, frequent design and facilitation of organizational interventions, and serving as technical director of two major DoD Acquisition programs. Prior to founding the Mountain Quest Institute, Dr. Bennet was CEO, then Chairman of the Board and Chief Knowledge Officer of a professional services firm located in Alexandria, Virginia. He is a Phi Beta Kappa, Sigma Pi Sigma, and Suma Cum Laude graduate of the University of Texas, and holds degrees in Mathematics, Physics, Nuclear Physics, Liberal Arts, Human and Organizational Development, and a Ph.D. in Human Development focused on Neuroscience and adult learning. He is currently researching the nexus of Science, the Humanities and Spirituality.

Dr. Arthur Shelley is a capability development and knowledge strategy consultant with over 30 years professional experience. He has held a variety of professional roles including managing international projects in Australia, Europe, Asia and USA and has facilitated professional development program with organisations as diverse as NASA, Cirque du Soleil, World Bank, government agencies and corporates. He has facilitated courses in Masters programs on Executive Consulting, Leadership, Knowledge Management, Applied Research Practice and Entrepreneurship in face to face, blended and on-line modes. Arthur is the author of three books: *KNOWledge SUCCESSion (2017) Being a Successful Knowledge Leader (2009)*; *The Organizational Zoo, A Survival Guide to Workplace Behavior (2007)*. In 2014 he was awarded with an Australian Office of Learning and Teaching citation for "Outstanding contributions to student learning outcomes". Arthur is a regular invited speaker and workshop facilitator at international conferences to discuss his writing or to share experiences as the former Global Knowledge Director for Cadbury Schweppes. He is founder of The Organizational Zoo Ambassadors Network (a professional peer mentoring group), creator of the RMIT University MBA mentoring program and co-facilitator of the Melbourne KM Leadership Forum. Arthur has a PhD in Project Management, a Master of Science in Microbiology/Biochemistry, a Graduate Certificate in Tertiary Learning and Teaching and a Bachelor of Science. Arthur may be reached at arthur.shelley@rmit.edu.au

Dr. Theresa Bullard combines a Ph.D. in Physics with a life-long path of embracing the new paradigm of Science and Consciousness. Her passion and ability to bridge these worlds are her strengths and distinguish her as an exceptional teacher, speaker, leader and change-agent. Theresa is the founder of QLA Consulting Inc., President of the Board of Directors of Mysterium Center, an International Instructor with the Modern Mystery School, and co-founder of the Universal Kabbalah

Network. She has over 15 years of experience in science research, international speaking, and transformational training. Author of *The Game Changers: Social Alchemists in the 21st Century*, along with several guided meditation albums and audio tools for accessing Quantum conscious states, her mission is to help individuals and organizations thrive in a changing world. Theresa may be contacted at Theresa@quantumleapalchemy.com

Dr. John Lewis is a speaker, business consultant, and part-time professor on the topics of organizational learning, thought leadership, and knowledge & innovation management. John is a proven leader with business results, and was acknowledged by Gartner with an industry "Best Practice" paper for an innovative knowledge management implementation. He is a co-founder at The CoHero Institute, creating collaborative leadership in learning organizations. John holds a Doctoral degree in Educational Psychology from the University of Southern California, with a dissertation focus on mental models and decision making, and is the author of *The Explanation Age*, which Kirkus Reviews described as "An iconoclast's blueprint for a new era of innovation." John may be contacted at John@ExplanationAge.com

Dr. Donna Panucci comes from a clinical background as a Specialist in Orthodontics, "Creating Smiles in More Ways than One" in her private practice for 23 years. Donna began exploring the human psyche as an HBDI® Certified Practitioner, which assesses preferences in the four brain quadrants, as depicted by the Herrmann Whole Brain® Model. Her burning desire to empower her family, friends and patients to see their lives in a positive light led her to study with Doreen Virtue and become a Certified Angel Therapy Practitioner® (under Doreen Virtue), a Reiki Master, an Integrated Energy Therapy® Master-Instructor, a Pathway Prayer Process Akashic Records Practitioner (under the guidance of Linda Howe) and a Certified Energy Medicine Practitioner (under Donna Eden). She is passionate about teaching the importance of optimizing our personal energies to create mind-body shifts that promote overall whole body health and vitality. Donna is the founder of Blue Ray of Hope. She may be contacted at donna.panucci@gmail.com

Other Books by MQI Press (www.MQIPress.net)

MQIPress is a wholly-owned subsidiary of Mountain Quest Institute, LLC, located at 303 Mountain Quest Lane, Marlinton, West Virginia 24954, USA. (304) 799-7267

Other Bennet eBooks available from in PDF format from MQIPress (US 304-799-7267 or alex@mountainquestinstitute.com) and Kindle format from Amazon.

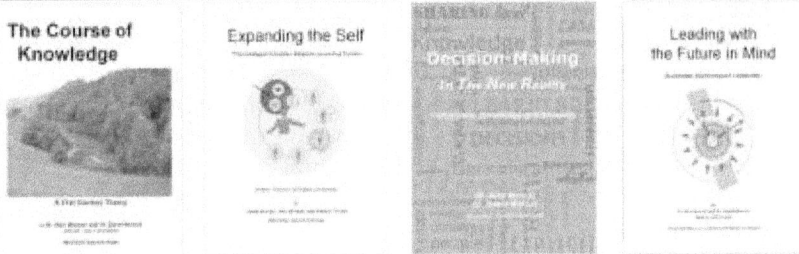

The Course of Knowledge: A 21st Century Theory
by Alex Bennet and David Bennet with Joyce Avedisian (2015)

Knowledge is at the core of what it is to be human, the substance which informs our thoughts and determines the course of our actions. Our growing focus on, and understanding of, knowledge and its consequent actions is changing our relationship with the world. Because **knowledge determines the quality of every single decision we make**, it is critical to learn about and understand what knowledge is. **From a 21st century viewpoint,** we explore a theory of knowledge that is both pragmatic and biological. Pragmatic in that it is based on taking effective action, and biological because it is created by humans via patterns of neuronal connections in the mind/brain.

In this book we explore *the course of knowledge*. Just as a winding stream in the bowls of the mountains curves and dips through ravines and high valleys, so, too, with knowledge. In a continuous journey towards intelligent activity, context-sensitive and situation-dependent knowledge, imperfect and incomplete, experientially engages a changing landscape in a continuous cycle of learning and expanding. *We are in a continuous cycle of knowledge creation such that every moment offers the opportunity for the emergence of new and exciting ideas, all waiting to be put in service to an interconnected world.* Learn more about this **exciting human capacity**! AVAILABLE FROM AMAZON in Kindle Format. AVAILABLE FROM MQIPress in PDF.

Expanding the Self: The Intelligent Complex Adaptive Learning System
by David Bennet, Alex Bennet and Robert Turner (2015)

We live in unprecedented times; indeed, turbulent times that can arguably be defined as ushering humanity into a new Golden Age, offering the opportunity to embrace new ways of learning and living in a globally and collaboratively entangled connectedness (Bennet & Bennet, 2007). In this shifting and dynamic environment, life demands accelerated cycles of learning experiences. Fortunately, we as a humanity have begun to look within ourselves to better understand the way our mind/brain operates, the amazing qualities of the body that power our thoughts and feelings, and the reciprocal loops as those thoughts and feelings change our physical structure. This emerging knowledge begs us to relook and rethink what we know about learning, providing a new starting point to expand toward the future.

This book is a treasure for those interested in how recent findings in neuroscience impact learning. The result of this work is an expanding experiential learning model call the Intelligent Complex Adaptive Learning System, adding the fifth mode of social engagement to Kolb's concrete experience, reflective observation, abstract conceptualization and active experimentation, with the five modes undergirded by the power of Self. A significant conclusion is that should they desire, adults have much more control over their learning than they may realize. AVAILABLE FROM AMAZON in Kindle Format. AVAILALBE FROM MQIPress in PDF.

Decision-Making in The New Reality: Complexity, Knowledge and Knowing
by Alex Bennet and David Bennet (2013)

We live in a world that offers many possible futures. The ever-expanding complexity of information and knowledge provide many choices for decision-makers, and we are all making decisions every single day! As the problems and messes of the world become more complex, our decision consequences are more and more difficult to anticipate, and our decision-making processes must change to keep up with this world complexification. This book takes a consilience approach to explore decision-making in The New Reality, fully engaging systems and complexity theory, knowledge research, and recent neuroscience findings. It also presents methodologies for decision-makers to tap into their unconscious, accessing tacit knowledge resources and increasingly relying on the sense of knowing that is available to each of us.

Almost every day new energies are erupting around the world: new thoughts, new feelings, new knowing, all contributing to new situations that require new decisions and actions from each and every one of us. Indeed, with the rise of the Net Generation and social media, a global consciousness may well be emerging. As individuals and organizations we are realizing that there are larger resources available to us, and that, as complex adaptive systems linked to a flowing fount of knowing, we can bring these resources to bear to achieve our ever-expanding vision of the future. Are we up to the challenge? AVAILABLE FROM AMAZON in Kindle Format. AVAILABLE FROM MQIPress in PDF.

Leading with the Future in Mind: Knowledge and Emergent Leadership
by Alex Bennet and David Bennet with John Lewis (2015)

We exist in a new reality, a global world where the individuated power of the mind/brain offers possibilities beyond our imagination. It is within this framework that thought leading emerges, and when married to our collaborative nature, makes the impossible an everyday occurrence. *Leading with the Future in Mind*, building on profound insights unleashed by recent findings in neuroscience, provides a new view that converges leadership, knowledge and learning for individual and organizational advancement.

This book provides a research-based *tour de force* for the future of leadership. Moving from the leadership of the past, for the few at the top, using authority as the explanation, we now find leadership emerging from all levels of the organization, with knowledge as the explanation. The future will be owned by the organizations that can master the relationships between knowledge and leadership. Being familiar with the role of a knowledge worker is not the same as understanding the role of a knowledge leader. As the key ingredient, collaboration is much more than "getting along"; it embraces and engages. Wrapped in the mantle of collaboration and engaging our full resources—hysical, mental, emotional and spiritual—we open the door to possibilities. We are dreaming the future together. AVAILABLE FROM AMAZON in Kindle Format. AVAILABLE FROM MQIPress in PDF.

Other books available from the authors and on Amazon..

The Game Changers: Social Alchemists in the 21st Century
by Theresa Bullard, Ph.D. (2013), available in hard and soft formats from Amazon.
Just about everywhere we look right now change is afoot. What is all this change about? Why now? And how do we best adapt? Many have called this time a "quickening", where the speed with which we must think, respond, and take action is accelerating. Systems are breaking down, people are rising up, and there is uncertainty of what tomorrow will bring. This book is dedicated to times such as these, times of great transformation. It can be seen as a companion guide on how to navigate the tumultuous tides of change. It aims to put such current events into a possible context within the evolutionary and alchemical process that humanity is going through. In it, author, physicist, and change-agent, Theresa Bullard, Ph.D., discusses emerging new paradigms, world events, future trends, and ancient wisdom that help reveal a bigger picture of what is happening. She offers insights and solutions to empower you, the reader, to become a more conscious participant in these exciting times of change. With this knowledge you will be more equipped to harness the *opportunities* that such times present you with. AVAILABLE FROM AMAZON in Kindle Format ... Paperback

The Organizational Zoo: A Survival Guide to Work Place Behavior
by Arthur Shelley (2006), available in hard and soft formats from Amazon.
Organizational Zoo is a fresh approach to organizational culture development, a witty and thought-provoking book that makes ideal reading for students and management. When you think of your organization as containing ants, bees, chameleons, and other creatures on through the alphabet, your work world becomes more manageable. Discover the secret strengths and weaknesses of each distinct animal so that you can communicate more productively—or manipulate more cunningly. Your choice! AVAILABLE FROM AMAZON in Paperback

The Explanation Age
by John Lewis (2013) (3rd Ed.), available in hard and soft formats from Amazon.
The technological quest of the last several decades has been to create the information age, with ubiquitous and immediate access to information. With this goal arguably accomplished, even from our mobile phones, this thought-provoking book describes the next quest and provides a blueprint for how to get there. When all organizational knowledge is framed as answers to our fundamental questions, we find ubiquitous and visual access to knowledge related to who, where, how, etc., yet the explanations are still buried within the prose. The question of "why" is arguably the most important question, yet it is currently the least supported. This is why business process methodologies feel like "box-checking" instead of "sense-making." This is why lessons learned are not actually learned. And this is why the consequential options and choices are captured better within a chess game than within the important decisions faced by organizations and society. With implications for business, education,

policy making, and artificial intelligence, Dr. Lewis provides a visualization of explanations which promotes organizational sense-making and collaboration. AVAILABLE FROM AMAZON in Paperback

KNOWledge SUCCESSion: Sustained Capability Growth Through Strategic Projects
by Arthur Shelley (2016), available in hard and soft formats from Amazon.
KNOWledge SUCCESSion is intended for executives and developing professionals who face the challenges of delivering business benefits for today, whilst building the capabilities required for an increasingly changing future. The book is structured to build from foundational requirements towards connecting the highly interdependent aspects of success in an emerging complex world. A wide range of concepts are brought together in a logical framework to enable readers of different disciplines to understand how they either create barriers or can be harvested to generate synergistic opportunities. The framework builds a way to make sense of the connections and provides novel paths to take advantage of the potential synergies that arise through aligning the concepts into a portfolio of strategic projects. AVAILABLE FROM AMAZON. Kindle Format ... Paperback

Knowledge Mobilization in the Social Sciences and Humanities: Moving from Research to Action
by Alex Bennet and David Bennet (2007), available in hard and soft formats from Amazon.
This book takes the reader from the University lab to the playgrounds of communities. It shows how to integrate, move and use knowledge, an action journey within an identified action space that is called knowledge mobilization. Whether knowledge is mobilized through an individual, organization, community or nation, it becomes a powerful asset creating a synergy and focus that brings forth the best of action and values. Individuals and teams who can envision, feel, create and apply this power are the true leaders of tomorrow. When we can mobilize knowledge for the greater good humanity will have left the information age and entered the age of knowledge, ultimately leading to compassion and—hopefully—wisdom. AVAILABLE FROM AMAZON. Kindle Format ... Paperback
AVAILABLE FROM MQIPress in PDF and Softback.

Being a Successful Knowledge Leader: What Knowledge Practitioners Need to Know to Make a Difference.
by Arthur Shelley (2009). AVAILABLE FROM AMAZON. Paperback
Being a Successful Knowledge Leader explores the challenges of leading a program of knowledge-informed change initiatives to generate sustained performance improvement. The book explores how to embed knowledge flows into strategic development cycles to align organizational development with changing environmental conditions. The high rate of change interferes with the growth of organizational knowledge because what is relevant only generates a competitive advantage for a short

time. Also the people who possess this knowledge are more mobile than previously. Combined, these factors can have a detrimental impact on performance and need to be mitigated against to ensure capabilities are built rather than diluted overtime. The characteristics for success that a knowledge leader needs to possess are explored from a unique perspective to stimulate creative thinking around how to develop and maintain these in emergent times.

Organizational Survival in the New World: the Intelligent Complex Adaptive System
    by Alex Bennet and David Bennet (Elsevier, 2004), available in hard and soft formats from Amazon.
In this book David and Alex Bennet propose a new model for organizations that enables them to react more quickly and fluidly to today's fast-changing, dynamic business environment: the Intelligent Complex Adaptive System (ICAS). ICAS is a new organic model of the firm based on recent research in complexity and neuroscience, and incorporating networking theory and knowledge management, and turns the living system metaphor into a reality for organizations. This book synthesizes new thinking about organizational structure from the fields listed above into ICAS, a new systems model for the successful organization of the future designed to help leaders and managers of knowledge organizations succeed in a non-linear, complex, fast-changing and turbulent environment. Technology enables connectivity, and the ICAS model takes advantage of that connectivity by fostering the development of dynamic, effective and trusting relationships in a new organizational structure. AVAILABLE FROM AMAZON in Kindle Format ... Hardback ... Paperback

Other MQIPress books available in PDF format at www.MQIPress.net (US 304-799-7267 or alex@mountainquestinstitute.com**) and Kindle format from Amazon.**

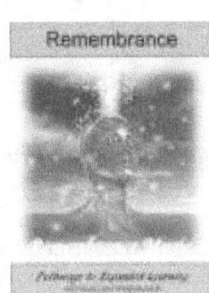

REMEMBRANCE: Pathways to Expanded Learning with Music and Metamusic®
    by Barbara Bullard and Alex Bennet (2013)
Take a journey of discovery into the last great frontier—the human mind/brain, an instrument of amazing flexibility and plasticity. This eBook is written for brain users who are intent on mining more of the golden possibilities that lie inherent in each of our unique brains. Begin by discovering the role positive attitudes play in learning, and the power of self affirmations and visualizations. Then explore the use of brain wave entrainment mixed with designer music called Metamusic® to achieve enhanced learning states. Join students of all ages who are creating magical learning outcomes using music and Metamusic.® AVAILABLE FROM AMAZON in Kindle Format.

The Journey into the Myst (Vol. 1 of The Myst Series)
    by Alex Bennet and David Bennet (2012)

What we are about to tell you would have been quite unbelievable to me before this journey began. It is not a story of the reality either of us has known for well over our 60 and 70 years of age, but rather, the reality of dreams and fairytales." This is the true story of a sequence of events that happened at Mountain Quest Institute, situated in a high valley of the Allegheny Mountains of West Virginia. The story begins with a miracle, expanding into the capture and cataloging of thousands of pictures of electromagnetic spheres widely known as "orbs." This joyous experience became an exploration into the unknown with the emergence of what the author's fondly call the Myst, the forming and shaping of non-random patterns such as human faces, angels and animals. As this phenomenon unfolds, you will discover how the Drs. Alex and David Bennet began to observe and interact with the Myst. This book shares the beginning of an extraordinary *Journey into the Myst*. AVAILABLE FROM AMAZON in Kindle Format. AVAILABLE FROM MQIPress in PDF.

Patterns in the Myst (Vol. 2 of The Myst Series)
by Alex Bennet and David Bennet (2013)

The Journey into the Myst was just the beginning for Drs. Alex and David Bennet. Volume II of the Myst Series brings Science into the Spiritual experience, bringing to bear what the Bennets have learned through their research and educational experiences in physics, neuroscience, human systems, knowledge management and human development. Embracing the paralogical, patterns in the Myst are observed, felt, interpreted, analyzed and compared in terms of their physical make-up, non-randomness, intelligent sources and potential implications. Along the way, the Bennets were provided amazing pictures reflecting the forming of the Myst. The Bennets shift to introspection in the third volume of the series to explore the continuing impact of the Myst experience on the human psyche. AVAILABLE FROM AMAZON in Kindle Format. AVAILABLE FROM MQIPress in PDF.

The Profundity and Bifurcation of Change Part I:
Laying the Groundwork

by Alex Bennet and David Bennet with Arthur Shelley, Theresa Bullard and John Lewis

This book lays the groundwork for the **Intelligent Social Change Journey** (ISCJ), a developmental journey of the body, mind and heart, moving from the heaviness of cause-and-effect linear extrapolations, to the fluidity of co-evolving with our environment, to the lightness of breathing our thought and feelings into reality. Grounded in development of our mental faculties, these are phase changes, each building on and expanding previous learning in our movement toward intelligent activity. As we lay the groundwork, we move through the concepts of change, knowledge, forces, self and consciousness. Then, recognizing that we are holistic beings, we provide a baseline model for individual change from within.

The Profundity and Bifurcation of Change Part II:
Learning from the Past

by Alex Bennet and David Bennet with Arthur Shelley, Theresa Bullard and John Lewis

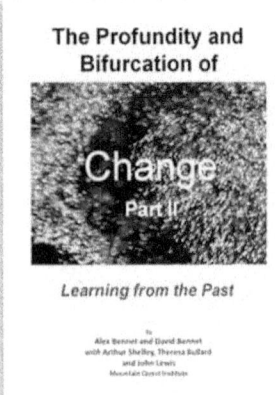

Phase 1 of the Intelligent Social Change Journey (ISCJ) is focused on the linear cause-and-effect relationships of logical thinking. Knowledge, situation dependent and context sensitive, is a product of the past. **Phase 1 assumes that for every effect there is an originating cause.** This is where we as a humanity, and as individuals, begin to develop our mental faculties. In this book we explore cause and effect, scan a kaleidoscope of change models, and review the modalities of change. Since change is easier and more fluid when we are grounded, we explore three interpretations of grounding. In preparation for expanding our consciousness, a readiness assessment and sample change agent's strategy are provided.

The Profundity and Bifurcation of Change Part III:
Learning in the Present

by Alex Bennet and David Bennet with Arthur Shelley, Theresa Bullard and John Lewis

As the world becomes increasingly complex, Phase 2 of the Intelligent Social Change Journey (ISCJ) is focused on **co-evolving with the environment**. This requires a deepening connection to others, moving into empathy. While the NOW is the focus, there is an increasing ability to put together patterns from the past and think conceptually, as well as extrapolate future behaviors. Thus, we look closely at the relationship of time and space, and pattern thinking. We look at the human body as a complex energetic system, exploring the role of emotions as a guidance system, and what happens when we have stuck energy. This book also introduces Knowledge Capacities, different ways of thinking that build capacity for sustainability.

The Profundity and Bifurcation of Change Part IV:
Co-Creating the Future

by Alex Bennet and David Bennet with Arthur Shelley, Theresa Bullard and John Lewis

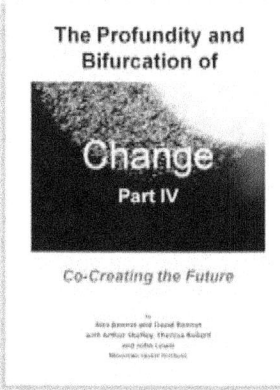

As we move into Phase 3 of the Intelligent Social Change Journey (ISCJ), **we fully embrace our role as co-creator**. We recognize the power of thought and the role of attention and intention in our ever-expanding search for a higher level of truth. Whether we choose to engage it or not, we explore mental discipline as a tool toward expanded consciousness. In preparing ourselves for the creative leap, there are ever-deepening connections with others. We now understand that the mental faculties are in service to the intuitional, preparing us to, and expanding our ability to, act in and on the world, living with conscious compassion and tapping into the intuitional at will.

The Profundity and Bifurcation of Change Part V: Living the Future

by Alex Bennet and David Bennet with Arthur Shelley, Theresa Bullard, John Lewis and Donna Panucci

We embrace the ancient art and science of Alchemy to **explore the larger shift underway for humanity** and how we can consciously and intentionally speed up evolution to enhance outcomes. In this conversation, we look at balancing and sensing, the harmony of beauty, and virtues for living the future. Conscious compassion, a virtue, is introduced as a state of being connected to morality and good character, inclusive of giving selfless service. We are now ready to refocus our attention on knowledge and consciousness, exploring the new roles these play in our advancement. And all of this—all of our expanding and growth as we move through the Intelligent Social Change journey—is giving a wide freedom of choice as we approach the bifurcation. What will we manifest?

Available in PDF format from www.MQIPress.net

Available in Kindle format from www.amazon.com

www.ingramcontent.com/pod-product-compliance
Lightning Source LLC
Chambersburg PA
CBHW080728230426
43665CB00020B/2663